GUILTY

GUILTY

LIBERAL "VICTIMS" AND THEIR
ASSAULT ON AMERICA

ANN COULTER

THREE RIVERS PRESS
NEW YORK

Library of Congress Cataloging-in-Publication Data
is available upon request.

ISBN 978-0-307-35347-4

Printed in the United States of America

10 9 8 7 6 5 4 3 2 1

First Paperback Edition

TO

KIMBERLY LLOYD COULTER

AND

CHRISTINA HART COULTER

CONTENTS

1

LIBERAL MOTTO:
SPEAK LOUDLY AND CARRY
A SMALL VICTIM

Liberals always have to be the victims, particularly when they are oppressing others. Modern victims aren't victims because of what they have suffered; they are victims of convenience for the Left. There's no way to determine if an action is offensive by looking at the action. One must know who did it to whom, and whose side the most powerful people in America will take. Republican senator Trent Lott committed a hate crime when he praised former segregationist Strom Thurmond at a birthday party, but a year later, Democratic senator Chris Dodd did nothing wrong when he praised a former Ku Klux Klanner, Senator Robert Byrd—who was also a sort of "community organizer."

Playing the game of He Who Is Offended First Wins, the key to any political argument is to pretend to be insulted and register operatic anger. Liberals are the masters of finger-wagging indignation. They will wail about some perceived slight to a sacred feeling of theirs, frightening people who have never before witnessed the liberals' capacity to invoke synthetic outrage. Distracted by the crocodile tears of the liberal, Americans don't notice that these fake victims are attacking, advancing, and creating genuine victims.

Just as we're always told that schoolyard bullies are actually deeply insecure, liberals rationalize their own ferocious behavior by claiming to have been wounded somehow. What about the little guy our poor, insecure bully is beating the living daylights out of? How's his self-esteem coming along? That is the essence of liberals: They viciously attack everyone else, while wailing that they are the victims.

Liberals' infernal habit of accusing others of what they themselves are doing distracts attention from who is really being attacked. No one is victimized by a mouse: Real victims are those who are called the oppressors by the powerful. Just as Nazi mythology made ordinary working Germans believe they were victims of Jewish oppressors—in order to oppress the Jews—today's media-certified victims are the true oppressors, and the alleged aggressors are the real victims. To find the authentic victims in most situations, one can simply refer to the people the mainstream media urge us to hate, beasts such as George Bush, the Duke lacrosse players, Joe McCarthy, Jesse Helms, Tom DeLay, the Swift Boat Veterans, and Sarah Palin. But often the victims are nameless, faceless victims of repellent liberal policies that are promoted on behalf of counterfeit victims, such as single mothers or "the poor." Media-anointed victims inevitably create actual victims who became so the old-fashioned way: They earned it.

Fake victims have become so crucial to liberal argument that you need a pathos-meter to follow politics in modern America. Every policy proposal is launched or opposed on the stories of victims. When Senator Hillary Clinton sought more federal money for New York City in 2007, she made a big show of attending Bush's January 2007 State of the Union Address with the son of a New York City police officer, Cesar A. Borja, who had died that very day of a rare lung disease he had allegedly acquired from working "16-hour shifts" at the World Trade Center after the 9/11 attacks.

The New York *Daily News* had told the tear-jerking story of Cesar Borja a few weeks earlier in an article claiming that "when the twin towers fell," Borja "rushed to ground zero and started working long days there." Now he was dying of a rare lung disease, a result, the *Daily News* suggested, of his having "volunteered to work months of 16-hour shifts in the rubble, breathing in clouds of toxic dust."[1]

Senator Hillary Clinton seized on the 9/11 victim's story, parading Officer Borja's twenty-one-year-old son at the State of the Union Address. She even sent President Bush a letter—made available to the press—inviting him to meet Officer Borja's son, at the same time requesting more federal funding for New York's emergency workers. The federal money allocated thus far, she said, was "only a down payment in repaying our debt to those who came to assist us in our hour of need." She asked the president to "honor" Officer Borja's memory and those who had "lost loved ones as a result of the 9/11 attacks."[2]

Bush met with Officer Borja's son and agreed to the additional federal funding for those suffering nonspecific health problems related to the 9/11 attack. Senator Clinton then released another letter noting "our responsibility to take care of those who took care of us"—those who, she said, "selflessly risked their lives and their health at Ground Zero."[3]

Then it turned out the story of Officer Borja's glorious heroism on 9/11 was a complete hoax. Borja had not "rushed" to the disaster site after the attack. He only started working there, directing traffic, near the end of December 2001, by which time much of the rubble had been cleared away. He was not a volunteer—this was his job. Indeed, the only reason he was working sixteen-hour days was to boost his pension just before he retired. In all, Borja had worked seventeen days at the World Trade Center, most of them in 2002.[4] Borja retired in June 2003 and did not begin to develop pulmonary fibrosis until 2005. There were other possible explanations for his rare lung disease, such as his pack-a-day cigarette habit until five or six years before the 9/11 attack.[5] Officer Borja had done nothing dishonorable, but he had not selflessly risked his life at Ground Zero, as Hillary Clinton claimed in order to beg for more taxpayer money for New York City.

Asked about its make-believe reporting on Borja's undaunted heroism, the *Daily News* observed that "the paper had never explicitly said Officer Borja had rushed there soon after Sept. 11, only that at some point he had rushed there."[6] No matter—he had served his purpose and New York City got its federal funding.

All the Left's seminal imagery keeps turning out to be a hoax. Daddy was diving repeatedly into ground zero—when he was nowhere near the place. The *New Republic*'s "Baghdad Diarist" told sickening tales about the brutish behavior of American troops in Iraq—and then he signed an affidavit admitting he made it all up. John Edwards was the loyal husband to his cancer-stricken wife—except it turned out he was carrying on an extended affair with Rielle Hunter. The Democrats dredge up victim after victim, but it's hard to find one real story.

Why do liberals keep coming up with hoaxes for our edification? Time and again, liberals transform themselves into chaste Victorian virgins fainting over the suffering of their victim du jour—but then the facts come out, and liberals react like Emily Litella on *Saturday Night Live:* "Never mind."

You know you've really made it in America when the Left weeps for you. But this much-sought-after victim status is evanescent, lasting only as long as the fake victim's bellyaching advances the liberal agenda. Poor, long-suffering Valerie Plame, Joe Wilson, Scott Ritter, Cindy Sheehan, the Jersey Girls, Scott McClellan—all putative victims of the Republicans—weep alone these days. The liberal establishment has moved on.

It's so popular to be a victim in modern American society that people are constantly faking their own hard-luck stories—and not just in the "personal statement" essay in their Harvard applications. Among the recent hoax memoirs was one in 2008 by "Margaret B. Jones" called *Love and Consequences: A Memoir of Hope and Survival.* Jones claimed to be a half-white, half–Native American girl who grew up in a foster home in South Central Los Angeles, raised by an African American mother. She said she ran drugs for the Bloods in the middle of the deadly crack wars of the 1980s, losing her foster brother to the gang wars. Jones gave interviews using an urban black patois, referring to her fellow gang members as her "homies." In her book she passed on urban wisdom, such as "Trust no one. Even your own momma will sell you out for the right price or if she gets scared enough."

But then it turned out Margaret Jones was really Peggy Seltzer, a suburban Valley Girl, who grew up with her biological family in affluent Sherman Oaks, California, where she attended a private day school. The closest she had come to the projects was watching *Project Runway* on Bravo. Her hoax was exposed when her sister, Cyndi Hoffman, called the publisher after seeing Seltzer's photo by a book review in the *New York Times*—which praised the book as a "humane and deeply affecting memoir."

Even when caught red-handed, Seltzer claimed to be serving a greater good: "I thought it was my opportunity to put a voice to people who people don't listen to." She said others had told her "you should speak for us because nobody else is going to let us in to talk." Admitting it was "an ego thing," she explained, "I don't know. I just felt that there was good that I could do and there was no other way that someone would listen to it."[7]

Also in 2008, a Holocaust memoir published in 1997 was exposed as a hoax. In the book, *Misha: A Mémoire of the Holocaust Years,* Misha Defonseca described her parents being arrested and deported by the Nazis when she was six years old. She wrote that she went to live with the De Wael family, who gave her the name "Monique," but she so missed her parents that she embarked on a trans-European trek to find them. Wandering alone throughout Europe, she said she killed a German soldier, was sheltered by a pack of wolves, and saw a train full of Jews headed for the death chamber. So her story was believable.

The memoir was a smash bestseller in Europe and Canada and was on its way to a triumphant success in the United States with both Oprah and Disney expressing interest in the book. But a money dispute with the publisher delayed negotiations—and in the meantime the book was exposed as a fraud.

Defonseca really had been born "Monique De Wael," a Belgian Catholic, whose parents were arrested and later executed by the Nazis for being part of the Belgian Catholic resistance. Defonseca had never gone in search of her parents. To the contrary, she renounced the name of her brave Nazi-resisting parents, saying she had "wanted to forget" her real name since she was four years old because she had been called "daughter of a traitor" after her parents were arrested. She added that all her life she "felt Jewish . . . it was my reality, my way of surviving."[8] In short, she did everything she could think of to sound more Jewish but complain about being seated too close to the air conditioner.

Another award-winning Holocaust memoir, Benjamin Wilkomirski's *Fragments: Memories of a Wartime Childhood,* was published in 1995 and—although it was never an official selection of Oprah's Book Club— was exposed as a hoax by 1999. Wilkomirski claimed to have survived Nazi concentration camps as a small boy, drawing gruesome tales of watching his mother die, rats crawling out of dead bodies, and children eating their own fingers. Genealogists later established that he was the illegitimate child of a Protestant woman, and he had spent the war years safely ensconced in Switzerland with his adoptive parents.

This literary Munchausen syndrome produces Jewish girls trying to be black and gentiles claiming to be Jewish Holocaust survivors. So naturally, when a con artist threesome sought fame and fortune in America, they invented a young fiction author by the name of JT LeRoy, who was a cross-dressing child prostitute, drug addict, vagrant, and AIDS victim. Among the fake transgendered prostitute's celebrity entourage were Lou Reed, Courtney Love, Winona Ryder, Carrie Fisher, Tatum O'Neal, Debbie Harry, Madonna, and Liv Tyler—all of whom, when assembled under one roof, conveniently constitute a quorum for a 12-step meeting.

The con artist LeRoy explained his attraction to celebrities, saying, "Artists want to hang out with other artists because that's the language they talk"[9]—which may have been the truest thing "he" said. The nonexistent LeRoy was celebrated in a glamorous write-up in *Vanity Fair,* a glowing profile in the *New York Times,* and a song, "Cherry Lips," by Shirley Manson—a trio of honors known in the Hamptons as a "hat trick." A fawning piece in the *Boston Globe* said of LeRoy's hard-luck stories, the "perversity of religious fundamentalists is a near constant in American gothic writing."[10] Everything always changes, except the avant-garde, which is always the same.

But the love from Hiplandia came to a crashing halt when it was discovered that there was no JT LeRoy. The books were written by Laura Albert, a middle-class woman in her forties. Savannah Knoop, the half-sister of Albert's boyfriend, had been enlisted to play LeRoy in public. Is it possible that trendy airheads would have swooned over these con artists had they instead impersonated a brave U.S. Marine? How would a Horatio Alger type do in Hollywood these days?

Even grifters know that to be embraced by the cool people in America, you must claim to be a victim, preferably abused by religious fundamentalists.

In a related phenomenon, various half-black celebrities insist on representing themselves simply as "black"—the better to race-bait their way to success. Actress Halle Berry, singer Alicia Keys, and matinee idol Barack Obama were all abandoned by their black fathers and raised by their white mothers. But instead of seeing themselves as half-white, they prefer to see the glass as half-black. They all choose to identify with the fathers who ditched them, while insulting the women who struggled to raise them.

In 2002, Berry engaged in wild race-baiting to win her Oscar and then ate up most of the awards show with an interminable acceptance speech claiming that her award was "so much bigger than me." People who say "it's bigger than me" always mean it's just about them. During the 2008 campaign, Barack Obama repeatedly said the exact same thing: "This election is bigger than me."[11] Would they be able to pawn off their personal victories as transformative events for the nation if they were not claiming to be doing it for the blacks?

The mediocre-sounding, award-winning songstress Keys casually mentioned in a March 2008 interview with *Blender* magazine that the government had instigated shoot-outs between rappers Biggie Smalls and Tupac "to stop another great black leader from existing." Keys boasted of wearing a necklace made of metal from an AK-47 machine gun, the weapon of choice for drive-by shooters—"to symbolize strength, power and killing 'em dead"—and of reading numerous bi-ographies of "Black Panther leaders."[12]

Her black father abandoned Ms. Keys's Italian-American mother, who raised Keys, sacrificed to give her classical piano lessons, but evidently isn't important enough to register in her daughter's sense of her own ethnicity. This is a strange twist on the "one drop" rule, once used by white racists to denigrate those of mixed race but now seized upon by celebrities eager to acquire Victim Chic.

The downward spiral into liberal insanity began when liberals adopted blacks as their special victims. What had started as a legitimate cause—no racial discrimination—was soon being used as a battering ram by feminists, gays, illegal aliens, and "people of color." I reached my limit when Asians started complaining about being called "model minorities." They were victims of other people's esteem for them!

For decades, the Democratic Party had ferociously enforced legal race discrimination. So they wanted a do-over, allowing them to cast themselves as the heroes the next time around. This is why the Left is constantly trying to gin up phony racial crises in a nation where none exist. They were finally willing to take a stand against racism at the precise moment in time when no one was for racism.

Today there are more men who are sexually aroused by women in stiletto heels crushing live frogs to death while talking erotically to the frog than there are members of the Ku Klux Klan. And that's in the en-tire nation—in New York City the frog fetishists probably outnumber the Klan by 500 to 1.[13] (Philosophy professor Richard C. Richards of California State Polytechnic University in Pomona told the *New York Times* that there are about a thousand "crush fetishists" in the country, adding, "I think it's wrong to demonize these things.")[14]

And yet students at Columbia University claim to be seized by a paralyzing terror of white supremacists. In 2007, a psychology and edu-cation professor at Columbia who specialized in racial issues was em-broiled in a plagiarism investigation. The professor defended herself by claiming that the charges themselves were evidence of the "structural racism that pervades this institution," saying that as "one of only two tenured black women full professors at Teachers College, it pains me to conclude that I have been specifically and systematically targeted."

In an amazing coincidence, just as the investigation was heating up, a noose was found hanging on the professor's office door. The apparent hate crime roiled the city and made national news for weeks. Eventually, the noose investigation quietly disappeared, unsolved, but the professor was fired for plagiarism the following year.[15]

The only shocking fact about a noose showing up on a university campus would be if an actual racist put it there. Example after example of the racism allegedly sweeping the nation's campuses keeps turning out to be a fraud. While liberals go around physically assaulting conservatives, they pretend to live in terror of jackbooted racist thugs.

In 2007, vicious anti-Muslim flyers were posted all over the George Washington University campus—by leftists, of course, including a member of Iraq Veterans Against the War. When it was thought the leaflets were from the conservative group Young America's Foundation (YAF), the university president called the flyers "reprehensible" and the university demanded that YAF officers sign a statement disavowing "hate speech." The executive vice president of the student association called for the expulsion of the culprits. But when it turned out leftists had distributed the flyers, the university dropped the matter.[16] Only because of the uproar from conservatives did the university, one month later, put the liberal students on "probation" and ask them to pay a $25 fine.

In 2004, dormitory walls at the College of Wooster in Ohio were defaced with obscenity-laced racist and anti-Semitic messages, some nearly as graphic as the lyrics on the new Kanye West CD. Included among the obscenities was the message "Vote Goldwater"—which was the first clue the graffiti was written by liberals, since Goldwater died in 1998. According to the student government president, most of the campus believed the perpetrators were "drunk, white males"—or as another student put it, a "typical white male." But eventually it emerged that the real culprits were a group of leftist students led by a black studies major.[17]

Also in 2004, a white, Catholic visiting professor at Claremont

McKenna College claimed her car had been vandalized with racist and anti-Semitic graffiti, with the words "Shut Up!" spray-painted on the hood of her car. This—at the very moment she was giving a talk on intolerance! It was just a little too ironic. But the suggestion that the hate crime was a hoax sent liberals into further depths of self-despair. One student angrily told the *Los Angeles Times* that anyone thinking it could be a hoax was "so sick, they are in denial. People don't want to accept that a well-educated, liberal community can have hate."[18]

Classes were canceled and demonstrations swept the campus. The professor was not black or Jewish, but was converting to Judaism and was an outspoken opponent of racism—which takes guts on a college campus. Far from being "silenced," this anonymous mountebank was given a national microphone to bore us with her race-gender-culture theories. Can you guess what happened next? Yes, the vandalism turned out to have been perpetrated by the professor herself when eyewitnesses identified her as the one who had spray-painted her own car.[19]

In 2002, vile racial epithets and other racist graffiti were scrawled on dorm room doors at Ole Miss, producing mass protests and a "Say No to Racism" march—just in time to counter the proposed "Say Yes to Racism" rally at Ole Miss. A university police official gravely warned that the offending parties could be prosecuted for "criminal charges, possibly a felony, or it could be a federal offense."[20]

Then the school learned that the graffiti had been written by black students. No criminal charges were brought.[21]

In 1997, at Duke University, a black doll was found hanging by a noose from tree at the precise spot where the Black Student Alliance planned to hold a rally against racism. Two black students later admitted they were the culprits and were immediately praised for bringing attention to the problem of racism on campus.[22] Which is why I'm thinking about knocking over a liquor store to focus attention on the problem of big-city crime.

Rather than "institutional racism," what we are witnessing is "institutional racial hoaxism" committed by liberals. Will anyone rally against that? In the future, I plan to checkmate liberals by claiming to have found a noose on my office door and wailing that I was shocked, nauseated, appalled, dizzy. I will not be silenced! In fairness, I wasn't particularly silenced before. But what the heck—everyone else gets people to treat them nicely for a few weeks after "discovering" nooses they hung themselves.

Meanwhile, when real victims of racism and sexism appear on the very same campus, liberals lead the lynch mob against them. In 2006, a group of white Duke lacrosse players was falsely accused of gang raping a black stripper. Despite the fact that the evidence against the players quickly unraveled, the *New York Times* doggedly refused to tell the truth about the case. At the university itself, professors and administrators attacked the victims of the false accusation, both publicly and privately. In an open letter that presumed the innocent players guilty, gender and ethnic studies professors droned on about the "racism and sexism" that students "live with every day"—mostly thanks to the professors who signed that letter and never apologized, even after the players were completely exonerated. Liberals love nothing more than these constant self-righteous-athons—as if they would ever have the courage to stand up for any cause not universally supported by everyone around them.

Elizabeth Edwards acknowledged the value of being a certified victim in politics by ruefully complaining during the 2007 Democratic primary, "We can't make John black, we can't make him a woman."[23] (Well, they can't make him black.) Even if they can't be black—in fact, even if they are the opposite of black, like Jacob Weisberg—liberals love to speak for the blacks. Denouncing racism, which no one defends, allows them to borrow from blacks to portray themselves as victims. Throughout the 2008 campaign, white liberals issued dire warnings that the only thing that could prevent Obama from becoming the next president was racism. Writing in the liberal *Slate* magazine, Weisberg said that only if Obama won would children in America be able to "grow up thinking of prejudice as a nonfactor in their lives." But if Obama lost, "our children will grow up thinking of equal opportunity as a myth. His defeat would say that when handed a perfect opportunity to put the worst part of our history behind us, we chose not to."[24]

Fortuitously for the liberal Weisberg, Obama also happened to be the most left-wing person ever to run for president in the United States on a major-party ticket. If Republicans were running black Republicans Michael Steele, Ken Blackwell, or Condoleezza Rice for president, would liberals tell us that only racism could prevent them from becoming president? Say—do we need to send federal civil rights monitors into Maryland and Ohio right now, on account of the fact that Steele and Blackwell lost recent elections in those states?

Policymaking by victim status inevitably creates real victims. For openers, being a media-certified victim does not bring out the best in people. Once you are a victim, you can do anything—lord your victimhood over others, behave abominably, tell lies, commit crimes, slander willfully—and liberals will give you a standing ovation.

This is why the O.J. murder trial was the best thing that ever happened to blacks in America. As it happens, the one thing even certified victims can't do is wildly cheer the acquittal of a double murderer. That is what finally ended the patience of ordinary people for liberal patronization of blacks.

By that point, tender liberal ministrations toward the black community had nearly destroyed it. The black illegitimacy rate was through the roof and the criminal behavior that flows from such a massive social breakdown was on full display. And yet people would still listen in rapt attention to pompous liberal blowhards at dinner parties opining that the reason blacks committed crimes was white racism. Even after decades of racial quotas and set-asides, and endless rallies, sit-ins, demonstrations, and chitchat about racism in America, white people were still so guilty about how blacks had been treated by a minority of thugs three or four decades earlier most people would respond, "Gosh, that's so profound."

It wasn't black people's job to tell whites to stop being pussies, it was white people's job to stop being pussies.

The O.J. verdict finally did that. At last, reasonable people began to roll their eyes when white liberals and professional blacks droned on about racism. The shocking images of law students at Howard University cheering a black man who had just gotten away with two heinous murders was the end of the infantilization of blacks in America.

But it was a good run, which is why from college campuses, to the literary world, to public discourse, to politics—everyone wants to be a victim.

LIBERALS LIVE IN A WORLD IN WHICH EVERYONE IS EITHER AN oppressor or a victim. In this rather extreme morality play, they control the casting: They are always the victims, and conservatives are always the oppressors. These dramatic productions are brought to you by network television, the *New York Times*, and NPR, with the Greek chorus backing them up on cable. The plots are so well known that liberals of various stripes have memorized their parts and take the stage eagerly, hoping to deliver a best-supporting actor performance, for which they might win, say, a Pulitzer, a university chair, or a Sunday morning interview with Tom Brokaw.

The rest of us are forced to live in liberals' fantasy lives, inasmuch as liberals command a monopoly on the writing of these morality plays. Naturally, they are irredeemably hostile to outsiders such as Fox News and Rush Limbaugh, who would audaciously suggest that Joe Wilson has been fatally miscast in the role of Victim. Nobody likes a critic.

The establishment media are the most powerful force in the nation and yet they are constantly claiming to speak up for the little guy and berating those whom they call "the powerful." In this affectation, they are like the fake blind guy asking for spare change and then beating street urchins when no one is looking.

The media are irreducibly powerful because they produce everything we know about the world outside of our personal experience. And these are people whose morality is so perverse that, as Brent Bozell of the Media Research Center pointed out, "they showed more outrage at John McCain featuring a picture of Paris Hilton in a commercial for two eye blinks than for Edwards catting around on a dying spouse."

How the media report stories, which stories they report, and which they don't report create the universe of accepted facts. As Newman said of the post office in the sitcom *Seinfeld*, "When you control the mail, you control information." Even sports columns have a political agenda, such as Robert Lipsyte's pompous denunciation of Cold War politics in a 1995 *New York Times* sports page column. Remarking on Mickey Mantle's liver disease, Lipsyte said:

> And like America in the 50s, he was burdened with a distant sense of doom. For America it was the threat of atomic attack by the Soviet Union. . . . The threats to both America and Mantle ultimately proved empty, but they dominated the psyche of the country and the center fielder and gave each an urgency and a poignancy that affected behavior in often destructive ways. America abused itself with the cold war. Mantle had booze.[25]

You could hear a pin drop. When Lipsyte announced he was leaving the sports page to write about politics full-time, his editor stopped him just in the nick of time: *Don't do it, Robert! You'll hurt yourself—you're not smart enough!*

What keeps people reading the *New York Times*—to the extent people still are reading the *Times*—is not the paper's brave editorial stance on Iraq. It is the massive coverage that can only be provided by more than a thousand reporters, editors, photographers, and newsroom staff. A newspaper with the vast resources of the *Times* that had a reputation for editorial evenhandedness would do even better. But the relentless censorship and partisanship of the major media made alternative media sources such as Fox News not only possible, but necessary.

The expansion of the alternative media in the last decade has allowed a breach in the wall of sound of the one-party establishment media, at least for those who take the trouble to seek out commentary to the right of V. I. Lenin. So now the big complaint from the Left is that people can pick their own news sources—also known as "choice." Liberals fret that people will only be exposed to "Me-zines" and "The Daily Me"—as if the *New York Times* were not exactly that. This represents a crisis: No one can be forced to read the *New York Times* anymore! What will become of us?

Liberals carry on so about Fox News Channel that one almost forgets how much power the establishment media still have. After half a century of being attacked by every possible news outlet, Republicans have the Stockholm syndrome. They're so tickled to have one fair and balanced cable channel in an ocean of liberal advocacy that it doesn't even cross their minds to be shocked when the Democratic candidates for president refuse to participate in a debate on Fox News—the highest-rated news station on cable TV—on the grounds that the channel is "conservative." These same Democrats were, however, willing to submit to questions from a talking snowman on the CNN/YouTube debate. If any TV station were treated like this during the mythical "McCarthy era," I would admit that liberals' claims of blacklisting were not entirely imaginary.

It is impossible to imagine Republicans self-righteously spurning a debate sponsored by CBS News—the station that once employed left-wing conspiracy nut Dan Rather. Indeed, for reasons that remain obscure, Republican candidates for president submitted to partisan harangues from Chris Matthews in a debate on unfair and mentally unbalanced MSNBC, which incidentally has about one-third the viewers of Fox News.

By any objective standard, Fox News is a more respected and respectable news outlet than MSNBC—to say nothing of CNN, ABC, CBS, and NBC. It has a greater variety of opinion, including liberal hosts Chris Wallace, Shep Smith, Greta Van Susteren, and Geraldo Rivera, and even its one clearly conservative host, Sean Hannity, is balanced by his liberal cohost Alan Colmes. Hannity also happens to preside over the second-most-watched program on all of cable news. Fox News has never been caught promoting a fraud—unlike CBS (Bush National Guard story), ABC (tobacco industry report),[26] NBC (exploding GM trucks),[27] CNN (Tailwind),[28] and MSNBC (Keith Olbermann).

In 2008, the Democratic governor of Pennsylvania, Ed Rendell, said that "starting in Iowa and up to the present—Fox has done the fairest job, and remained the most objective of all the cable networks."[29] Even Hillary Clinton agreed that Fox News had the fairest political coverage, citing an independent study showing that. Noting the "pattern of demeaning comments" made on NBC networks, Hillary remarked that MSNBC hadn't issued apologies for commentary "that might have merited one."[30]

But reality is irrelevant. Fox News does not ferociously promote a left-wing agenda, so liberals do not consider it real news. That Fox News is "partisan" has been agreed upon by the establishment media and they have determined that they determine what reality is. It's as if we're speaking French and they're speaking Urdu. Instead of responding to the smashing success of Fox News by becoming more balanced and thereby winning more viewers, the establishment media have apparently decided to wait Fox out. Roger Ailes can't live forever.

Seized by their Stockholm syndrome, Republicans had to be forced by livid rank and file conservatives to register a mild objection when it was revealed that the moderator of the vice presidential debate, Gwen Ifill—of the totally nonpartisan Public Broadcasting Service—was writing a book titled *The Breakthrough: Politics and Race in the Age of Obama*.[31] Only because the author of the Sweetness & Light blog happened to be searching Amazon for another Obama book was this startling fact discovered before the debate. The book was scheduled to be released on Inauguration Day, so its prospects obviously depended to a great degree on Obama's being elected. There wouldn't be much of a "breakthrough" if he lost.

In no other circumstance would anyone conceive of allowing a self-interested party to mediate such a contest. It would be as if a Miss America judge had a book coming out titled *The Breakthrough: Beauty Contests in the Age of Miss South Dakota* before the winner had been chosen. Would anyone consider permitting a sports referee to bet on the game or a judge to have a financial interest in a case's outcome? No, of course, not—it's utter madness. But when it comes to the media, even after the explosion of alternative news sources, nonliberal news sources are still the redheaded stepchild.

Accustomed to being abused by the media, Americans meekly submit to boring debates focusing on the political fetishes of people living in Manhattan and Los Angeles. The difference between the forum moderated by Rick Warren of the Saddleback Church and the debates moderated by the dinosaur media was like the difference between great literature and *Screw* magazine.

Warren asked the candidates about abortion, their moral failings, the wisest people in their lives, taxes ("Define 'rich'"), what's worth dying for, war, AIDS, religious persecution, and human trafficking.

The mainstream media moderators asked questions like "Who would you name as your Treasury secretary?" It was as if all the big questions had been resolved by PBS and the *New York Times,* and now we just needed to know about staffing decisions. How about illegal immigration? Guns? Taxes? None of that interested liberals. Gwen Ifill asked the vice presidential candidates about global warming. A series of *Washington Post* polls from 2007 to 2008 found that global warming was the most important issue for 0 percent of voters.[32] No matter. Liberals with beachfront haciendas are scared to death of global warming's effect on beach erosion, so that's what the candidates were asked.

This is still how we choose the leader of the free world!

But liberals blandly deny that there is a liberal establishment. After decades of angrily denouncing the reams and reams of evidence that the media were massively left-wing, one day, liberals began admitting that the media had once been liberal—but those days were long past. On a typical night of CNN coverage during the 2008 Republican National Convention, CNN had conservative commentators Alex Castellanos, Tara Wall, Leslie Sanchez, and Bill Bennett. Balancing out the four conservatives were eight liberals—Donna Brazile, Roland Martin, Paul Begala, James Carville, Gloria Borger, Dana Bash, David Gergen, and Jeffrey Toobin.

It's as if Fox News never happened.

On evenly balanced CNN that night, the insipid David Gergen claimed to be baffled by Mitt Romney's reference to a "liberal establishment" in his convention speech.

DAVID GERGEN: Mitt Romney tried to argue last night about some liberal establishment, which doesn't exist anymore. . . .

ALEX CASTELLANOS: In all honesty, I think if David Gergen thinks the liberal establishment does not exist anymore, I

think he has become a part of it. I think Republicans at
this convention will have a very different view of that. . . .

GERGEN: . . . [I]f there has been a liberal establishment, it
shrunk a lot and it's not right in Washington. That's a '70s
concept, Alex. You know that.[33]

Obviously, it doesn't take much to be a professor at Harvard's
John F. Kennedy School of Government, where the students are willing
to spend $50,000 to have their names associated with the most low-
brow of the Harvard degrees.

If there used to be a liberal establishment, how have things
changed? There's Fox News, talk radio, and the Internet. Meanwhile,
liberals plotting to undermine Fox News are itching to bring back the
"Fairness Doctrine" to destroy talk radio and invoke campaign finance
laws to restrict speech on the Internet.

Consider that the first small breach in the liberal media behemoth
came about only because Ronald Reagan's Federal Communications
Commission repealed the "Fairness Doctrine" in 1987. The Rush Limbaugh show premiered on August 1, 1988. Illustrating the irony of its
name, the "Fairness Doctrine" does not apply to TV stations, newspapers, magazines, or Hollywood movies. Only on the radio is the government required to enforce "fairness."

By mandating that any political views disseminated over the radio
be counterbalanced by the opposing view, the "Fairness Doctrine" not
only requires radio stations to give boring crackpots airtime, it also creates a conceptual and administrative nightmare. What is fair? There are
conservative and liberal views—but there are also libertarian, Green
party, Federalist, and Marxist views. (Though the liberals will tend to
have the Marxist arguments covered.) The problem isn't just the paperwork stations would have to fill out. It's also that radio stations would
have to start balancing three hours of Rush Limbaugh (20 million listeners) with three hours of Randi Rhodes (6 listeners) every day. Reim-
plementation of the "Fairness Doctrine" spells the end of talk radio.

So naturally Democrats are itching to bring it back! Democrats
have already passed two bills reinstating the "Fairness Doctrine" since

its merciful repeal—both vetoed, by Republican presidents Reagan and George H. W. Bush.[34] Congresswoman Nancy Pelosi and Senators Jeff Bingaman, Richard Durbin, Dianne Feinstein, John Kerry, and Chuck Schumer—all Democrats—have said they want to reinstate the "Fairness Doctrine."

A Clinton-appointed judge has found that speech on the Internet is also subject to federal control. In 2004, U.S. District Court judge Colleen Kollar-Kotelly ordered the Federal Election Commission (FEC) to consider extending the McCain-Feingold speech restrictions to the Internet, saying that exempting the Internet has allowed the "rampant circumvention of the campaign finance laws."[35] Evidently, excluding Hollywood movies and TV shows, magazines, newspapers, and the broadcast and cable networks from federal speech restrictions poses no such threat to the campaign finance laws.

Once the government has muzzled speech on talk radio and the Internet, we can happily return to a world called "1984." The establishment media will heave a sigh of relief and say, "Thank God that's over!" Then they can go back to insisting that the idea of the "liberal establishment" is a kooky conservative conspiracy theory. There's your liberal establishment that Gergen says "doesn't exist anymore."

THE MEDIA ARE SO PARTISAN THAT MANY PEOPLE ARE UNDER the impression that they must take their marching orders directly from the Democratic National Committee. But journalists aren't merely the willing recipients of information from campaign consultants: They are active participants in Democratic campaigns. As difficult as it is to separate them, the Democratic Party is beholden to the media, not the other way around.

It wasn't the Kerry campaign calling in the Bush National Guard hoax in to CBS News. It was the reverse: Dan Rather's producer at CBS, Mary Mapes, called Kerry campaign official Joe Lockhart about Bush's fake National Guard scandal, imploring him to call CBS's trusted source and proven liar Bill Burkett.[36]

And it wasn't House Democrats who launched the Mark Foley e-mail scandal,[37] that was ABC News. House pages had complained about receiving inappropriate e-mails and instant messages from Republican representative Mark Foley as far back as 2000 or 2001. House Democrats didn't care. The media did—precisely one month before a hard-fought midterm congressional election and one day after the deadline for removing Foley's name from the Florida ballot. (All I can say is, thank God a good, faithful Democrat took Foley's old seat so there won't be any more sex scandals in Palm Beach County!)

True, the Democrats and the media are generally fighting for the same thing: the total destruction of the United States of America. But when their interests collide, as they did when Hillary was in a primary against spine-tingler Obama, we see who wins.

In the 2008 election season, it wasn't the Obama campaign but the *New York Times* that put a thinly sourced article about an alleged John McCain affair on its front page. It wasn't the Democratic National Committee but a newspaper reporter, David Singleton of the *Scranton Times-Tribune,* who invented the story about Republican crowds yelling "Kill him!" about Obama at a Palin rally.[38] It wasn't the Obama campaign but the *Times* that put an angry, and yet still pointless, Alaska ethics report on Governor Sarah Palin on its front page.

On the main charge against Palin, the firing of her public safety commissioner, the investigators found it "was a proper and lawful exercise of her constitutional and statutory authority" to fire her own department head. Though the report doesn't dwell on it, this particular public safety commissioner was badly in need of firing. In the midst of the Palin family's formal complaints about state trooper and former Palin brother-in-law Mike Wooten for threatening her family, drinking on the job, and Tasering Palin's nephew, the public safety commission asked the governor to sign a photo of a state trooper, in uniform, saluting the flag for the purpose of turning the photo into a poster. The trooper chosen for this photo was none other than . . . Mike Wooten![39]

But the report also accused Palin of "abuse by inaction" for not preventing her husband from complaining about Wooten. Notwithstanding Palin's stated fear of the trooper, the report concluded that this was not a genuine fear because according to the geniuses on the investigating panel, getting Wooten fired would not make him any less dangerous. "On the contrary," the report advised, "it might just precipitate some retaliatory conduct on his part."

So whatever you do, do not complain about abusive cops: They might retaliate! Though I still think it might make them a little less dangerous to take away their badges and guns.

Out of more than forty newspaper and wire stories on the legislature's report the day after it was released, most with banner headlines declaring Palin GUILTY, only twenty documents even mentioned that the trooper in question had Tasered his ten-year-old stepson. The *New York Times* was not among them.

Instead, *Times* reporter Serge F. Kovaleski described the Palin family's interest in the trooper as resulting from "a harsh divorce and child-custody battle" with Palin's sister.[40] This would be like describing Justin Volpe's sodomitic broomstick attack on Abner Louima as an "enhanced interrogation."

One imagines a normal person trying to grasp what happened after reading the *New York Times* version of the story:

NORMAL PERSON: Why was Palin trying to fire this guy?

REPORTER: Because she's a horrible person.

NORMAL PERSON: Yeah, but what was her reason? She must have had a reason.

REPORTER: Don't worry, it's not important.

NORMAL PERSON: If you don't tell me, I'm going online to find out.

REPORTER: He Tasered her ten-year-old nephew, threatened to kill his father-in-law, and drank on the job, but anyway, she's a horrible person!

NORMAL PERSON: HE WHAT!

No wonder the establishment media are so frustrated with the Internet.

In any other connection, a woman going through a divorce from a cop who had made threats against her father and Tasered her son would be a Lifetime TV (for women) movie. The media had to do a highly unusual 180-degree turn on cops to make Sarah Palin the villain in this story. My own position is that sometimes cops are innocent and sometimes they are guilty, but I need to know the facts. It's good to know that the Left's new default position is: "We always believe the cop." That represents a major policy shift.

The smear tactics used by the media against McCain and Palin show the absurdity of the Left's claims of perpetual victimization at the hands of the Republican Attack Machine. While Republican "attacks" went out on little Web videos and in campaign stump speeches—just like the Democratic attacks on Republicans—liberal attacks on McCain and Palin went out in AP wire reports, *Saturday Night Live* sketches, and CBS News interviews.

Again: it wasn't the Democrats who started calling Sarah Palin a racist: It was the media. On October 5, the objective, nonpartisan Associated Press reported that Palin's statement that Obama was "palling around with terrorists"—referring to the white, privileged, cretinous member of the Weather Underground Bill Ayers—"was unsubstantiated and carried a racially tinged subtext that John McCain himself may come to regret."[41] The following week, Democratic politicians joined the media bandwagon, when Representatives Gregory Meeks, Ed Towns, and Yvette Clarke all called Palin a racist.

Apparently, in addition to raising Obama's fraternizing with a white domestic terrorist, Palin had used the racist code words "Joe Six-Pack" and "Hockey Mom." If those were code words, they were extremely subtle. In fact, I think the NAACP would give you a pass on "Joe Six-Pack" and "Hockey Mom."

But Representative Clarke demanded to know "Who exactly is Joe Six-Pack and who are these hockey moms?" The same people who said they couldn't have a conversation that didn't include the phrase "lipstick on a pig" now claimed they had never heard the expression "Joe Six-Pack." Clarke continued, "Is that supposed to be terminology that is of common ground to all Americans? I don't find that. It leaves a lot of people out."[42] Many had hoped that the nomination of the first black man for president would end the playing of the pinot noir card, but it was not to be.

It's a symbiotic relationship the Democrats and the media have, with the media sometimes concocting their own rogue attacks on Republicans and sometimes getting their arguments directly from Democratic talking points. Take the *New York Times*'s Katherine Q. Seelye, for example.

On October 15, 2008, the Obama campaign's internal predebate talking points were inadvertently released to the media. They said:

- This is John McCain's last chance to turn this race around and somehow convince the American people that his erratic response to this economic crisis doesn't disqualify him from being president.
- Just this weekend, John McCain vowed to "whip Obama's you-know-what" at the debate, and he's indicated that he'll be bringing up Bill Ayers to try to distract voters.
- So we know that Senator McCain will come ready to attack Barack Obama and bring his dishonorable campaign tactics to the debate stage.
- John McCain has been erratic and unsteady since this crisis began, staggering from position to position and trying to change the subject away from the economy by launching false character attacks.[43]

Katharine Q. Seelye's October 15, 2008, *New York Times* article, "What to Watch for During the Final Debate," included the following points in her news analysis—observations that were uncannily similar to the Obama campaign's talking points:

- "Tonight's debate provides Senator John McCain with his last, best hope of reversing the tide that appears to be running against him."
- "Mr. McCain has already vowed to 'whip' Mr. Obama's 'you-know-what' tonight. At the same time, watch to see if Mr. McCain raises the matter of Mr. Obama's past association with William Ayers, the former 1960s radical."
- "Watch for the degree to which Mr. McCain dials back his attacks, as he has on the campaign trail."

■ "His behavior during the current crisis—from announcing a brief suspension of his campaign to offering a plan during the last debate for buying up bad mortgages—appeared to have the effect of undermining voter confidence and driving away independents."

One would hope that professional journalists wouldn't typically reprint Democratic talking points as news. More often, what professional journalists do is manufacture their own mock outrages against Republicans and then hand-deliver the fake scandal to the Democrats, who act dutifully shocked.

According to his devoted media claque, Obambi was a victim of "guilt by association" whenever anyone mentioned his two-decade association with a racist preacher or his ties to an unrepentant domestic terrorist. Being offended by "guilt by association" was another new posture for liberals, who heretofore had specialized in making guilt-by-association charges.

Republican politicians who had given speeches to a conservative group, the Council of Conservative Citizens (CCC), were branded sympathizers of white supremacists because some of the directors of the CCC had, decades earlier, been leaders of a segregationist group, the Citizen Councils of America, which were founded in 1954. There is no evidence on its Web page that the modern incarnation of the CCC supports segregation, though its "Statement of Principles" offers that the organization opposes "forced integration" and "efforts to mix the races of mankind." But mostly the principles refer to subjects such as a strong national defense, the right to keep and bear arms, the traditional family, and an "America First" trade policy.[44]

Apart from some aggressive reporting on black-on-white crimes—the very crimes that are aggressively hidden by the establishment media—there is little on the CCC website suggesting that the group is a "thinly veiled white supremacist" organization, as the *New York Times* calls it in one of its more charitable descriptions. At least the crimes reported on the CCC's Web page actually happened, as opposed to the Reverend Jeremiah Wright's claim that the U.S. government invented AIDS to kill blacks.

Republicans Senator Trent Lott and Representative Bob Barr did nothing more than give speeches to the CCC, yet they were forever damned by their association with it. Neither man even belonged to the CCC, nor did they attend CCC meetings once a week for twenty years. They certainly didn't have their daughters baptized by CCC activists.

But according to the establishment media, Lott and Barr were fully responsible for the decades-old affiliations of some of the directors of a group . . . because they spoke at the CCC. As the media's hysteria about the CCC reached a fever pitch, a *Times* editorial howled about "fresh evidence of the persistence of racism" on the part of Lott based on his "links to the white separatist group called the Council of Conservative Citizens." The *New York Times* was shocked by the group's "thinly veiled white supremacist agenda," but was somewhat more accepting of the completely unveiled racism of Obama's preacher.[45] One surmises that the CCC's thin veil of white supremacy would have become a bit thicker had Democratic congressman Dick Gephardt ever been a serious candidate for president. In the 1970s, he had spoken to a branch of the related, but more outré, Citizen Councils of America.[46] That, and the fact that he's a preposterous boob, are probably the only two things that kept Dick Gephardt out of the White House.

After the initial flurry of articles, editorials, and news stories in the *Times* excitedly reporting that Barr had spoken to the CCC, Democratic representative Bob Wexler introduced a resolution in Congress for the sole purpose of denouncing the Council of Conservative Citizens.[47] Other than the 9/11 terrorists, the CCC may be the only group ever singled out for denunciation in a congressional resolution. How about a resolution from Obama pom-pom girl Wexler on Obama's Trinity United Church of Christ?

When Barr later gave a speech on the House floor favorably citing President John F. Kennedy, Senator Ted Kennedy's son, Representative Patrick Kennedy, got in Barr's face, shouting, "How dare you! Anybody who has been to a racist group has no right invoking my uncle's memory!"[48] Liberals are now reserving the right to tell us which former presidents we can mention by name.

Barr had given a speech to a group that, even assuming everything that the Southern Poverty Law Center says about it is true, does not hold a candle to the racism of Obama's Trinity United Church of Christ. Obama was married by the Reverend Wright, his daughters were baptized by the Reverend Wright, Obama gave his second autobiography the title of one of the Reverend Wright's sermons. And yet after decades of majoring in Guilt by Association, liberals were indignant when an ad on cable television linked Obama and the Reverend Jeremiah Wright Jr. The *Times* produced a blistering editorial decrying the "hate mongering" and calling the ads "the product of a radical fringe that has little regard for rational debate."[49]

Liberals, who will attack with whatever is available because they have no principles, were also appalled by any attempt to link Obama to Bill Ayers. In an op-ed so clever she couldn't stand herself, *New York Times* columnist Gail Collins wrote that if Obama was responsible for Ayers's actions then she was responsible for the banking scandals of the eighties by virtue of the fact that savings-and-loan king Charles Keating had spoken at her high school thirty years earlier. Collins's satirical chain of causation did not, however, apply to Republicans speaking to a group containing members who had belonged to a segregationist group thirty years earlier, which, come to think of it, pretty much describes Collins's connection to the banking scandals.[50]

Can Trent Lott and Bob Barr get an apology now?

THE ESTABLISHMENT MEDIA'S MOST COMICAL DOUBLE STANdard appears in their treatment of gays. Liberals claim to love gays when it allows them to vent their spleen at Republicans. But disagree with liberals and their first response is to call you gay. Liberals are gays' biggest champions on issues most gays couldn't care less about, like gay marriage or taxpayer funding of photos of men with bullwhips up their derrieres. But who has done more to out, embarrass, and destroy the lives of gay men who prefer to keep their orientation private than Democrats? Who is more intolerant of gays in the Republican Party than gays in the Democratic Party?

Speaking of very gay people, take *New York Times* columnist Frank Rich. In a blind rage at Karl Rove, Rich announced that Rove's late father was gay, citing a book by the Rove-obsessed authors of *Bush's Brain*, one a columnist for the *Huffington Post*.

First, let's pause to appreciate the irony of being called gay by Frank Rich and a columnist on the *Huffington Post*. Here is a case study for the psychoanalysts. One of Rich's friends needs to take him aside and tell him to stop taking the lead on outing gays. Let someone else do it, Frank—you're not exactly the butchest guy on the planet. Meanwhile, the *Huffington Post* is made possible because such an un-calculating, simple person as Arianna Huffington acquired millions of dollars by marrying a very rich gay man.

These are the people Frank Rich cites in the Newspaper of Record to announce that Karl Rove's father was gay. Rich justifies his postmortem attack on Rove's father by accusing Rove of "dealing the gay card, dating back to the lesbian whispers that pursued Ann Richards." This is like accusing Rove of being the guy who started the rumor that Jerry Nadler was fat.

The Richards rumor required no instigation from Rove. It grew out of Governor Richards's own peculiar habit of announcing the sexual preference of her political appointments: *And today, I announce Texas's first openly gay utility commissioner!* Gay encomiums coming out of the governor's office were so persistent that years later, at the opening of Houston's Museum of Gay, Lesbian, Bisexual and Transgender History, the exhibit included Governor Ann Richards's letter of commendation to a former Health Department caseworker, aka the drag queen "Lady Victoria Lust."[51]

It's a weird thing with Democrats: They love telling complete strangers about their sexual proclivities—or even the sexual proclivities of people they know. At the 1996 Democratic National Convention, the Florida delegation decided to trumpet their diversity by enumerating the gay delegates, including one very much closeted gay man.[52] *Hey! Wait a minute!*

Texans didn't care if government employees were gay, but they didn't need to know about every appointee's sexual preferences. Richards's insistence on telling them was a strange enough habit to ignite rumors without Rove's intervention. In any event, the only person ever to complain about Richards's constant gay alerts was a liberal Republican, state senator Bill Ratliff—as admitted by Rich's own source, the Rove-obsessed *Huffington Post* columnist.[53] I realize that in the world of the Bush-haters, anything any Republican ever says must have come on direct orders from Karl Rove. But back in the Euclidian world, there's no evidence that Rove had anything to do with any rumors that Richards was gay. Frank Rich hates Rove, ergo he calls Rove's father gay.

There is nothing liberals love more than vicious gay-baiting, which they disguise as an attack on "hypocrisy." They throw it out whenever a Republican is caught engaging in any sort of bad behavior, never bothering to check to see if any actual hypocrisy is involved.

When Senator Larry Craig pleaded guilty to disorderly conduct after he was accused of making a foot-tapping proposition to an undercover cop in a Minneapolis Airport bathroom, the media jeeringly gay-baited Craig for a week—and then accused Republicans of being homophobic for not insisting that Craig stay in office and run for reelection so their gay-baiting could continue unabated. Liberals accused Larry Craig of leading a double life, but they are the ones who constantly want to have it both ways. They wanted to be hysterical about Larry Craig—and hysterical about Republicans for not standing by Larry Craig. They wanted to gay-bait Republicans—and accuse Republicans of gay-baiting.

The *Washington Post* ran thirty items on Craig in the month after the story broke. The *New York Times* ran thirty-seven items—and then continued to provide *Times* readers with monthly *Larry Craig: Deviant* updates after that. In five separate columns, Frank Rich sneered about Craig—this from the newspaper that thinks we're wallowing in 9/11 anniversary coverage.

MSNBC's Chris Matthews opened his *Hardball* program on August 28, 2007, "The big story tonight, dirty politics. Idaho senator Larry Craig, cultural warrior of the right, stands naked tonight, exposed as both a sexual deviant and a world-class hypocrite."[54] Normally, using the word "deviant" in reference to a gay person would be a linguistic offense worse than calling college basketball players "nappy-headed hos," but fortunately for Matthews, no one watches *Hardball*.

Naturally, the media claimed that Larry Craig was a hypocrite because he opposed gay marriage—and yet he propositioned an undercover cop in a public bathroom! Hypocrite!

But unless Craig proposed marriage to the undercover cop in the airport bathroom, I'm not seeing the hypocrisy. If Democrats were claiming that Craig was simply a bad person—but not a hypocrite—for living in a sham marriage for political gain, I note that Democrats voted for someone with those credentials for president in 1992 and 1996.

The Craig disorderly conduct charge also allowed *Newsweek*'s Jonathan Alter to resurrect a long-ago-disproved hoax sex scandal out of Nebraska. Claiming that the "conservative-hypocrisy angle goes way back," Alter cited "the Franklin child-sex ring, which ensnared more than a dozen officials in the Reagan and first Bush administrations."[55] It was odd that the rest of the mainstream media had failed to take note of a "child-sex ring" involving "more than a dozen officials in the Reagan and first Bush administrations," but since *Newsweek* tries to pass off Alter as a serious journalist, this required a quick Nexis check.

The "Franklin child-abuse sex scandal" grew out of a 1988 federal embezzlement investigation of Lawrence King, manager of the Franklin Community Federal Credit Union, in Omaha. This was in the midst of the child sex-abuse hysteria of the 1980s, so naturally, state and federal investigators were soon investigating child sex-abuse charges that somehow involved the embezzled money. According to the *New York Times*, two teenagers alleged that as foster children, they had been flown to hotels around the country where they participated in sex orgies attended by prominent Republicans. One teenager claimed she was forced to stand naked in the middle of a party and auctioned off as a sex slave to the highest bidder. A "child care specialist" began telling reporters that one teenager described a party that involved sex between "more than two people, same sex and opposite sex."[56]

Granting that teenagers tend to exaggerate, what part of that story could possibly have been true? Even the *Times* must have smelled a rat, because after one story mentioning the investigation, there were no further articles on foster child sex orgies until July 1990, when the *Times* reported that the story was a hoax. "Lurid reports of child sex abuse, drug trafficking, pornography and political intrigue that have held Omaha enthralled for nearly two years," the *Times* article began, "were a 'carefully crafted hoax,' a county grand jury in Nebraska has concluded."[57]

The two teenagers who concocted the story were indicted for perjury by the grand jury, and two months later a federal grand jury reached the same conclusion and indicted one of the same two accusers on eight counts of perjury.[58]

That was "the Franklin child-sex ring" that Jonathan Alter dramatically rolled out in 2007 to prove Republican "hypocrisy" on family values. Alter's next exposé on Republican hypocrisy on sex? Tawana Brawley! Didn't Brawley accuse a Republican prosecutor of raping her? And how about the Duke lacrosse case? Some of the falsely accused Duke lacrosse players must have been Republicans. This was the equivalent of a column on the mendacity of the Jews that cited the Dreyfus case as proof.

Inasmuch as Alter surely has all back issues in the *New York Times* carefully filed in plastic folders, it appears that he intentionally cited bogus information in a deliberate attempt to reintroduce a hoax into the public bloodstream. At least Dan Rather was actually stupid. Alter's invocation of "the Franklin child-sex ring" may be the most vile lie ever spread by the establishment media. No right-wing radio host has ever propagated such a fraud.

On the bright side, at least his lie appeared only in the pages of *Newsweek* (circulation: 1,123). If Alter were any less physically repellent, he might have said it on TV, and millions more people could have been hoodwinked by this farce.

Meanwhile, just a few years ago, there was a sex story about Bill Clinton that turned out to be true, but it was killed by a magazine called—HEY! That magazine was called "*Newsweek,*" too!

To be fair, in the "Franklin child-sex ring" article, Alter did not rest his case on the hoax scandal. He also cited two gay Republicans exposed in sex scandals a quarter-century earlier. One was a one-term representative from Mississippi, Jon Hinson—yes, *that* Jon Hinson—and the other was the great Maryland Republican Bob Bauman. Alter called Bauman "arguably the single most anti-gay and sanctimonious right-winger in town"—which is liberal-speak for "conservative." Bauman was in fact a strong social conservative who promoted family values. Only liberals consider it offensive for a gay person to have strong morals.

Correction: Earlier in this chapter, in comments on Frank Rich, I was operating under the impression that Rich is gay and castigated him for sneering at gay men. Based on Rich's speaking style and manner, I simply assumed that he was gay, just as I assume that Little Richard is gay. Apparently he is not, and although I consider it a matter of indifference, I apologize if there was any offense taken. In my defense, I submit any video of Frank Rich talking on TV. I insist on an all-black jury.

IT'S A PERVERSE WORLD WHEN THE MOST AGGRESSIVE PEOple are always wailing about their victimhood. In what other place or time have people boasted about how wretched they are? Isn't it more natural to claim to be better than you are than to claim to be worse than you are? But instead of falsely claiming to be rich or of royal lineage, in modern America people seek rewards by falsely asserting they are victims—of homophobes, hypocrites, Karl Rove, racists, Republicans, and oppressive Alaska governors.

Liberals seem to have hit upon a reverse Christ story as their belief system. He suffered and died for our sins; liberals make the rest of us suffer for sins we didn't commit. Their claims of how awful "we" are never seems to encompass themselves in the "we." Saying America is a racist nation is never meant to suggest that the speaker is a racist—it's his neighbors who are the racists. (Especially in Congressman John Murtha's district in Pennsylvania, apparently.) That's not a "mea culpa," it's a "theya culpa."[59]

Ironically, liberals' victim strategy works in this country precisely because of Americans' boundless tenderheartedness and generosity. Sailing to the New World in 1630 on the ship *Arabella*, the Puritans' leader, John Winthrop, announced that they had entered into a covenant with God to create a "city upon a hill." He said if they kept the covenant, "We shall find that the God of Israel is among us, when ten of us shall be able to resist a thousand of our enemies." Noting that "in all times some must be rich, some poor, some high and eminent in power and dignity, others mean and in subjection," Winthrop set forth the principles of Christian charity. He quoted from, among other things, the Book of Isaiah to proclaim the new citizens' obligation to "loose the bands of wickedness, to undo the heavy burdens, and to let the oppressed go free, and . . . break every yoke."[60]

That charitable American instinct has never left us. Even with greedy liberals Krazy-Gluing their wallets shut, Americans give more to charity than the citizens of any other country. After the deadly 2004 tsunami struck, the U.S. government gave $350 million to the victims, which was less than the $800 million given by the German government. But American citizens privately donated $2 billion, while the citizens of other countries gave virtually nothing, allowing their governments' aid to suffice.[61]

The United States government bears most of the cost of NATO, military protection, refugee programs, and even useless international organizations such as the United Nations. But mere governmental figures are the least of it. Americans individually contribute more to charities than any other country—seven times more than Germans and fourteen times more than Italians.

Americans just adore disasters. They love to go in and clean up the mess, get turkeys out to the poor, take up a collection, make sandwiches, build shelters, and raise extravagant amounts of aid. On 9/11, there were more volunteers and more donated blood than the Red Cross could handle. Whether it's a flood in Mississippi, a hurricane in Louisiana, or a little girl falling down a pipe in Texas, Americans are almost greedy for a full-fledged disaster so they can all pitch in and help.

Liberals prey on this deep-seated American instinct to aid the afflicted by constantly bellyaching that they have been mortally offended. They are not offended, they are offending. They are not wounded victims, they are the marauding oppressors. They are not innocents, they are the guilty.

2

VICTIM OF A CRIME?
THANK A SINGLE MOTHER

The most worshiped figure in modern America is the "single mother." Politicians tout their programs by explaining how they will help single mothers. At campaign stops, a sure way to draw applause from the crowd is to introduce single mothers in the audience. No news report on a matter of national importance is complete unless it includes a sound bite from a single mother, preferably one bravely struggling to juggle a career and child-rearing obligations. Christian ministers cite the single mother in their sermons as the personification of selfless virtue. Jesse Jackson—at last count personally responsible for at least one single mother—compares single mothers to Mary the mother of Jesus. Even Superman's girlfriend Lois Lane is a single mother in the 2006 movie *Superman Returns,* in which the Man of Steel plays a superhero deadbeat dad.

Single mothers are not only "Unsung Heroines," as the title of a recent book puts it, they are perennial victims—the unwitting victims of sex with men they're not married to. Over and over again, we are told that this or that policy will result in "single mothers being hit hardest." Newspapers must have a macro on their computers: "single mothers hardest hit."

Bankruptcy reform: "Single mothers especially, are among those hardest hit by bankruptcy reform."[1]

Home oil prices: "Hardest hit by the heating hike will be people like Dena Terrano, 28, an unemployed single mother who has lived with her mother in their Bellevue home for 20 years."[2]

Shift work: "Often working women, particularly single mothers, suffer the most from shift work because the household activities and child-care duties still fall to them, experts said."[3]

Health insurance: "Those hardest hit are women—especially single mothers—and children."[4]

A slowing economy: "Women, and especially single mothers, have been the hardest hit by this economic downturn."[5]

Housing woes: "Single mothers with children are among the hardest hit by the state's shortage of affordable homes and apartments."[6]

Hurricane Katrina: "The most vulnerable populations in New Orleans—the elderly, people with physical and mental disabilities, and single mothers out of the labor market—arguably were hit hardest by Katrina."[7]

Immigration fees: "Single mothers, battered women, the homeless . . . will suffer the most."[8]

Day care: "Hardest hit are single mothers."[9]

Global warming: "The rise of energy prices affects energy accessibility and its usage by the poorest, particularly elderly women and single mothers."[10]

Parents abused by children: "Single mothers appear to suffer the most from child violence."[11]

Grocery stores relocating: "Hardest hit by the exodus are single mothers, the elderly and residents without cars."[12]

The minimum wage: "The minimum wage needs to be raised, and the group it hits the hardest are single mothers."[13]

Workfare rules: "Republican efforts to tighten America's chief welfare plan could drive poor single mothers deeper into poverty, according to a new report."[14]

There is no better example of phony victims who are actually victimizers than single mothers. We're not living in Dickensian England, with husbands dropping like flies from cholera, plague, and industrial accidents, creating blameless single mothers. Charles Dickens's England had single mothers because the average life span for males, circa 1830, ranged from forty-four years for the middle and upper classes down to twenty-two years for laborers. That isn't the reason we have an explosion of single mothers in twenty-first-century America.

We have "single mothers" because more than a million women choose to have children out of wedlock every year in America, and do not then wed or give the babies up for adoption. By their own choices, they consign their children to starting life with second-class status.

Of all single mothers in America, only 6.5 percent of them are widows, 37.8 percent are divorced, and 41.3 percent gave birth out of wedlock.[15] The 6.5 percent of single mothers whose husbands have died shouldn't be called "single mothers" at all. We already have a word for them: "widows." Their children do just fine compared with the children of married parents.[16] Liberals refer to widows as "single mothers" to try to class up the category, much as they do with their infuriating description of the GI Bill as a form of "welfare" or the U.S. military as a successful "government program."

We can't blame mothers who get divorced for being single mothers: We should blame both mothers and fathers. Divorce typically proceeds from adultery, abandonment, or abuse—and there are only two suspects, both of whom are the parents of the children whose lives will forever be harmed by the dissolution of a marriage. After interviewing nearly one hundred children of divorce, Linda Bird Francke, a divorced mother who wrote the book *Growing Up Divorced*, said almost all were sad and virtually all were angry.[17] In any event, divorced mothers should be called "divorced mothers," not "single mothers." We also have a term for the youngsters involved: "the children of divorce," or as I call them, "future strippers." It is a mark of how attractive it is to be a phony victim that divorcées will often claim to belong to the more disreputable category of "single mothers."

Far more cruel than bequeathing your children a broken family through divorce is to raise children out of wedlock. True "single mothers" are women who, by their own volition, have done everything in their power to ruin their children's lives before they're even born. It makes no difference if the pregnancy was unplanned, unwanted, or accidental. And many aren't any of those. Getting pregnant isn't like catching the flu. There are volitional acts involved—someone else explain it to Dennis Kucinich. By this purposeful act, single mothers cause irreparable harm to other human beings—their own children—as countless studies on the subject make clear. Not only do single mothers hurt their children, they also foist a raft of social pathologies on society. Look at almost any societal problem and you will find it is really a problem of single mothers.

IS IT CRUEL TO DESCRIBE THE LIFE CHANCES SINGLE MOTHERS are giving their children? How about compared with actually doing that to children at a rate of about 1.5 million a year?

If a child in the womb could choose one fact about his parents— rich, good-looking, intelligent, easygoing, athletic, went to Harvard, black, or white—the one factor that would improve his life chances more than any other is that they be married. (Or at least the second choice, right after "Mother is not 'pro-choice.'") The only thing a baby shouldn't want is parents who divorce or—worst of all—were never married. That's starting life with a losing hand.

Liberal think tanks denounce efforts to promote marriage, deceptively chirping, as Mary Parke of the Center for Law and Social Policy did, that most children in single-parent homes "grow up without serious problems."[18]

Yes, and most smokers won't die of lung disease.

The evidence of the damage of single parenthood is so blindingly obvious even liberals have started to admit it. A 2004 *New York Times Magazine* article on welfare families by Jason DeParle said, "Mounds of social science, from the left and the right, leave little doubt that the children of single-parent families face heightened risks." Calling a single-parent family "a double dose of disadvantage,"[19] the *Times* article cited as "the definitive text" a book by sociologists Sara McLanahan and Gary Sandefur that concluded, back in 1994, "In our opinion, the evidence is quite clear: Children who grow up in a household with only one biological parent are worse off, on average, than children who grow up in a household with both of their biological parents, regardless of the parents' race or educational background."[20]

That's an understatement. The eminent social scientist Charles Murray says, "Illegitimacy is the single most important social problem of our time—more important than crime, drugs, poverty, illiteracy, welfare or homelessness because it drives everything else."[21]

Here is the lottery ticket that single mothers are handing their innocent children by choosing to raise them without fathers: Controlling for socioeconomic status, race, and place of residence, the strongest predictor of whether a person will end up in prison is that he was raised by a single parent.[22] By 1996, 70 percent of inmates in state juvenile detention centers serving long-term sentences were raised by single mothers.[23] Seventy-two percent of juvenile murderers and 60 percent of rapists come from single-mother homes.[24] Seventy percent of teenage births,[25] dropouts, suicides,[26] runaways, juvenile delinquents, and child murderers involve children raised by single mothers.[27] Girls raised without fathers are more sexually promiscuous and more likely to end up divorced.[28] A 1990 study by the Progressive Policy Institute showed that after controlling for single motherhood, the difference between black and white crime rates disappeared.[29]

Various studies come up with slightly different numbers, but all the figures are grim. According to the Index of Leading Cultural Indicators, children from single-parent families account for 63 percent of all youth suicides, 70 percent of all teenage pregnancies, 71 percent of all adolescent chemical/substance abuse, 80 percent of all prison inmates, and 90 percent of all homeless and runaway children.[30]

A study cited in the *Village Voice* produced similar numbers. It found that children brought up in single-mother homes "are five times more likely to commit suicide, nine times more likely to drop out of high school, 10 times more likely to abuse chemical substances, 14 times more likely to commit rape (for the boys), 20 times more likely to end up in prison, and 32 times more likely to run away from home."[31] Single motherhood is like a farm team for future criminals and social outcasts.

With new children being born, running away, dropping out of high school, and committing murder every year, it's not a static problem to analyze. But however the numbers are run, single motherhood is a societal nuclear bomb.

Many of these studies, for example, are from the 1990s, when the percentage of teenagers raised by single parents was lower than it is today. In 1990, 28 percent of children under eighteen were being raised in one-parent homes (mother or father), and 71 percent were being raised in two-parent homes.[32] By 2005, more than one-third of all babies born in the United States were illegitimate. That's a lot of social problems coming.

Imagine an America with 70 percent fewer juvenile delinquents, 70 percent fewer teenage births, 63 to 70 percent fewer teenage suicides, and 70 percent to 90 percent fewer runaways and you will appreciate what the sainted single mothers have accomplished. Even in liberals' fevered nightmares, predatory mortgage dealers, oil speculators, and Ken Lay could never do as much harm to their fellow human beings as single mothers do.

The problem is not confined to the United States. With a welfare state similar to America's,[33] Britain leads Europe in the proportion of single mothers—and also is ranked by UNICEF at the bottom of all industrialized nations in the well-being of its children. Britain tops the European Union in crime—including violent crime—alcohol and drug abuse, obesity, and sexually transmitted diseases, though some are ties.[34] Citing these statistics in a 2007 article in *Maclean's* magazine, British journalist Martin Newland said, "Increasingly, but belatedly, politicians are beginning to identify the decline of marriage and the family as the major cause of . . . social dysfunctions including ill health, crime, rampant promiscuity and welfare dependency."

Family breakdown is not spread evenly throughout the population. America has more than twice as many teenage births as other developed nations,[35] 80 percent of which are out of wedlock.[36] Only 4 percent of college graduates have illegitimate children. Sixteen percent of college graduates will get divorced, compared with 46 percent of high school dropouts, despite the fact that high school dropouts are less likely to get married in the first place.[37]

This rash of single motherhood is breeding a huge underclass. Half of the single mothers in the United States are below the poverty line, making their children six times more likely to be in poverty than children with married parents.[38] Single mothers account for 85 percent of homeless families.[39] Ninety percent of welfare recipients are single mothers.[40] According to Isabel V. Sawhill of the liberal Brookings Institution, almost all of the increase in child poverty since the 1970s is attributable to the increase in single-parent families.[41] The 2004 *New York Times Magazine* article describing the world of welfare families hinted at the problem, saying that if you dig down deep in the world of the underclass "you hit a geyser of father-yearning."[42]

The English doctor who writes under the pen name "Theodore Dalrymple" says the conceptual framework of the underclass is to see themselves as the passive victims of circumstances, with no control over their own lives. This is a worldview unique to two groups—derelicts and liberals. Dalrymple reports that three murderers in the prison he serves used the exact same words to describe their crimes: "The knife went in." As Dalrymple says, "That the long-hated victims were sought out, and the knives carried to the scene of the crimes, was as nothing compared with the willpower possessed by the inanimate knives themselves, which determined the unfortunate outcome." Murderers view their arrests for murder a matter of bad "luck." All their life choices are things that happen to them, these "marionettes of happenstance."[43]

It's the same thing with battered women who act as if they could not possibly have foreseen the violent tendencies in their boyfriends.

This, Dalrymple says, "serves to absolve them of all responsibility for whatever happens thereafter, allowing them to think of themselves as victims alone rather than the victims and accomplices they are." And yet Dalrymple demonstrates that they knew exactly what they were getting into with the men who beat them. He ascertains this by asking battered women two questions: (1) Do you think I could have guessed by looking at your boyfriend that he would beat you? (Answer: Yes); and (2) What do you think I noticed about your boyfriend that would cause me to know he would beat you? (Answer: the tattoos, the scars, the shaved head, etc.). Thus, Dalrymple concludes that they knew it, too, but acted as if their boyfriends' beating them was a bolt out of the blue in order to hold themselves blameless for hooking up with abusive men.[44]

How much stranger is it to act as if unwed pregnant women have nothing to do with their circumstances? Getting pregnant isn't like getting cancer. Single mothers don't occur randomly in the population. As any kindergartner in today's public schools can tell you, pregnancy is the result of having sex without using a condom.

And yet a 1992 *New York Times* article about single mothers on welfare used the exact same passive voice of the criminal described by Dalrymple. According to the *Times,* the women became pregnant out of wedlock when "their youth was overtaken by motherhood."[45] External factors caused their dilemmas, not their own free will: "Being black and from the inner city also raised the likelihood of dependency." Adopting the language of irresponsibility that has done so much for the poor, the fifteen-year-old son of an unwed mother told the *Times,* "My mother ain't got the money. . . . That's the kind of stuff that makes you sell drugs. You want something, and you ain't got nothing in your pocket."[46] A *Times* editorial explained that the "true enemy" is "poverty."[47]

For half a century, American welfare policy was premised on the insane idea that being poor causes single motherhood and crime, rather than that single motherhood causes criminal behavior and poverty. The result of treating a symptom rather than the cause was that all three—poverty, single motherhood, and crime—skyrocketed.

A single mother in West Virginia explained her unwed pregnancy to *The Economist*, saying, "It just happened."[48] Our entire political class and popular culture seem to agree: Single motherhood just happens. We must all pretend that single women are passive victims of their own incredibly stupid choices and then extol them for their pluck.

A book praising single mothers denounces those in middle-class America who "implicitly assume that girls and young women would have more control over their lives if they deferred motherhood." Apparently, deferring motherhood until marriage is impossible for the poor because the knife went in— Wait, no, because they "rarely see such choices" as marriage "as open to them at all."[49] Perhaps they would see such choices more clearly if the entire liberal establishment were not constantly praising single mothers and sneering at the unhip, drab middle class with their bourgeois prejudices against having children out of wedlock.

Having money doesn't make you middle-class. The secret to being middle-class in America is: Keep your knees together before marriage and graduate from high school. That's it! Anyone who does those two things has a smaller chance of being in poverty than a boy from the Dalton School has of being in the Navy SEALs. We could wipe out chronic poverty in America tomorrow if women could just manage to get married before having children—and to stay married after having children.

But reinforcing the idea that single motherhood is just a matter of rotten luck on the order of a brick falling on your head—or, apparently, knifing someone in a pub—liberals respond to the crisis of single motherhood by demanding yet more instruction in birth control. It's society's fault that teenagers are getting pregnant.

We've already run that experiment. It was precisely the advent of the pill that precipitated the gusher of illegitimate births in the first place. As with Dalrymple's battered women, if it was just bad luck, why were conservatives able to predict that the wide availability of birth control would lead to more illegitimate children? Teaching proper condom use in government schools sends what we call a "mixed message": *Never, under any circumstances, have sex before you're married. Now, here are the precautions you'll want to take before having premar-*

ital sex. . . . It doesn't matter if twice as many unwed girls are using birth control if 10,000 times more unwed girls are having sex.

Our public schools are drowning in condoms. More seventh-graders know how to put on a condom than can name the first president—although kids who are really good with a condom all seem to know the name of the 42nd. If public schools were required to offer any more birth control classes, they might not have time for their "plan a jihad" lessons. The idea that mastering the use of birth control is information adolescents are lacking is nonsense. They're running transcontinental drug rings and complicated welfare frauds. But they need instruction in how to put on a condom?

Apparently it wasn't society's failure to provide birth control classes that led to a spike in unwed mothers at Gloucester High School in Massachusetts in 2008. *Time* magazine revealed that nearly a dozen adolescent girls had entered a pregnancy pact, agreeing to get pregnant on purpose. After seventeen high school girls—none older than sixteen—got pregnant that year, four times more than the average, the school nurses remarked that they had noticed a surge in sophomores coming in for pregnancy testing. The girls walked out sullen if the test came back negative, but ecstatic if it was positive. For some, it was the first test they had ever passed.

Under questioning, the girls "confessed to making a pact to get pregnant and raise their babies together." One girl had gotten herself pregnant with a homeless man who reportedly wooed her with free rides in his shopping cart. "They're so excited," one unwed teenaged mother said, "to finally have someone to love them unconditionally."[50] Another classmate explained, "No one's offered them a better option." Admittedly, a "better option" than being impregnated by a guy who sleeps under an overpass and collects cans for a living is hard to imagine. But the point is: It's our fault. These girls are just victims of a society that hasn't "offered" them something better—other than living in the most prosperous, free nation on earth.

I know from reading the *New York Times* that it's madness to ask people to wait until marriage to have sex. Why should people worry about the kind of life they are giving a child when they have a shot at fleeting sexual pleasure? Even Sidonie Squier, head of President Bush's marriage-promotion project in the Office of Family Assistance, stoutly assured *The Economist* that her office did not "take a view on whether people should have pre-marital sex."[51] So I guess, as with global warming, the debate is over.

But Americans used to be able to care about the circumstances of their children's births: The illegitimacy rate has gone up by more than 300 percent since 1970.[52] Moreover, even assuming that, sometime around the year 1969, the entire human race lost the ability to defer gratification, there's still the wholly volitional decision not to give the baby up for adoption.

In 1979, only about 600,000 babies were born out of wedlock and one-quarter of them were put up for adoption. By 1991, the number of illegitimate births had doubled to 1,225,000 annually, but only 4 percent were allowed to be adopted[53]—and most of those babies were snapped up by either Angelina Jolie or Mia Farrow. By 2003, 1.5 million illegitimate babies were born every year, but only about 14,000 of them, less than 1 percent, were put up for adoption.[54] Not surprisingly, unwed mothers who care enough to give their children up for adoption also come overwhelmingly from responsible backgrounds. They tend to have higher education and income levels and to come from intact upper-middle-class families with highly educated parents.[55]

You will note that we do not read about adopted children filling up the prisons, welfare rolls, and runaway shelters. Adopted children are no worse off—and, indeed, are generally better off—than nonadopted children. There aren't a lot of studies about adopted children, because they aren't constantly mugging us and creating social disorders, but one four-year study by the Search Institute in Minnesota looked at the mental and psychological well-being of 881 teenagers who had been adopted as infants. The study found that adopted teenagers had greater empathy, higher self-esteem, and more close friends than nonadopted teenagers in public schools.[56] They were less likely to engage in high-risk behavior, such as stealing or excessive drinking, than nonadopted teenagers.[57] In all, they scored higher than the control group of nonadopted children on sixteen indicators of well-being.[58] They were less than half as likely to have divorced parents than nonadopted teenagers (11 percent to 28 percent) and were as strongly attached to their parents as their nonadopted siblings. Ninety-five percent of the adoptive parents were strongly attached to their adopted child. The majority of adopted teenagers rarely even thought about the fact that they were adopted.[59]

Adopted children of a different race from their family did just as well.[60] The only important factor in adoption is that the child be adopted within the first fifteen months of his life. "We cannot overstate," the study's authors said, "the power of early placement."

The blessed "single mothers" we are required to idolize had a choice of placing their children in the best of all possible worlds for their children (adoption) or the worst of all possible worlds (single-mother families). To satisfy their own selfish interests, they chose the worst of all possible worlds. Couldn't newspapers start telling us how global warming, government programs, and hurricanes are going to affect a more desirable group, like drug dealers?

Obviously, adoptive parents are the people who deserve all the praise, admiration, and *Oprah* appearances, not "single mothers." But they're merely saving children's lives. They're not sad-sack victims selfishly destroying their children's lives and depending on society to support them.

Contrary to popular mythology, there is no shortage of parents ready to adopt. There are waiting lists of parents who want to adopt babies with Down syndrome, spina bifida, and AIDS. In 2004, the head of Adoption Rhode Island, Jeff Katz, said, "I have seen children who were victims of torture adopted. I know an adoptive mother who grew up in foster care who was able to recognize the cigarette burns on her adopted son's body because she, too, had those scars. I have seen countless children whom 'nobody wanted' become treasured members of their new families. I have seen all of these children thrive and I have seen their families thrive." Katz implored, "Don't ever, ever let anyone tell you that these children wait because no one wants to adopt them."[61] Unable to adopt babies in this country, Americans adopt from abroad—more than 20,000 babies in 2003.[62]

■ ■ ■

BACK IN THE DAYS WHEN WE WEREN'T REQUIRED TO CON-
stantly praise single mothers, a New York University study found single mothers to be "overtly dominant, aggressive, narcissistic and bitterly hostile."[63] And yet all of society has been trained to have nothing
but sympathy for these aggressors.

Not surprisingly, Hollywood has taken a leading role in portraying
single mothers as victims, while relentlessly promoting promiscuity,
single motherhood, prostitution, and divorce to the detriment of the
most vulnerable members of society. But if anyone makes a peep of
criticism, suddenly it's 1939 Germany and overpaid writers from *Murphy Brown* are the Jews.

Hollywood movers and shakers are as rich as any oil company
CEO, but the role they love to play the most is victim. There was un-
mitigated joy when Dan Quayle said in 1992, "It doesn't help matters
when prime-time TV has Murphy Brown—a character who supposedly
epitomizes today's intelligent, highly paid, professional women—mocking the importance of fathers by bearing a child alone and calling it
just another lifestyle choice."

At the Emmy Award ceremony that year—they're always giving
awards to one another, these martyrs—the creator of the *Murphy
Brown* show, Diane English, was showered with awards. English took
the occasion to say, "I would like to thank our sponsors for hanging
in there when it was getting really dangerous." Inasmuch as the entire awards program was a Quayle-bashing festival, it's hard to believe
any of them were ever in much "danger" from Dan Quayle. TV producer Gary David Goldberg said, "I've never seen a time where people have responded this viscerally and taken the attacks so much
to heart." Bob Burkett, vice president of a film production outfit, said,
"No question that a gauntlet has been laid down to this community.
We've decided to pick it up." Marge Tabankin, executive director
of the Hollywood Women's Political Committee, said, "The community feels targeted. It's created a chill and fear reminiscent of the
'50s. Let's face it: We feel we're being used as whipping boys."[64] Yes,

Hollywood liberals have got balls to spare and that's why I admire them so much.

The starring victims, single mothers, were almost completely forgotten in the Hollywood sobfest. Liberals invoked their own mythical victim status to censor any criticism of Hollywood's celebration of illegitimacy.

The *New York Times* denounced Quayle's Murphy Brown speech in an editorial, sniffing, "He seems seriously to believe that what poor people most need is moral fiber."[65] Obviously, what poor people really need is free housing, food stamps, and yet another government program designed to treat them like passive, helpless children.

Despite the fact that a majority of illegitimate children in America are whites of European descent, soon Jesse Jackson was getting into the victimhood act, attacking conservative criticism of single motherhood as "racist." In a debate about Quayle's remarks between Jackson and Pat Robertson on ABC's *Good Morning America*, Robertson discussed the scourge of single motherhood, saying he had lived in Bedford-Stuyvesant, "one of the worst black slums in America, and I know the plight of the poor and I've committed my life to help them, but you're not going to help black people unless the black men stop siring children out of wedlock."

Fortunately, Jackson did not threaten to "cut his nuts off" as he would years later to B. Hussein Obama. Instead, Jackson retorted, "That's a racist statement! That's a racist statement!"[66]

Then at the 1992 Democratic National Convention that year, Jackson said:

Lastly, a lot of talk these days about family values, even as we spurn the homeless on the street. Remember, Jesus was born to a homeless couple, outdoors in a stable, in the winter. Jesus was the child of a single mother. When Mary said Joseph was not the father, she was abused and questioned. If she had aborted the baby, she would have been called immoral. If she had the baby, she would have been called unfit, without family values. But Mary had family values. It was Herod—the Quayle of his day—who put no value on the family.[67]

I wonder if that's the line Jackson used on Karin Stanford, the mother of his illegitimate child.

Needless to say, the Democratic Convention erupted in applause at Jackson's lunatic comparison of single mothers to Mary the mother of Jesus. In the Democrats' defense, they could not be accused of applauding a sacrilegious speech, because the delegates were unfamiliar with the original story.

Just quickly: Mary and Joseph were married before Jesus was born. They were not homeless, they were traveling to Bethlehem to register for the census. No one ever "abused and questioned" Mary about being pregnant. Mary did have the baby, so—luckily—we dodged the bullet of her aborting the Son of God. No one called Mary "unfit, without family values." The only people who knew who the real Father was came to worship Jesus. Also, Mary was a virgin. I am fairly certain that we are not witnessing the miracle of 1.5 million virgin births every year. As David Reinhard wrote in *The Oregonian*, perhaps at the next convention Jackson would "be likening Jesus' disciples to the Crips and Bloods."[68]

Finally, to compare someone to Herod is like comparing him to Hitler—or whoever the current head of Planned Parenthood is. Herod ordered the slaughter of all children under two years old in Bethlehem. He did not give a speech criticizing Hollywood elites for glamorizing single motherhood.

But apart from that, the Reverend Jackson had all his biblical points right. For example, Jesus was, in fact, a "Hymie."

Not only was Jackson not laughed into obscurity, but his inane remarks turned him into the Democrats' most respected speaker since William Jennings Bryan. The *Boston Globe* hailed the speech as "a powerful reminder of his importance to the party, as its conscience, its goad and its spokesman for those too often ignored as the Democrats move relentlessly toward the middle."[69] I couldn't have said it better myself. Jesse Jackson: not just an unintelligible, skirt-chasing shake-down artist, but the Conscience of the Democratic Party.

After the massive, coordinated attack on Dan Quayle for his Murphy Brown speech, no politician again dared to speak up on behalf of the 1.5 million children consigned to starting life on the back bench each year in America. They might be accused by Bryant Gumbel, then of CBS's *Early Show*, of using "family values" as a "code word" for "intolerance"[70] and "less inclusion."[71] As Brent Bozell of the Media Research Center said, even after the 2004 election, when voters chose "moral values" as the most important issue, Republicans refused to campaign on issues of morality. "Republican strategists," Bozell said, "pull muscles just thinking about Dan Quayle scorning the 'Murphy Brown' single-mom plot in 1992."[72] A phalanx of professional victims—oppressed Hollywood multimillionaires, single mothers, and black agitators—swept the real victims, children raised without fathers, under the rug.

As Time Warner's surprisingly large-circulation magazine *Babytalk* put it in 2007, "Just 15 years ago, then Vice President Dan Quayle publicly scolded a fictional television character, Murphy Brown, from the prime-time sitcom of the same name, for choosing to have a child on her own. Today, the 2008 Presidential hopefuls from both parties recognize that single moms are a force to be reckoned with and would be more likely to send Brown a baby gift than to question her choices."[73] And so they do.

When President Bush gave the commencement address at Miami Dade College in 2007, he singled out two members of the graduating class for special mention, both immigrants. One had enlisted in the United States Marine Corps out of high school, served in Iraq, and returned to go to college. The other, from Trinidad and Tobago, was a single mother of four.[74] Did America lose some sort of immigration lottery?

That same year, President Bush's daughter Jenna wrote a book about a seventeen-year-old single mother who was HIV-positive: *Ana's Story: A Journey of Hope.*

As a presidential candidate, John Kerry was constantly touting single mothers, using them in his campaign ads and giving them speaking time at campaign rallies. The week he announced he was running for president, Kerry held a campaign event at Faneuil Hall in Boston. Three eminences spoke on his behalf: the mayor of Boston, Senator Ted Kennedy, and . . . a twenty-year-old single mother.[75] It's hard to say whose reputation suffered the most from this joint appearance.

In 1994, President Bill Clinton held an emotional press conference at the White House to promote his crime bill, which was going to end crime in America by providing for midnight basketball and banning so-called "assault weapons," defined as "Semi-Automatics That Look Scary to Liberals." Three crime victims spoke in favor of one or another aspect of the bill, including Janice Payne of New Orleans, whose nine-year-old son James had been shot and killed in his neighborhood. In an eerie coincidence, just days before he was shot, James had written a letter to Clinton saying, "I want you to stop the killing. People is dead and I think somebody might kill me."[76]

In this particular case, however, there were other risk factors in James's life that arguably superseded the availability of guns. For example, he lived with a single mother in a crack house—or as the Realtors call it, a "shooter-upper." His mother had pleaded guilty to possession of painkillers and crack cocaine.[77] These facts came to light after Louisiana law enforcement saw Ms. Payne standing next to the president during the Rose Garden ceremony and arrested her for parole violations[78]—which, by the way, was about the extent to which Clinton's crime bill stopped crime.

In 2008, the city commissioner of Opa-locka, Florida—a single mother herself—hosted "A Salute to Single Mothers," with cash prizes for the single mother with the most affecting story.[79] They "struggle to cope." Give them prizes! One single mother said, "It would be easy to be single by myself, but I would rather have my kids with me and struggle with them." If someone said that about a pet, he'd be charged with animal cruelty. The attendees got gift bags, cash prizes, and information on taxpayer-funded goodies available to single mothers. The commissioner said she hoped the next "awards ceremony" for mothers who intentionally harm their children to be even bigger!

In 2004, the *New York Times* attacked the Bush tax cuts by quoting a retired coal miner from southern Illinois who complained, "My daughter is a single mother," and she didn't get a tax cut.[80] Admittedly, in this case, the problem may have less to do with the absence of a husband and more to do with Democrats' maddening inability to understand that you have to pay taxes in order to get a tax cut. But notice how the man, a Democrat according to the *Times*, self-righteously announced the embarrassing circumstances of his own daughter, as if it were a badge of honor that she was a single mother. People used to brag about their children getting into an Ivy League school or joining the Marines. Now they brag about their kids having children without being married.

That same year, discussing the alternative minimum tax on National Public Radio, David Cay Johnston, then a tax reporter for the *New York Times*, illustrated the unfairness of it by saying, "It now applies to very few people who make multimillion-dollar incomes, but it can apply to a single mother who only makes $30,000."[81] How about we double the tax on single mothers to create a disincentive to illegitimacy, so that fewer children's lives will be ruined?

Sociologist Ruth Sidel was a little late to the party when she wrote that single mothers should be "celebrated and indeed applauded" for their "courage, determination, commitment to others, and independence of spirit." This was in her book, *Unsung Heroines: Single Mothers and the American Dream*, which is not to be confused with Louise Sloan's book *Knock Yourself Up: No Man? No Problem: A Tell-All Guide to Becoming a Single Mom*, or Jane Mattes's book *Single Mothers by Choice: A Guidebook for Single Women Who Are Considering or Have Chosen Motherhood*, or Colleen Sell's book *Cup of Comfort for Single Mothers: Stories That Celebrate the Women Who Do It All*, or Rosanna Hertz's book *Single by Chance, Mothers by Choice: How Women Are Choosing Parenthood Without Marriage and Creating the New American Family*, or Ellie Slott Fisher's *Mom, There's a Man in the Kitchen and He's Wearing Your Robe: The Single Mom's Guide to Dating Well Without Parenting Poorly*. And of course there's the soon-to-be classic by me: *What to Expect When You're Expecting Because You're an Irresponsible Little Tramp*.

Single motherhood is the apotheosis of the feminist vision: women

without men! Except they're not without men. They're without one specific man with an interest in their particular children. But men—and
women—across the country have been forcibly enlisted in the job of
feeding, housing, and clothing single mothers and their children. The
rest of us have to be constantly attuned to the needs of single mothers.
Government policies are designed to support single mothers, rather
than to stop them. Churches, corporations, and nonprofit organizations
are required to chip in to make up for single mothers' lack of husbands. *I am woman, hear me roar! Hey, what's the holdup with my government check?*

A 2008 study led by Georgia State University economist Benjamin
Scafidi found that single mothers—unwed or divorced—cost the U.S.
taxpayer $112 billion every year. We could have had two Iraq wars at
that price. Ken Starr gave us more than a dozen high-level felony convictions and a presidential impeachment for a mere $40 million.
Scafidi underestimated single mothers' burden to society by using the
lowest estimates of single mothers in poverty and excluding additional
costs of single mothers to programs such as the Earned Income Tax
Credit and remedial education programs in public schools.

Scafidi's study did not even consider the burden single mothers
place on law enforcement because of their higher likelihood to neglect
or kill their children in order to spend more time with their boyfriends.
A huge percentage of law enforcement resources are spent dealing with
the behavior of white trash in America, of which single motherhood is
a major part. Eighty-five percent of mothers who kill their children
through neglect are single mothers.[82] Consider some of the more newsworthy child murder cases over the past few years:

- In the fall of 2008, single mother Casey Anthony was indicted
  for the murder of her two-year-old, Caylee Marie Anthony. However the trial comes out, the child is gone.
- In 2004, twenty-eight-year-old single mother Tammy Huff beat
  to death her eight-year-old son, Jose Torres, with the assistance
  of her boyfriend, Bradley Dial.[83]
- In 2003, single mother Amanda Hamm, twenty-seven years old,

drowned her three young sons, aged six, three, and twenty-three months, so she could move to St. Louis with her boyfriend. It would have been a lot of trouble to bring the boys with them. Apparently, the prospect of hearing "are we there yet?" for eight hours was just too daunting for Amanda.[84]

- In 2001, twenty-one-year-old single mother Jennifer Cisowski killed her eight-month-old illegitimate son, Gideon Fusscas, by repeatedly throwing him down a flight of stairs at her grand-mother's swank Florida home. The case was especially unusual because Cisowski came from a wealthy, albeit broken, Connecticut family.[85]

- In 1998, twenty-five-year-old single mother Tami Lynn Richards left her two children, three and one and a half years old, alone in their apartment while she went to a bar to drink and listen to a band. One of the boys set a fire when he was playing with matches he found in the apartment. Both boys died. On the other hand, from what I hear, the bar band was pretty awesome.[86]

- In 1995, single mother Jennie Bain Ducker, twenty-one years old, left her two sons, aged one and two, buckled in their car seats with the windows rolled up outside a motel while she partied all night in a Nashville motel room with her boyfriend and three other men. When Ducker returned to the car in the morning, the boys were dead from the heat. It was estimated that the temperature in the car reached 120 degrees.[87]

- In 1994, twenty-four-year-old separated single mother Susan Smith strapped her two sons into their car seats before sending the car to the bottom of a lake in Union, South Carolina. Her boyfriend had just broken up with her, telling her he didn't want to marry a woman with children.

If single mothers killing their children were any more common, Hallmark would have to introduce a card: "Honey, you were so sweet . . . [open card] . . . to murder your children for me."

What makes these cases exceptional is that the mothers weren't teenagers and most of the children were older than one—having passed the most likely time period for a mother to kill her child. And also contrary to the norm, these cases seem to involve the idealized, Murphy Brown–style single mothers—mostly middle-class white women. But unfortunately for their children, they were still single mothers.

Even when they kill their children, single mothers are portrayed as victims. In the book *Mothering and Ambivalence,* author Wendy Hollway defended the mothering instincts of Susan Smith and Jennie Bain Ducker by noting that before drowning or cooking their children to death, the "children were strapped into *safety* seats"—emphasis hers—thus demonstrating the mothers' "concern with the children's safety."[88] Yeah, you wouldn't want to drown a child who's running around loose in the car. He might bump his head—or try to escape.

An article criticizing the "maternal myths" promoted in news reports about women who kill their children explained that women "may kill their children because of economic stress, to avoid the social stigma of an out-of-wedlock pregnancy, [or] because they feel isolated or depressed about a romantic relationship"[89]—all factors that limit the suspects to single mothers. Sadly, the alleged "stigma" of single motherhood is not nearly so powerful as the real stigma against criticizing single mothers, even the ones who murder their own children.

After thirty-three-year-old single mother Danielle Blais drowned her six-year-old autistic son in a bathtub in 1996,[90] the president of the Quebec Autism Society, Peter Zwack, leapt to the murderous mother's defense by explaining that an autistic child would be especially hard on a single mother: "She was all alone and that would have made things even more impossible."[91] Yes, even for someone with the parenting skills of a Danielle Blais!

How many crimes went unsolved in Orlando, Florida, while Casey Anthony led the police on one wild-goose chase after another? How many criminals escaped detection and capture in Union, South Carolina, while the police were tied up searching for Susan Smith's children when she knew they were at the bottom of a lake? Massive police resources were wasted, locally and nationally, looking for Smith's children for nine days, while she refused to tell the police that she had killed her children herself. What emergencies was the Westminster, Colorado, fire department unable to respond to while they were putting out the fire set by Tami Lynn Richards's children while she was at a bar? What crimes did the Nashville police fail to stop while they were dealing with children who died after being left in their mother's sweltering car overnight?

IT'S BAD ENOUGH THAT SINGLE MOTHERS ARE A GIANT DRAIN on society, but it is really too much to be constantly asked to feel sorry for them. Instead of being grateful, these societal parasites whine about being victimized. In 2006, the liberal magazine *In These Times* complained that from "Reagan's 'welfare queens,' Quayle's criticism of Murphy Brown and now Bush's dramatic slashing of social programs—single mothers have been under attack over the last 20 years."[92]

Also in 2006, participants at a National Women's Studies Association meeting raged about the untold cruelties visited upon single mothers. Even Hillary Clinton had thoughtlessly "jumped on the marriage promotion bandwagon," according to one speaker. These harpies demanded that single motherhood be affirmed as "the right of women."[93] Analysis that insightful is usually heard from people dressed in multiple layers of filthy clothing on a hot summer's day and pushing a grocery cart full of bottles and cans down an alley. But the idea that society owes single mothers has become conventional wisdom in America.

Even single mothers who became that way through artificial insemination are celebrated as deserving victims, which, unless they're claiming to have tripped and landed on top of a turkey baster full of semen, is not true.

Liberals view single women having babies by artificial insemination as a feminist success story. In an upbeat article about artificially inseminated single mothers, a *New York Times* reporter happily observed that a woman "can now select the father of her child from her living room and have his sperm sent directly to her doctor. It is faster and cheaper than adoption, and allows women to bear their own genetic offspring."[94]

But it's not all sunshine and song. Some intolerant people make remarks that are hurtful to women who have made the difficult, deeply personal choice to ruin their own child's life. As *Babytalk* magazine somberly reported, "Unmarried moms do feel the sting of prejudice."[95]

The *New York Times* noted that the "most common accusation" is that intentional single mothers are "selfish," which the *Times* explained was based on a "widely held belief that two-parent homes are best for children." One of the single mothers by artificial insemination indignantly reported that a friend had suggested that she "channel" her nurturing instincts into working at a children's hospital instead of becoming a single mother. To this impertinent remark, she retorted, "Can you say 'condescending'??"[96]

Another single mother by artificial insemination said that "the child was more important than the partner."[97] She might want to check with the child on that one. But the *Times* explained that these women have seen friends in unhappy marriages. What does the child's life chances matter when a woman is "not willing," as the *Times* article said, "to settle for 'Mr. Almost Right' in order to have a baby"?[98]

The *Los Angeles Times* quoted another single mother by artificial insemination, who said, "You're paying for it, so you kind of want the best of the best."[99] Call me old-fashioned, but when someone is promoting eugenics like that I prefer it in the original German. So she got the best sperm to create a child that she will raise in the worst possible environment for the development of a well-adjusted human being: fatherless. One member of Single Mothers by Choice sacrificed premarital sex while she was pregnant, which I gather is considered a herculean feat these days. "You go through an awful lot of trouble to get pregnant," she said. "You don't want to blow it on one night of fun."[100] Perhaps she'll be able to use that years later to browbeat her kid when he misbehaves. "I didn't sacrifice countless hours of casual sex to have you so you could live like a pig! Now go clean your room!"

In one of several pieces over the years celebrating single mothers by choice, *Marie Claire* magazine ran stories of various such heroes, including one artificially inseminated single mother who bravely confronted society's "belief" that a child should have a father. She recounted an e-mail exchange with a colleague after he found out she was pregnant:

"I didn't know that you were married," he wrote.

"I'm not," I replied, annoyed.

"Who's the father?" he pressed.

"I don't know his name," I shot back.[101]

Next, the artificially inseminated single mother let a post office worker have it for being confused when she gave "none" as the father's name: "The clerk at the crowded post office couldn't fathom it. 'Every child has a father!' she kept insisting. Finally, I shouted back, 'Well, mine has a sperm donor!' The room fell silent."[102] And to think people used to say single mothers are "overtly dominant, aggressive, narcissistic and bitterly hostile."[103]

These women are inflicting social pathologies on their own children for which society will pay and all we get are upbeat articles about how nice it is that single women were able to conceive. "I could not have imagined my life without being a mother," one artificially inseminated single mother said. "This wasn't a hard decision for me. For me it was an absolute."[104] Isn't that nice for her? Isn't it an "absolute" for car thieves that they take the car? At least she has the one trait that makes for a great mother: a narcissistic obsession with self-indulgence. It's as if society were under attack by a pack of wolves, while the blabocracy praises the wolves, builds them habitats, and publishes books on how to breed more wolves.

SOCIETY LOVES SINGLE MOTHERS SO MUCH WE KEEP CREATING more and more of them. In 2003, there were more than 10 million single mothers in the United States, up from about 3 million in 1970.[105] How did this happen? The plague of single motherhood isn't merely an inevitable decay brought on by stupid choices of the underclass. It is the active social policy of liberals. After winning a Pulitzer Prize, the Left's author laureate Toni Morrison told *Time* magazine in 1989, "The little nuclear family is a paradigm that just doesn't work. It doesn't work for white people or for black people. Why we are hanging on to it, I don't know."[106] (Of course, Toni Morrison was also under the impression that Bill Clinton was a black man.) Gloria Steinem's most dazzling accomplishment was coming up with the saying "A woman needs a man like a fish needs a bicycle"—proving that a woman has to be twice as stupid as a man does in order to be recognized as stupid. The National Organization for Women sells a bumper sticker with the motto "One Nuclear Family Can Ruin Your Whole Life."[107]

Barbara Ehrenreich, a columnist for *Time* magazine in the 1990s, wrote that the family is "personal hell," a "nest of pathology and a cradle of gruesome violence," where "we learn nasty things like hate and rage and shame."[108] To paraphrase Pat Buchanan's response to Hillary Clinton's comparison of the family to slavery: Speak for yourself, Barbara. She cites a "long and honorable tradition of 'anti-family' thought" that, oddly enough, includes nothing from C. S. Lewis, Paul Johnson, John Dos Passos, Flannery O'Connor, Thomas Sowell, or any other conservative favorites.

Ehrenreich wrote:

The French philosopher Charles Fourier taught that the family was a barrier to human progress; early feminists saw a degrading parallel between marriage and prostitution. More recently, the renowned British anthropologist Edmund Leach stated that "far from being the basis of the good society, the family, with its narrow privacy and tawdry secrets, is the source of all discontents."[109]

I guess these are household names among liberals. Ehrenreich, who, surprisingly enough, is divorced, sneers at "a culture that fetishizes the family as the ideal unit of human community."[110] She claims that "for a woman, home is, statistically speaking, the most dangerous place to be."[111]

There's wrong and then there's crazy wrong. According to the U.S. Justice Department crime statistics, domestic abuse is virtually nonexistent for married women living with their husbands. From 1993 to 2005, the number of married women victimized by their husbands ranged from 0.9 to 3.2 per 1,000. Domestic violence was about 40 times more likely among divorced or separated women, ranging from 37.7 to 118.5 per 1,000. Even never-married women were more than twice as likely to be victims of domestic violence as married women.[112] Evidently, the safest place for a woman to be is at home with her husband.

In another passage suggesting that Ehrenreich was raised on a different planet, she says, "The larger culture aggrandizes wife beaters, degrades women or nods approvingly at child slappers."[113] True, domestic violence skyrocketed the first year of Clinton's presidency and again the year of the Monica Lewinsky scandal.[114] But not to worry— Caligula is gone! Even Democrats rejected his wife as their presidential nominee in 2008. Of course, he would have been gone a lot sooner without liberals like Ehrenreich denouncing the "sexual Puritanism" of those of us trying to impeach him.

Ehrenreich says she is merely brave enough to state what "we all know." As proof that "we all" loathe the traditional family, she cites the public interest in O.J.'s murder of his ex-wife, the Menendez brothers' murder of their parents, and Lorena Bobbitt's attack on her husband's private parts. "Our unseemly interest in O.J. and Erik, Lyle and Lorena," she says, "allow us, however gingerly, to break the silence on the hellish side of family life."[115] I guess our unseemly interest in the missing Natalee Holloway case allowed us to break our silence on the hellish side of summer vacations and our unseemly interest in the Martha Moxley murder allowed us to break our silence on the hellish side of Greenwich, Connecticut.

In another upbeat article for *Time* magazine, Ehrenreich airily announced that society should concern itself with encouraging "good divorces." The goal, she says, should be "to de-stigmatize divorce" and to "concentrate on improving the quality of divorces." She suggests that couples be forced by the government to plan for divorce before marriage by "requiring prenuptial agreements specifying how the children will be cared for in the event of a split."[116] Children of divorce "already face enough tricky interpersonal situations," she said, without everyone acting as though divorce is a bad thing. Surely a society that smiles upon divorce will compensate for Mommy and Daddy not living together. While we're at it, if society would stop harping about drunk driving, I think it would really perk up paraplegics who became that way by driving drunk.

This is mainstream liberal thought. Ehrenreich wrote these inanities not on the Daily Kos blog but in *Time* magazine. She has been regularly featured in the *New York Times, The New Republic,* and *The Atlantic Monthly.* As Irving Kristol said, "Rot and decadence [are] no longer the consequence of liberalism but [are] the actual agenda of contemporary liberalism."[117]

Still, the Left's transformation of society from family-based to single-mother-based has been accomplished with astonishing speed. Author Maggie Gallagher, who, as an erstwhile single mother, speaks with some authority, says the problem is that people shrink from addressing the social disasters of their friends. People are mum about the horror of single motherhood—if they know a single mother. They refuse to condemn divorce—if they know a divorcee. They can't think of a single objection to gay adoption—if they know a gay couple that has adopted. Gallagher says this allows "upscale conservatives to hurl stigmas at unwed moms"—but not divorced single mothers—"without having to insult anyone they actually know."[118]

That would help explain how marriage, the central force in transmitting civilization, has unraveled with such alacrity. Starting only a few decades ago, liberals launched a three-front attack on marriage through the courts, the welfare system, and popular culture. With each incremental gain, their advances grew geometrically as people lost the ability to condemn what their family, friends, and neighbors were doing. By now, as G. K. Chesterton said, "The act of defending any of the cardinal virtues has . . . all the exhilaration of a vice."[119]

Welfare bureaucrats paid single women money just for having children out of wedlock, liberal justices on the Supreme Court stripped away the legal benefits of marriage, and pop culture glamorized single motherhood far more than cigarette companies have ever dreamed of glamorizing smoking. While masquerading as socially conscious do-gooders speaking for society's victims, liberals created a world where there would be a constant supply of new victims in need of their merciful aid. An illegitimate child might or might not be better off by having contact with his biological father. But social workers would definitely be better off with a lot more illegitimate children.

Time and again, organizations purporting to speak for the children urged the courts to abolish the legal protections of marriage. To quote Irving Kristol again, liberalism "aims simultaneously at political and social collectivism on the one hand, and moral anarchy on the other. It cannot win, but it can make us all losers." The problem with liberalism, he says, "is liberalism."[120]

The idiocy of paying single women to have illegitimate children has been so thoroughly explored, especially by Charles Murray in his groundbreaking book *Losing Ground,* that even President Clinton was compelled to sign the welfare reform bill that Newt Gingrich's Republican Congress sent him in 1996. No liberals resigned in protest over Clinton's getting oral sex from a White House intern, but Peter Edelman and other liberals resigned from the Department of Health and Human Services to protest Clinton's signing of the welfare reform bill. Liberals all swear to believe in evolution, but their own development since the 1930s is an example of devolution: Frances Perkins, FDR's secretary of labor, strenuously opposed granting welfare benefits to unwed mothers on the grounds that it would encourage women to have children out of wedlock. She had worked in a home for unwed mothers, and had seen up close the damage wrought by illegitimacy.[121]

To eliminate the pain of illegitimacy, liberals set out to destroy the stigma attached to illegitimacy, rather than to reduce its incidence. They turned a small problem into a national crisis by attacking laws that supported the idea that children should be born within marriage. Stigma or no stigma, the damage done to children born outside of marriage is the same.

From various Supreme Court decisions stripping marriage of its legal benefits, through Hillary Clinton's comparison of marriage and the family to "slavery and the Indian reservation system,"[122] right up to the Left's freakish obsession with gay marriage today, liberals have never been able to grasp the point of marriage. The only interest society has in marriage is its ability to harness men's energy and direct it to the upbringing of particular children, allowing children to grow up in a secure environment and not become rapists and serial killers. Because of the vital importance of marriage to creating half-decent human beings, civilized society has traditionally accorded a man no rights to his children—and the mother few or no claims upon the father—in the absence of marriage. Fathers of illegitimate children in colonial times would be pursued for minimal child support only to prevent the children from becoming wards of the state.

Ironically, the legal abolition of marriage was facilitated not by single mothers but by the archetypal villain in most liberal fairy tales: white men. Malingering unemployed white men, but white men nonetheless. Once again eclipsing women's accomplishments, men busting up the adoptions of their biological children may have done more damage to children in America than even single mothers. Unwed men began demanding rights to their biological offspring in the seventies, and this gave other men on the Supreme Court an excuse to destroy the legal protections of marriage.

From the beginning of history up until April 3, 1972, the law generally presumed that unwed fathers were not fit to raise their children. It was this statutory presumption that the U.S. Supreme Court struck down in *Stanley v. Illinois* (1972). (The *Stanley* case was argued by attorney Patrick T. Murphy, who not only persuaded the U.S. Supreme Court to ditch the legal benefits of marriage in *Stanley*, but years later would help persuade a state agency to return a three-year-old to his abusive mother, who later hanged the boy. Calling him a "Defender of Chicago's Children," the *New York Times* hailed Murphy for believing that children should stay with their biological parents whenever possible[123]— apparently, even violent, unwed, and unfit biological parents.)

Despite there being nothing in the Constitution about fathers' rights to children sired out of wedlock, the Supreme Court in *Stanley* found that it had the authority to nullify Illinois's statutory presumption that unwed fathers were unfit parents pursuant to the Due Process Clause of the Fourteenth Amendment. Peter Stanley had sought legal guardianship of his three biological children after their mother died and Illinois initiated a hearing to find legal guardians for them. Such a proceeding, obviously, would have been unnecessary had Stanley been married to their mother. But in eighteen years with her, Stanley had never sought a legal relationship either with her or their children together. After the mother died, he turned the children over to another couple, who also had no legally enforceable obligations to the children. Though Stanley apparently had no interest in obtaining actual custodianship of the children, he was particularly concerned, as Justice Warren Burger said in his dissent, "with the loss of the welfare payments he would suffer as a result of the designation of others as guardians of the children."

The U.S. Supreme Court found that the Illinois law on unwed fathers violated "substantive due process" by requiring unwed fathers to establish their fitness as parents in legal proceedings, while married fathers had to make no such proof. The "substantive due process" construct allows the Court to jettison the considered judgment of elected state representatives as well as thousands of years of human history in order to enshrine the crackpot ideas of liberals as the law of the land. The Court discovered it had this power sometime in the 1960s. For the first two centuries of the nation's history, we had small governing units across the nation called "states." These "states" would pass laws to govern people within their boundaries. The rulers of these governing units were elected by the people in a briefly popular system of government known as "democracy."

A few years after *Stanley*, the Supreme Court was required to issue opinions further explaining an unwed father's rights. In *Quilloin v. Walcott* (1978) and *Caban v. Mohammed* (1979), the Court held that the Constitution required courts to examine the level of interest the sperm donor had shown in his child before allowing him to disrupt an adoption, including long hearings into "the best interests of the child"— hearings that anyone could see were unquestionably not in the best interests of the child.

It was only a matter of time before the new rights the Court had accorded unwed fathers would involve an adulterer claiming rights against the cuckolded husband. In *Michael H. v. Gerald D.* (1989), the

Court acknowledged the concept of "marriage"—eighteen years too late—and denied the male mistress rights to the child he conceived with a married woman. But the opinion rejecting the adulterer's claims to his biological child was a shockingly narrow 5–4 decision. All five justices who ruled against the adulterer were appointed by Republican presidents. One more vote for the dissent and courts would be forcing innocent husbands to leave their homes every other weekend so that the men who cuckolded them could have visitation time with the kids.

Justice William Brennan's blistering dissent was the perfect distillation of liberal thinking: The wisdom of all previous ages—circa 4500 B.C. to 1989—amounted to mere "prejudices and superstitions." The traditional idea of a "family" as comprising a husband, a wife, and their children, Brennan said, would turn the Constitution into "a stagnant, archaic, hidebound document steeped in the prejudices and superstitions of a time long past." Brennan claimed to be arguing for "tolerance" of those with "idiosyncrasies"—that is, people who enjoy pursuing adulterous liaisons. He pretentiously cited the "freedom not to conform." But as Justice Antonin Scalia pointed out in the majority opinion, one way or another, somebody loses rights. Rights are a zero-sum game. If the Court were to grant the male mistress his "freedom not to conform," it would rather severely constrict the husband's "freedom to conform." Brennan's dissent is like one of those snowy globes filled with floating flakes of liberal fantasies in an imaginary landscape. It's a perfect encapsulation of the sweet little dreams . . . of those who are barking mad.

Although Brennan claimed to be interpreting a new, hip Constitution, it was a Constitution that existed only in his head. In every one of these cases, the Supreme Court was being asked to overrule lower courts that had upheld state laws reflecting the traditional view of marriage. The justices who argued against overruling long-standing laws warned of what would be lost. In *Caban*, for example, Justice John Paul Stevens wrote—in dissent, "All of these children have an interest in acquiring the status of legitimacy; a great many of them have an interest in being adopted by parents who can give them opportunities that would otherwise be denied; for some, the basic necessities of life are at stake." He was right. And no one, not even Justice Stevens, can remember his argument today.

In a couple of decades' time, Brennan's view had completely triumphed. It seems as though it was a million years ago that there were privileges and obligations that flowed from marriage—and marriage alone. Marriage may have won a nail-biting victory over adultery in *Michael H. v. Gerald D.*, but it was too little too late. In short order, courts and legislatures would be giving unwed mothers rights to the bank accounts of the fathers of children born out of wedlock, giving unwed fathers rights to their biological children living with adoptive parents, and giving illegitimate children inheritance rights to their biological fathers' estates.

Illegitimacy increased not because of neglect or accident but because of an idiotic idea aggressively pursued by self-righteous people who had worked it all out on paper. Then they returned to their exclusive doorman buildings or lush suburbs where they would never personally experience the consequences of the traditional family's destruction. It wasn't inevitable social decay that destroyed the family, it was a plan.

At least the social workers are thriving.

With the Supreme Court having augustly ruled that a one-night stand gives a man a constitutional right to disrupt his biological child's life, in no time at all cads were enjoying their new rights. By the 1990s, unwed—and frequently unemployed—biological fathers were ripping the products of their sexual conquests from the homes of loving adoptive families.

Perhaps the most infamous case involved "Baby Richard," as the courts called him, born in 1991. Baby Richard's mother, the pregnant, unwed Daniela Janikova, ditched the father, Otakar Kirchner, after he returned to their native Czechoslovakia and allegedly started dating another girl. With Kirchner still out of the country, Janikova moved into a home for abused women, saying she had been physically abused. She gave the baby up for adoption four days after his birth and later told Kirchner the baby had died. The adoptive parents, fireman Jay Warburton and his wife Kimberly, legally adopted the boy, named him Danny, and raised him as their own along with an older biological son.

Months later, Kirchner returned to America, found out Janikova had given up their illegitimate son for adoption, and decided he wanted the child back. Under thousands of years of Anglo-Saxon law, this would have been ludicrous. If Kirchner wanted rights to his child, he had better have been married to the mother when the child was born. But since the Supreme Court had declared marriage just a smelly old hidebound institution, Kirchner was in the game!

Pursuant to our new Brennan-invented traditions, when Danny was almost four years old, Illinois Supreme Court justice James Heiple ordered that the terrified child be torn away from the only parents he had ever known and handed over to a biological father he had never met. For people who hysterically denounce the influence of genetics on personality and intelligence, liberals seem to have a supernatural belief in the genetic attachment of a man to his sperm. During the court-ordered wrenching on April 30, 1995, Danny cried to his parents, "Please, Mommy, no! I'll be good. Don't make me leave. I'll be good."[124]

Danny's adoptive parents appealed to the U.S. Supreme Court, but the court refused to hear the case. To return Danny to his adoptive parents would have been to defer to the "stagnant, archaic, hidebound" tradition of marriage firmly rejected by the Court years earlier. Janikova and Kirchner eventually married, but less than two years after taking Danny from his adoptive parents, Kirchner left again, leaving his son behind. Although he returned sometime later, during the period he absconded on his wife and biological son an interesting legal wrinkle appeared. Mrs. Kirchner had no independent parental right to Danny since she had relinquished that right when she gave him up for adoption.

Nonetheless, the Warburtons never saw Danny again. The last time Danny's mother spoke to him was the night he was taken away from them. He called from Otakar Kirchner's house and told her, "I love you, Mommy. I'm coming home now."[125]

A few years later, Danny's psychologist Karen Moriarty, who had been hired by the biological father, sued *Chicago Tribune* columnist Bob Greene for suggesting that she planned to write a book about Baby Richard. She claimed not only that she had no intention of writing a book about Baby Richard, but that it was defamatory per se for Greene to imply that she had any idea of writing a book.[126] In 2003, Moriarty published *Baby Richard: A Four-Year-Old Comes Home.* In the book, she assured readers that Baby Richard had turned out just fine and bore no emotional scars from the court-ordered transfer that she had supported. Brain twister: Do we have to wait for Moriarty to claim it is defamatory per se to say Danny has emotional scars to know for sure that he has emotional scars?

In another case at about the same time, the "Baby Jessica" case, an unwed mother in Iowa, Cara Clausen, gave her baby up two days after the child's birth in 1991. She listed her then-boyfriend as the father on the child's birth certificate and both parents formally agreed to the adoption. A married couple from Michigan drove to Iowa to take custody of the baby girl and began the process of adoption. But a few weeks later the mother broke up with the boyfriend she had named as the father and resumed relations with an ex-boyfriend, Dan Schmidt, who she now said was the real father. Schmidt decided he wanted the baby. Two and a half years later, "Baby Jessica" was ripped away from the only parents she had ever known and given to the biological father.

Naturally, the unwed fathers taking their biological children from adoptive families portrayed themselves as . . . victims! To win in America, one must always be the first to claim victim status. Fathers' rights groups battled with women's rights groups over who was the greater victim, and in the process created real victims out of their children. The only point both sides seemed to agree on was that marriage is irrelevant. The institution that had protected children for thousands of years was gone. Just twenty years after *Stanley,* it was as if the concept of marriage had never existed.

The Supreme Court's destruction of marriage is the perfect example of Chesterton's remark that "When you break the big laws, you do not get freedom; you do not even get anarchy. You get the small laws."[127] Having decided in *Stanley* that being married to the mother was not necessary for a man to have rights to his children, the Supreme Court, together with lower courts and state legislatures, spent the subsequent three and a half decades trying to formulate substitute rules to govern unwed parents. But without the concept of marriage, this is like trying to rewrite the rules of baseball without a ball. Courts and legislatures have simply crafted a patchwork of new rules that are a pale imitation of the traditional law of marriage.

After a raft of these adoption cases in the early nineties, with unwed fathers being lied to by their pregnant girlfriends, leading to stomach-turning scenes of children being ripped from happy adoptive homes, states responded by trying to re-create the benefits of marriage—without marriage. Most states now have some form of paternity registry, requiring unwed fathers to stake their claim to illegitimate children within six months of the child's birth to have standing to bring lawsuits upending the child's life. Marriage used to do that without vast phalanxes of social workers having to maintain a "paternity registry."

Say, you know what would be great? It would be great if we had some way of determining who the father is, by law, at the moment a child is born. Also mothers should try to get some sort of commitment from the father to stay with her and raise their child together before bringing a child into the world. Maybe couples planning on having children together could have one of those "commitment" ceremonies the gays have. Justice Brennan might respect a "commitment" ceremony. Just don't call it "marriage."

It never occurs to anyone to simply return to the original rule: Unless a man is married to a woman when she gives birth to his child, he has no rights to that child, and unless a woman is married to a man when she gives birth to his child, she has no right to his paycheck or his time.

Surveying the wreckage wrought by the destruction of the legal incidents of marriage, a columnist in the *New York Times* exulted, "Surely this change is a welcome corrective to the injustice of traditional marriage laws and family values that stigmatized 'bastards' for life."[128] Except that one can't help noticing how many more "bastards" there are now that the stigma has been removed.

■ ■ ■

IT ONLY TOOK A FEW INANE SUPREME COURT RULINGS IN THE
1970s to make the idea of marriage fly completely out of the head of
Illinois Supreme Court justice James Heiple and his cohorts in various
courts across the nation. How much more vulnerable to the loss of this
idea are young, stupid women?[129]

Inasmuch as broken families are almost entirely a problem of the
underclass in America, it is fatuous to imagine that popular culture
doesn't influence these most feckless of citizens. Liberals believe that
the pathetic waifs with the "pregnancy pact" at Gloucester High
School are too stupid to know how to use a condom—as if they wanted
to—but are sophisticated enough to completely ignore a pop culture
that ferociously glamorizes single motherhood. We've got tabloids and
glossy magazines touting the unwed pregnancies of starlets, Christian
ministers referring to unwed mothers like they're Jesus on the cross,
and a popular culture that can conceive of no greater barbarity than
waiting for marriage to have sex. Hmmm, I wonder if that has had any
effect on the increase in illegitimate children being born to girls with
massively low self-esteem?

A real estate broker in Atlanta—not a teenage runaway—told the
New York Times she decided to become a single mother by in vitro fer-
tilization because she "concluded that it has quietly become a socially
acceptable choice, if only because so many are making it."[130] An adult
with a job in a major city can't resist the pop culture hype about single
motherhood. How much more vulnerable is a teenage girl from a broken family?

Among the movies featuring single mothers are *Look Who's Talk-
ing* (1989), *Stella* (1990), *Mermaids* (1990), *Gas Food Lodging* (1992),
Forrest Gump (1994), *Losing Isaiah* (1995), *As Good as It Gets* (1997),
Anywhere but Here (1999), *Tumbleweeds* (1999), *The Next Best Thing*
(2000), *Chocolat* (2000), *Erin Brockovich* (2000), *You Can Count on Me*
(2000), *The Princess Diaries* (2001), *Hearts in Atlantis* (2001), *White
Oleander* (2002), *Eight Crazy Nights* (2002), *Freaky Friday* (2003),
Secondhand Lions (2003), *SherryBaby* (2006), and *Superman Returns*
(2006).

I guess Hollywood got Dan Quayle back!

At the 2001 Academy Awards, three of the five women nominated for Best Actress played single mothers: Julia Roberts, who won the Oscar for her role in *Erin Brockovich*, as well as Juliette Binoche for *Chocolat* and Laura Linney for *You Can Count on Me*. (A fourth nominee, Ellen Burstyn, played a widow in *Requiem for a Dream*.) "This isn't a fad, it's a trend that reflects reality," said Jeff Sharp, a producer of *You Can Count on Me*. "There are increasing numbers of strong, successful women who are raising families and having a career without a partner."[131] Describing her role as a single mother in *Anywhere but Here*, Susan Sarandon, who has three children with two men to whom she has not been married, said, "It's just a very rich area to explore." Actress Janet McTeer, portraying a single mother in the movie *Tumbleweeds*, explained the prevalence of single mothers in Hollywood movies, saying, "It's more typical for a woman to have to raise children on her own. It's a theme that can be endlessly explored."[132]

We're constantly told that the underclass is trapped by circumstances, unaware of the option of waiting until marriage to have children. Maybe other choices would come into focus more clearly if Hollywood didn't have a new Hays standard prohibiting movies and TV shows from showing married people having children.

All sentient human beings know that single motherhood is ruinous for children, but meanwhile, the mainstream media and Hollywood studios are constantly issuing propaganda about the joys and triumphs of single motherhood. *Babytalk* magazine actually titled an article "Married vs. Single Moms: Who's Got the Better Deal?" The magazine warned that "having a partner to parent with isn't all wine and roses," adding that 22 percent of the married women they polled "agreed that it might sometimes be easier to be unmarried."[133] The magazine tepidly concluded that married mothers "probably win out in the end, just because they have Dad's extra assistance, emotional support, and income."[134] But it was a nail-biter.

Marie Claire seems to have updated the usual women's magazine formula—jealousy, envy, and love—to include regular paeans to the joys of single motherhood, even as the evidence pours in on its danger to children. The October 2001 issue featured an article about a single mother by choice: "I Made My Lifelong Dream Come True." In June 2005, it was an article titled "Why Should I Wait?," a happy story by an artificially inseminated unwed mother, who I predict will have trouble explaining to her child the concept of delayed gratification. And in 2008 it was "And Baby Makes Two," about heroic single mothers.

On NBC's megahit sitcom *Friends,* when the pretty, popular "Rachel" gets pregnant out of wedlock, two of the three male stars fall madly in love with her. On *Sex and the City,* unwed mother Miranda acquires her most impressive boyfriend of the series, a handsome doctor, after giving birth to an illegitimate baby, but then dumps him to marry the father of her child and end up happily ever after. Back on Planet Earth, one's chances of finding Mr. Right do not tend to improve after having a baby out of wedlock. A Cornell University study found that unwed mothers are 30 percent less likely to marry than other single women—and, I would venture, 100 percent more likely to have received sex education and condoms in schools that don't believe abstinence works. "Both the likelihood of marriage and the quality of marital partners," said the study's author, Daniel Lichter, "are adversely affected by out-of-wedlock childbearing."[135]

Us Weekly celebrated single motherhood with an article titled "The New Single Moms and How They Do It," delusionally proclaiming, "Sisters are doing it for themselves." No they're not. They're "doing it" at a colossal, unwelcome cost to every man, woman, and child in America.

Hollywood actresses have dropped sex tapes and moved on to single motherhood as a way to promote their careers. Among the current celebrity unwed mothers are Jessica Alba, Halle Berry, Minnie Driver, Bridget Moynahan, Nicole Richie, Jamie Lynn Spears, and Michelle Williams. There was also Shar Jackson, the ex-girlfriend of Kevin Federline, who was briefly married to Britney Spears, but if we're including people associated with Britney Spears, there's no telling how long the list would be. Starlets who have adopted children while unmarried include Sheryl Crow, Calista Flockhart, Camryn Manheim, Meg Ryan, and Angelina Jolie. Apparently, busting up tribal wars to adopt foreign babies has become the latest form of Hollywood autoeroticism.

In 2004, *Vanity Fair* gushed about single mother Angelina Jolie, "Splashed all over the tabloids as the temptress who came between Brad Pitt and Jennifer Aniston, Angelina Jolie sounds more like a stressed-out single parent than a screen siren."[136] *People* magazine quoted single mother Jolie saying, responsibly, "that she engages in 'adult relationships' with 'men who were already very close friends of mine,' lasting a few hours and promising no commitment. 'I can feel like a woman,' said Jolie, 28, 'but it's not a relationship that interferes with my family.' She stresses it's not casual. 'I've never had a one-night stand in my life—these are people I know very well.'"[137] How Angelina Jolie manages to lure men into brief, no-strings-attached sexual encounters is anybody's guess.

Meg Ryan was described in *People* as "raunchy in a new film—but keeps life as a single mom low-key." The magazine reported that she was dating another single parent, little-known actor William Keane—who shared custody of a daughter with an ex-girlfriend.[138]

After a single mother from the ghetto, Fantasia Monique Barrino, became the 2004 *American Idol* winner, she released her debut album, including the song "Baby Mama." For unknown reasons, some narrow-minded people thought the song celebrated single motherhood—solely because it includes lines like "nowadays it's like a badge of honor to be a baby mama" and "B-A-B-Y M-A-M-A. This goes out to all my baby mamas!" So everything will work out fine in the end for single mothers, provided they become *American Idol* winners.

A child has no control over whether his parents are married, but society can create incentives that will dramatically increase the odds of children having married parents. So why all the reverence for "single mothers" but not for married men and women raising their kids in the traditional way? Parents who had shotgun marriages, or who relinquished illegitimate children to adoptive parents, or who stuck it out through tough times for the sake of their children—these are the ones who should be venerated, not somebody's "baby mama."

3

RAGE AGAINST OUR MACHINE

After global warming, the Republican Attack Machine is the imaginary phenomenon that scares liberals the most. The mainstream media are always bristling with warnings about Republican smear campaigns, with reporters fretting about "what the Republicans are going to do." During a one-year period from June 2007 to June 2008, there were more than 700 documents on Nexis referring to the "Republican Attack Machine." For that same period, Nexis produces only 16 documents using either the phrase "Democratic Attack Machine" or "Democrat Attack Machine."

What liberals mean when they complain about "attacks" is simply that it is unfair to point out the things the Democrats believe. Republicans telling the truth about them is dirty pool. *There they go, calling our name again!* Naturally, the Republicans' damnable habit of talking candidly about the Democrats is enraging to people who are constantly working on perfecting their fake-American costumes. They believe it is unsporting for Republicans not to blindly accept their lofty rhetoric about "hope" and "change."

The rare appearance of the phrase "Democratic Attack Machine" in the media mostly comes from conservative columnists pointing out: *Hey, there's a Democratic Attack Machine too!* That is absurd. There is only one attack machine and that is the mainstream media. The media don't recognize what they're doing as attacks because their beliefs are axiomatic, the default position, what all "knowledgeable and fair-minded people"[1] believe.

Both the Republican and Democratic Parties are penny-ante compared with the liberal media behemoth, which has been utterly unmoved by the smashing success of fair and balanced Fox News Channel. Mass mailings and "robo-calls" by political parties are like mosquitoes buzzing around the King Kong of the mass media as it stomps on cars and buses and terrifies Japanese extras. The only difference between the attack machines of the political parties is that the media will pick up and repeat the attacks produced by the Democrats but will vilify any attacks launched by Republicans.

Indeed, the media and the Democratic Party synchronize their work so closely, it's often impossible to tell them apart. Who's to say where a Clinton flack ends and *This Week with George Stephanopoulos* begins? But as Bill and Hillary Clinton found out during the 2008 Democratic primaries, it's the media that call the shots for the Left in America, not the Democrats. Without the mainstream media 100 percent behind the Clintons, suddenly Bill wasn't so sexy and Hillary wasn't so smart.

Liberals have nothing but admiration for criminal defense lawyers who lie remorselessly on behalf of child murderers, self-righteously informing us that this is "part of the process." Without these "Twinkie defense" champions, liberals tell us, our adversarial system of justice would collapse. They boast "someone's got to do it," as if they were Marines going into battle. (For any liberals reading, a U.S. Marine is . . . oh, never mind. It would take too long to explain.) But an adversarial system in politics drives liberals to distraction. It's one thing to vigorously defend a child molester, another thing entirely to vigorously defend a Republican. Giving two sides of the story in a child kidnapping case is part of the process; giving two sides of the story in a political race is a dirty trick of the Republican Attack Machine.

IN LIBERALS' IMAGINARY WORLD, LONE BLOGGER MICHAEL Brodkorb is more powerful than the *New York Times*, the *Washington Post*, the *Minneapolis Star Tribune*, the *St. Paul Pioneer Press*, and the entire liberal blogosphere. As a hobby, Brodkorb started a blog called "Minnesota Democrats Exposed." In short order, he was uncovering stories the mainstream media somehow missed. In 2008, Brodkorb discovered that Democratic Senate candidate Al Franken owed about $70,000 in back taxes and had a $25,000 judgment against his corporation in New York for unpaid workers' compensation insurance. Franken's spokesman responded to these allegations by denouncing Brodkorb as "the right-wing noise machine."

In an Associated Press article about Brodkorb's repeatedly breaking news that the mainstream media had failed to uncover, the AP delusionally asserted that Brodkorb "has no real counterweight on the left."[2] No real counterweight? How about the Associated Press? The AP managed to file a decent report on Brodkorb. Why couldn't it report on Franken—not a conservative blogger, but a candidate for the U.S. Senate?

The Democratic base, not being particularly bright to begin with, has been infected with an almost paralyzing fear of Republicans. After Barack Obama sealed the Democratic presidential nomination in 2008, Bill Kownacki fired off an indignant letter to *The Oregonian*, huffing, "I don't know how they'll do it, but somehow Republicans are going to attack Barack Obama both for [supposedly] being a Muslim and for attending a Christian church with an outspoken pastor for 20 years. The real challenge: Can they do it in the same sentence?"[3] Republicans were being attacked for things they hadn't done, but they're the ones with an "attack machine."

Throughout the Thirty-Years'-War Democratic primary campaign, circa 2007–2008, all Democratic arguments were pitched in terms of the nonexistent, but still very frightening, Republican Attack Machine. Democrats accused one another of adopting Republican smear tactics, they bleated about being victims of imaginary Republican attacks, and, most impressively, they raised the specter of the Republican Attack Machine as a stalking horse to launch attacks on one another. *Really, I have no problem with Obama being a Muslim—but wait until Republicans get ahold of it!* It was a twofer for liberals: Attack your opponent and smear Republicans at the same time. Republicans could only watch in perplexity, thinking, *Wait a minute! We didn't say anything!*

This isn't normal politicking—unless you are a catty twelve-year-old girl. The Republicans held primaries in 2008, too, but they attacked one another's policies, records, and character. They didn't say, *Wait until the Democrats hear about this!* Indeed, judging by the candidate they chose, the Republicans appeared to be unaware of the existence of an opposing party. Even the smarmiest of Republican candidates never resorted to such a backhanded slime. When Mike Huckabee wanted to attack Mitt Romney, he innocently asked a *New York Times* reporter, "Don't Mormons believe that Jesus and the devil are brothers?" Unctuous? As Sarah Palin would say, You betcha! But at least Huckabee didn't say, *I don't have any problem with Mormons believing Jesus and Satan were brothers, but wait until the Democrats find out!*

The innovation of Democrats was to say, while putting the knife in a fellow Democrat, *Isn't it better to hear it from me than from the right-wing hate machine? Hey, don't blame me—I'm just giving you the printable version of what Republicans are going to say.* In a column on Reverend Jeremiah Wright—with long excerpts from his sermons—Clinton flack Lanny Davis wrote in the *Wall Street Journal,* "One thing is for sure: If Mr. Obama doesn't show a willingness to try to answer all the questions now, John McCain and the Republican attack machine will not waste a minute pressuring him to do so if he is the Democratic Party's choice in the fall."

Ah, the notorious Republican Attack Machine!

Jamie Rubin, assistant secretary of screwing up national security—oops, I mean "of state"—under Clinton, warned that "the Republicans are going to fight very, very hard and they're going to start looking to Senator Obama's record on a number of issues that really haven't gotten much attention so far."[4] In other words, Republicans were going to campaign.

Former Clinton White House assistant deputy fellatio apologist

Ann Lewis defended Hillary's attacks on Obama by warning that "in the fall election the Republicans are going to come after us with everything they've got."[5] As usual, Lewis was about a mile and a half off the mark. If only McCain had come at Obama with everything he had! Or even with everything I had. Hillary supporter Lisa Caputo explained that Hillary was talking about Obama's racist loon pastor, Jeremiah Wright, because "these are the kind of attacks that the Republicans are going to throw at Senator Obama."[6] Well, thanks for the heads-up!

Was the issue why Obama had sat through a deranged segregationist reverend's sermons for twenty years? No, of course not, you stupid racist. "The issue is," as Clinton hatchet man Harold Ickes said of Obama's Rev. Wright problem, "what Republicans [will do] . . . I think they're going to give him a very tough time."[7] *It's not a question of what Sirhan Sirhan did. That's beside the point. It's what Sirhan Sirhan's critics are going to do with it that concerns us.*

Warning of what Republicans would do with the Reverend Wright, an unnamed Clinton ally told the *New York Times,* "The Republicans made John Kerry look like a coward in 2004," and quoting Wright "wouldn't even look like 'Swift-boating.'"[8] For something called the "Republican Attack Machine," it sure seems to get used by a lot of Democrats. These are the lionhearted warriors who plan to lead us through the terror war? (I only raise the point of their collective, pants-wetting cowardice now because, if I don't, you can bet al Qaeda will!)

Clinton's New Hampshire campaign cochairman William Shaheen injected the idea that Obama had been a drug dealer into the race by raising What-the-Republicans-Will-Do: "The Republicans are not going to give up without a fight . . . and one of the things they're certainly going to jump on is his drug use." Shaheen continued, "It'll be, 'When was the last time? Did you ever give drugs to anyone? Did you sell them to anyone?'" Of course, Shaheen himself had no problem with Obama's being a major stoner, but there were "so many openings for Republican dirty tricks." America still awaits the first Republican to criticize Obama for his admitted drug use. Maybe their attack machine is in the shop or something.

In point of fact, the historical record shows that attacks on a politician for his marijuana use will come from the mainstream media—not the apocryphal Republican Attack Machine. In 1987, writing about the prior drug use of Reagan Supreme Court nominee Douglas Ginsburg, *New York Times* columnist Anthony Lewis said, "How could a President who talks about the need for law and order pick as a Supreme Court nominee someone who illegally used marijuana when he was a law professor?"[9] Yes, and how much more embarrassing would it be if it were the president himself who had smoked weed? Apparently, not so much if the pothead is a Democrat.

Anthony "Reefer Madness" Lewis continued, "There is no way of escaping the fact that having on the Supreme Court someone who had violated the drug laws as an adult would be embarrassing or worse." Or worse! Granted, Lewis knows from "embarrassing or worse," judging from his columns. He also hooted at Reagan's claim that Ginsburg's pot-smoking was a youthful indiscretion.

What *is* the cut-off point for "youthful indiscretions"? Ginsburg was thirty-three when he smoked pot. Bill Clinton was thirty-two when Juanita Broaddrick says he raped her. Michelle Obama was forty-four when she said America is a "downright mean" country.[10] And B. Hussein Obama was twenty-six to forty-six years old during the twenty years he was an enthusiastic member of the Reverend Jeremiah Wright's congregation.

The *Times* was forced to editorialize repeatedly about Ginsburg's "marijuana matter," in order to get the balance just right between self-righteous indignation about Ginsburg on one hand and condescending contempt for antipot Puritans on the other. For a few awkward moments it almost seemed as if the *Times* was opposed to the use of illegal drugs. In a single bipolar editorial, the *Times* complained that "public pieties haven't kept up with the change of attitude" toward pot, while also huffily announcing that Ginsburg's case was "not just a marijuana disclosure but one that involved a conservative President who talks militantly against drugs and for law and order."[11] No, that wasn't a typo: The *Times* thinks it's possible to be "militantly" against crime.

Not only was the only marijuana scandal in U.S. history a creation of the media against a Republican, but the media made absolutely clear, ab initio, that they would not hold Democrats to the same standard they hold Republicans to. As if anticipating Bill Clinton, Al Gore, and Obama, an op-ed in the *Washington Post* concluded, "A Democratic president could successfully name a former marijuana smoker to the court—indeed, a Democratic president could be a former marijuana smoker. But not a Republican president."[12] And to think some people say the media have a double standard! Sure enough, just five years later, the only protests about Clinton's admitted marijuana use were over his claim not to have inhaled.[13]

So Obama had nothing to fear about his admitted drug use, least of all from Republicans. The media wanted to screw him, but only in the sense that they literally wanted to have sex with him.

It wasn't just Clinton flacks neurotically fretting about the Republican Attack Machine. No one in the establishment media had the slightest interest in the facts about Obama that might be an issue for the voters. Obama's being ranked the most liberal member of the Senate, his attack on Americans who "cling" to God and guns, his spiritual mentor being a deranged racist, his associations with felons and domestic terrorists— none of these facts bothered the media any more than they bothered the Clinton campagin. Again, the only question was whether it might occur to the Republicans to mention any of it in the general election.

On MSNBC, Dan Abrams warned, "If Obama becomes the Democratic nominee, Republicans are going to attack him as too liberal."[14] (Even that bold, out-of-nowhere prediction wasn't enough to save Abrams his anchor job.) On CNN, Jeffrey Toobin raised the fact that Obama "was one of the most liberal members of the Illinois state senate" and "if Hillary Clinton doesn't say it, you can bet the Republicans are going to say it in the fall."[15] What else were they supposed to talk about? His big ears?

In an article titled "Insults Hit a New Low," the *Times* of London reported that McCain, "unprompted," had mentioned Obama's association with domestic terrorist Bill Ayers. "It was a clear sign," the article continued, "of how Republicans are going to attack the Illinois senator if he becomes the nominee."[16] Yes, indeed. The Republicans were prepared to stoop to out-and-out truth-telling! The *Washington Post* quoted a Clinton supporter saying, "The general election is not going to be like these primaries. The Republicans are going to really attack."[17]

Writing about a Democratic debate in 2008, *New York Times* columnist Maureen Dowd wrote that during some of Obama's answers, "you could see white letters on a black background scrawling across the screen of a Republican attack ad."[18] The *Times* summarized Dowd's column on the contents page: "Obama's gotta do more than get that dirt off his shoulder. Because the Republicans are going to keep it real, with attack ads and worse."[19] What could possibly be worse than sharing documented, factually correct information with voters about the potential leader of the free world?

LIBERALS' HYSTERICAL OBSESSION WITH THE "REPUBLICAN Attack Machine" turns Democratic primaries into a contest of: "Who's the Biggest Pussy?" Although I would have voted for "All of Them," inasmuch as none of the Democrats could face questions from Fox News's Brit Hume, the winner turned out to be Obama. Hillary claimed to be a victim of the Republicans, while Obama claimed to be a victim of Republicans, Hillary, and racists.

To make her case that she was the best candidate, Hillary said she was the biggest victim of Republicans. She got a round of applause during the South Carolina Democratic Debate, in January 2008, by saying, "If it is indeed the classic Republican campaign, I've been there. I've done that. They've been after me for sixteen years, and much to their dismay I am still here." Brave Hillary!

Obama countered Hillary's claim that he was too scrawny to withstand the Republican Attack Machine by saying Hillary had been weakened by the Republican Attack Machine. As Obama supporter Senator Sheldon Whitehouse put it, Obama "has not been worked over for years by the Republican smear machine. . . . Hillary carries a legacy of the Republican attack machine that took her and President Clinton on for a decade, really, with billions of dollars behind them—well, hundreds of millions anyway—and so it's a different thing."[20] This makes me very angry: If the fantasy Republican Attack Machine has billions, or at least hundreds of millions of dollars, where's my check?

Obama claimed to be a victim of Republicans, too. Blubbering on *60 Minutes* about the coming Republican attacks, he said, "The Republicans are going to come after me. There's no doubt that there will be attempts on the part of the Republican Party to demonize me in the general election."[21]

Both Hillary and Obama accused each other of adopting the smear techniques of the Republicans. Hillary said Obama was using tactics "right out of Karl Rove's playbook"[22]—an incongruous complaint from a candidate who boasted of her ability to withstand Republican attacks. Obama's team had the same complaint with Hillary—that she was as bad as the Republicans. When superdelegate and Indiana native Joe Andrew switched his allegiance from Hillary to Obama days before the Indiana primary, Evan Bayh, senator from Indiana and Clinton delegate, commented, "I don't think he's lived in our state for eight or nine years. I don't think he can even vote in Indiana."

This brutal attack was too much for Andrew, who went on MSNBC's *Countdown with Keith Olbermann* to complain, "What you're hearing now is the exact kind of language that came out from Republicans when I was defending Bill Clinton during the impeachment of the president."[23]

This was surprising to me, because if anyone was part of any Republican Attack Machine during Clinton's impeachment, I think I was, and yet I had never heard of Joe Andrew. Indeed, Keith Olbermann pompously introduced Andrew as "the most influential politician you probably had never heard of"—which is a big compliment coming from a TV show host most Americans have never heard of. Maybe when Andrew said Hillary's people were using "the exact kind of language that came out from Republicans," he meant English.

A search of Joe Andrew on Nexis turns up innumerable mentions of Andrew, who was the chair of the Democratic Party in 1999, reciting bland Democratic talking points, but there wasn't a lot of criticism from the Republican Attack Machine, perhaps because it can only attack objects large enough to be seen by the naked eye. Still, if Andrew says he was a victim of Republican attacks, then he must have been. So I tried searching Andrew's name near words like "lie" or "liar" or "lying" and finally got a hit: It was Andrew accusing his Republican counterpart of "lying on national television" for implying that Hillary knew what Bill was doing with Monica

Lewinsky. To this, Andrew responded, "Look, if you're going to lie on national television, at least you ought to be called on it occasionally."[24]

Joe Andrew: victim of the Republican Attack Machine.

While pretending to be bravely facing down an Attack Machine, in fact, Andrew was capitulating to an Attack Machine: the media. The mainstream media switched their allegiance from the Clintons to Obama, so Andrew did, too. Surely no one noticed the about-face more than the Clintons themselves.

For years, the media took a sadistic pleasure in reporting that Bill Clinton, a sociopathic sex offender and bully with a narcissistic disorder, was wildly popular. The media simply asserted that Clinton was beloved across the land—despite never being able to get 50 percent of the country to vote for him, even before the country knew about Monica Lewinsky. Democratic pollster Stanley Greenberg, who worked for Al Gore's 2000 presidential campaign, and was paid not to lie to his client, explained to *Vanity Fair* magazine that Clinton was banished from Gore's 2000 presidential campaign because research showed that whenever Clinton was mentioned, Gore's numbers plummeted. Greenberg said that if polls showed Clinton would have helped, he would have "had Bill Clinton carry Al Gore around on his back." Mind you, this was when one man could still actually carry Al Gore on his back.

But the mainstream media wouldn't quit. No matter how preposterous it was, liberals just kept telling us that the chubby kid with the big red nose whose greatest moment on the football field involved a wind instrument was "Elvis." According to Nexis, that appellation has been applied to Clinton approximately 1,000 times. In print, that is. There's no telling how many drunken cocktail waitresses have whispered it in Clinton's ear during late-night elevator assignations.

As late as 2006, Clinton could expect an exchange like this with Meredith Vieira on *The Today Show:*

VIEIRA: Where do you think [Osama bin Laden] is? Everybody's wondering where the heck he is. Where do you think he is?

CLINTON: I think he's probably in— I have no intelligence,
   okay? I think he's probably—

VIEIRA *(interrupting):* You have plenty of intelligence.

CLINTON: No, I mean government intelligence.

VIEIRA: I know, I'm kidding.[25]

But then Obama emerged from the clouds, and at long last, liberals were finished with the Clintons—which was as close to actual mainstream thinking as they'd been in years. Worst of all, the media turned on Clinton using the nastiest trick of the Republican Attack Machine: They told the truth about him.

If you've ever wondered how a Democrat would fare being treated like a Republican by the media, you'll still have to wait to see it. But at least liberals stopped aggressively lying for the Clintons. It took a decade, but journalists finally noticed that Clinton getting serviced by a White House intern whose name he couldn't recall may not have been the equivalent of the Gettysburg Address. "Bill's affair with Monica Lewinsky," liberal columnist Jonathan Chait wrote in the *Los Angeles Times*, "jeopardized the whole progressive project for momentary pleasure."[26] Chait also mentioned the Clintons' "lying and sleaze-mongering"—while still denouncing "frothing Clinton haters."

Having finally noticed the blindingly obvious, Chait asked, "Were the conservatives right about Bill Clinton all along?" He idiotically added, "Maybe not right to set up a perjury trap so they could impeach him, but right about the Clintons' essential nature?" Um. It wasn't a "trap." It was a "question." Try sending a bimbo with a thong into the Oval Office of any Republican president and feel free to ask him any questions about it later, under oath. President Bush would have probably taken the strumpet to church with him. This is where the "essential nature" issue comes in.

In a July 2008 *Vanity Fair* article about Bill Clinton by Todd Purdum, husband of Clinton's former press secretary Dee Dee Myers, consumers of the mainstream media would read for the first time about Clinton's "cavernous narcissism," his "blowups at television reporters," his cheating at golf, his "maladroit" campaigning for his wife, and his "repellent grandiosity."[27] Purdum stoutly stuck by the old lie, claiming that—until that very year!—Clinton "was among the most popular figures on the planet," which, assuming he was referring to the planet Earth, was preposterous. Demonstrating the irresistible charm for which he was famous, Clinton responded to the article by calling Purdum "sleazy," "dishonest," "slimy," and a "scumbag."

To avoid having to admit that the only thing that had changed about Bill Clinton was that the media were no longer lying for him, reporters began postulating a series of ludicrous explanations for why their earlier descriptions of him were so different. The most ambitious of these Rube Goldberg–type stretches of the imagination was Purdum's suggestion that it was perhaps "his quadruple-bypass surgery." Purdum noted that friends say "Clinton has never been the same." Yes, who doesn't know someone who, after open-heart surgery, suddenly became an egomaniacal, pathologically lying horndog? Clinton was exactly the same as he had always been.

But in an exciting new development, the establishment media began to notice the Clinton attack machine. Maybe the mainstream media had had open-heart surgery! In the entire eight years of the Clinton administration—through the attacks on Rush Limbaugh, Newt Gingrich, Paula Jones, Linda Tripp, Ken Starr, the fired White House Travel Office employees, and the "Vast Right-Wing Conspiracy"— there are only 28 documents on Nexis with the words "Clinton attack machine." But in the six months before Hillary dropped out of the primary campaign against Obama, Nexis records 54 mentions of the "Clinton attack machine." The same people who loved the Clinton attack machine when it was used against Republicans cried foul when it was turned on the new fair-haired boy B. Hussein Obama. It was hard to decide what was more fun—watching liberals discover the Clinton attack machine or watching Hillary discover affirmative action.

You can tell which candidate the Media Attack Machine has anointed the favored candidate by seeing which one gets treated like the biggest victim. Instead of asking the beloved Obama any tough questions, the media asked the Golden Boy to comment on Republicans' attacks—imagined attacks that hadn't materialized yet. Referring to Obama's admitted past drug use, Tom Brokaw's question to Obama was "Aren't the Republicans going to come after you on that?" (Obama: "You know, they already have.")[28]

Or consider the questions asked of presidential candidates appearing on CNN's *Late Edition with Wolf Blitzer* during the most crucial phase of the 2008 primaries (January for the Republicans and May for the Democrats). Excluding pointless chitchat, the first question asked of all Republicans—as well as disfavored Democrat Hillary Clinton—was a tough question about the economy. The angel Obama was asked if he was prepared for the Republican assault. As Blitzer himself described the coming interview, "And is he ready for an onslaught from the Republicans? Some tough questions for Senator Obama."

Blitzer's Question to Mitt Romney:
Let's talk about fears of a recession in the United States. There is now [speculation] the president might want to put forward some sort of economic stimulus package to try to create some jobs and avoid a recession. If you were president right now, Governor, what would be your immediate first step that you would take?[29]

Blitzer's Question to Fred Thompson:
All right. Let's talk about the economy right now. Assume you're the president, facing a recession, a lot of jobs being lost right now, especially in states like South Carolina and in Michigan. What do you do, if you're president right now?[30]

Blitzer's Question to Mike Huckabee:
Let's talk about fear of recession in the United States right now. There's some talk the president will announce a short-term economic stimulus package, try to create some jobs and try to improve the economy right now because there is a lot of fear that recession could take place later in the year.

If you were president right now, what would you do immediately to try to deal with this crisis?[31]

(John McCain was apparently not interviewed by Blitzer during the Republican primaries.)

Blitzer's Question to Hillary Clinton, who, as Obambi's opponent, was treated like a Republican:
Let's talk about some of the issues, the key issues, the economic issues, issue number one, the economy, gas prices right now. You've said in recent days you want to get tough with the major oil-exporting countries, OPEC, because of the huge cost per barrel, the resultant price of a gallon of gas.

But when you say get tough with OPEC, what does it mean when you have members of OPEC like Ahmadinejad of Iran or Hugo Chávez of Venezuela, or Qaddafi of Libya? How do you plan on getting tough with them?[32]

Blitzer's Question to Obambi:
You know they're going to paint you, the McCain camp, Republicans, as a classic tax-and-spend liberal Democrat, that you're going to raise the taxes for the American people and just spend money like there is no tomorrow when it comes to federal government programs.

Are you ready to handle that kind of assault?[33]
(Obama: "Absolutely.")

Follow-up question: You've been called "perhaps the greatest human being ever born." How do you respond? Is that too strong? Or are you, in point of fact, more of a god than a human being? Can you think of ANY flaws you have? Because I sure can't.

THE MEDIA USE THE IDEA OF A REPUBLICAN ATTACK MACHINE to bury negative information about a Democrat without actually refuting it. Whenever there's a glitch in the matrix and the public is accidentally exposed to actual facts about a Democrat, the media go to DEFCON 1 to neutralize the negative information with hysterical denunciations of Republican attacks.

Obama supporter Steven Cohen, public administration professor at Columbia University, warned, "It's clear how the Republicans are going to attack. . . . They're going to try to make him out like he's some kind of Middle East left-wing crazy."[34] Obama had said he would meet without preconditions with Iranian president Mahmoud Ahmadinejad, a mad Holocaust denier with a messianic complex trying to develop nuclear weapons. (Plus he has some other ideas that are just plain nuts.) Obama also said that, as president, he would immediately withdraw U.S. forces from Iraq. As the cherry on top, Obama had been endorsed by the Islamic terror group Hamas. Weren't those facts voters should be told?

On *The Charlie Rose Show*, Joe Klein of *Newsweek* said, "Republicans are going to want this to be about guns and about God and about homosexuality and all the other things."[35] Why shouldn't Republicans talk about those things? Those are at least actual issues, as opposed to having to listen to liberals fret about Republican attacks in every media outlet twenty-four hours a day.

Democrats have staged an all-out war on guns, God, and marriage. Liberal judges have banished any allusion to a higher being from the public square. They even ban the Pledge of Allegiance periodically because it mentions "God," whoever she is. Democratic legislators have enacted restrictions and all-out bans on gun ownership. Obama himself had dismissed gun owners and people of faith, famously sneering that they "cling" to God and guns because they're "bitter." And those sneaky Republicans were threatening to quote him!

Judges appointed by Democrats have forced gay marriage on the nation despite Americans' repeatedly rejecting the idea at the ballot box. Liberals treat the Boy Scouts like a hate group because they refuse to employ gay scoutmasters to take adolescent boys camping in the woods—a policy the Catholic Church wishes it had thought of years ago. In 2000, the U.S. Supreme Court barely upheld the Boy Scouts' First Amendment right to exclude gay scoutmasters—in a 5–4 ruling. That same year, Democratic congresswoman Lynn C. Woolsey introduced a House bill to revoke the Boy Scouts' nearly century-old congressional charter[36] and a Boy Scout troop was booed by the delegates at the Democratic National Convention.

Klein's statement is the equivalent of the Japanese complaining on December 8, 1941, that the Americans "want to make this about Pearl Harbor."

Just a few weeks before Jeremiah Wright's greatest hits collection hit the airwaves, Obama had said, "I don't think my church is actually particularly controversial."[37] But once Americans got a taste of Wright's sermons, it turned out most people found them fairly controversial. The clips were not—as Obama's defenders initially said—taken "out of context." What Democrats mean when they say something was "taken out of context" is that a third party heard it. That's the context: No one else was supposed to hear it. The Jeremiah Wright clips happened to have come from the Trinity United Church's own website, which was selling the videos as stand-alone gems from the Reverend Wright's oeuvre. Once it became clear that normal people were appalled by Obama's reverend damning America, denouncing "white arrogance," and saying America deserved 9/11, Obama distanced himself from whatever voters didn't like, saying, "All of the statements that have been the subject of controversy are ones that I vehemently condemn."[38]

And yet in his autobiography, *Dreams from My Father*, Obama wrote admiringly of the first sermon he heard the Reverend Wright give, in which the pastor blamed "white folks' greed" for "a world in need." Obama said of this talk, "I felt the tears running down my cheek." Indeed, he was so moved by the "white folks' greed" sermon, he joined the church immediately and even used the name of Wright's sermon, "The Audacity of Hope," as the title of his second book.

These were legitimate issues about the man running to be the most powerful person in the universe. But all liberals cared about was whether Republicans would run ads about Obama's crazy pastor. Thus, the *New York Times* earnestly reported on April 23, 2008, "Yet Mr. Obama also faces challenges ahead: According to Republican Party officials, party members in North Carolina . . . are considering running an advertisement against Mr. Obama that highlights his ties to controversial figures like his former pastor, the Rev. Jeremiah A. Wright Jr. That ad could have the effect of adding a racially divisive element to that Southern state's primary."[39] The North Carolina Republican Party ad showed Obama's pastor Jeremiah Wright screaming one of his classics: "God damn America!" The ad noted that two North Carolina Democrats had endorsed Obama for president and concluded, "Too extreme for North Carolina."

Evidently it is not racially divisive to accuse the U.S. government of starting AIDS to kill blacks or to preach about "white man's greed" creating a "world in need." It's only racist to quote a black man saying these things.

Liberals were ecstatic about the ad: The Republican Attack Machine had shown its ugly true colors! America's only fifty-three-year-old woman trapped in a man's body to host his own TV show, Keith Olbermann, called the North Carolina ad a "Republican hit job," a "Republican smear ad," and a "virulent racist anti-Obama ad."[40] Which I guess it was, if "hit job" is defined as "giving voters relevant information about a Democrat." The Reverend Wright matter wasn't a smear, it was a fact: Obama attended Wright's church for twenty years, listening to what the *Times* itself called "racist oratory."[41] If he didn't grasp the hatred in Wright's sermons, let's just hope he pays closer attention during national security briefings than he did during twenty years of the Reverend Wright's church services.

Alas, despite liberals' terrific fear of John McCain and the Republican Attack Machine, evidently McCain was more afraid of the real attack machine: the mainstream media. He wasted no time in denouncing the North Carolina ad. Obeying the media's command that Republicans not mention any facts unfavorable to Obama, McCain said, "There's no place for that kind of campaigning, and the American people don't want it." He promptly fired off a letter to the North Carolina Republican Party presuming to tell them not to run the ad.

Say, is it too late to nominate someone else for that "Who's the Biggest Pussy?" contest?

McCain even fired a "low-level staffer" who sent around a YouTube video on his personal Twitter account linking Obama to the Reverend Wright—Obama's own pastor, who married him, baptized his children, and gave him the title to his second book. "We have been very clear," a McCain campaign statement said, "on the type of campaign we intend to run and this staffer acted in violation of our policy. He has been reprimanded by campaign leadership and suspended from the campaign."[42] Rank-and-file Republicans began to fear an announcement from McCain that Reverend Wright would be joining his campaign.

Even faced with a Republican presidential candidate who stoutly refused to mention any negative information about his opponent in order to impress the media, liberals would not stop fretting about the Republican Attack Machine.

In the *New York Times*, Frank Rich paid the usual media homage to Obama by denouncing Hillary for "her ceaseless parroting of right-wing attacks." More of a man than McCain, Hillary was not afraid to mention Obama's friends. Or as Rich put it, she launched a "barrage of McCarthyesque guilt-by-association charges against [the media's] candidate, portraying him as a fellow traveler of bomb-throwing, America-hating, flag-denigrating terrorists."[43] True, Joe McCarthy named only Soviet spies and their witting accomplices, but when liberals use phrases like "McCarthyesque guilt-by-association charges," they mean something bad.

No one had accused Obama of guilt by association, but rather guilt *of* association—association with a bomb-planting, America-hating, flag-denigrating imbecile. Obama's pal Bill Ayers was cofounder of the domestic terrorist group the Weather Underground, which had bombed a dozen buildings, including the Pentagon, the U.S. Capitol, and various police stations. Ayers was utterly unrepentant, saying—in an interview published on September 11, 2001—that he wished he had set more bombs. In a 2001 issue of *Chicago* magazine, Ayers was photographed jumping on an American flag, and in another interview after the 9/11 attack, he said that this country makes him want to "puke." Those are facts. I am sure liberals like Frank Rich would like to embargo discussion of their favorite terrorists, but Obama's friends were not being "portrayed" as "bomb-throwing, America-hating, flag-denigrating terrorists." They *were* "bomb-throwing, America-hating, flag-denigrating terrorists."

It is also a fact that Ayers's wife, fellow Weatherman Bernardine Dohrn, praised the Manson family for murdering Sharon Tate and others, shouting at a 1969 rally, "Dig it. First they killed those pigs, then they ate dinner in the same room with them. They even shoved a fork into a victim's stomach! Wild!" In a better country, just saying "Dig it!" in public would get you twenty years in the slammer. At other rallies, Dohrn said, "Bring the revolution home, kill your parents—that's where it's at." It got to the point that the members of the Manson family had to distance themselves from Ayers and Dohrn.

Nor, as Obama and his adoring media claimed, were sociopaths Ayers and Dohrn just people who happened to live in his neighborhood: They were there at the inception of Obama's political career, hosting a fundraiser for Obama at their home back in 1995. Obama served with Ayers on the board of the radical Woods Fund, long after Ayers's 2001 wish that he had set more bombs. Obama shared a podium with Ayers at a University of Chicago event—organized by Michelle Obama, director of the university's Community Service Program.[44] In keeping with Obama's statements on his other friends, like Tony Rezko ("This isn't the Tony Rezko I knew")[45] or the Reverend Wright ("The person I saw yesterday was not the person that I met twenty years ago"),[46] perhaps Obama could have said, "The Bill Ayers I embraced at the kickoff party to my political career was not the same Bill Ayers who tried to murder hundreds of innocent Americans by blowing up the Pentagon and other buildings." That has a nice ring to it.

What was a candidate for the United States presidency doing being friends with these former terrorists, Ayers and Dohrn? Why not Timothy McVeigh? Would anyone have a problem with handing the presidency to a friend of McVeigh's?

Obama also tried to dismiss his friendship with Ayers in one of the Democratic debates, on the grounds that Ayers is a college professor—well, yes, but that's a whole other problem—and that he hadn't tried to bomb any government buildings for years. In the ABC debate in April 2008, Obama said Ayers is "a professor of English in Chicago . . . and the notion that somehow as a consequence of me knowing somebody who engaged in detestable acts forty years ago when I was eight years old, somehow reflects on me and my values, doesn't make much sense."[47] (Technically, Ayers is a professor of education, meaning that he is less qualified to teach than the entire population of the United States.)

Forty years was a long time ago, but not as long ago as slavery existed in this country and we never hear the end of that. But the real problem was, Ayers and his Weatherman wife not only had never repented, they wouldn't stop boasting about being revolutionaries. To the contrary, blowing up buildings was their greatest glory! They were like Bette Davis in the movie *What Ever Happened to Baby Jane?*—endlessly reliving their ridiculous youth. They've never accomplished anything else. Run a search of their names. All you will find are documentaries, books, memoirs, and interviews about their days as "revolutionaries"! Ayers finally produced a book in 2001. Guess what it was about? Nope, it was not a treatise on economics. Come on, have another guess!

Ayers's now-famous quote published on September 11, 2001—"I don't regret setting bombs. I feel we didn't do enough"[48]—was from an interview about . . . guess what? If you guessed the history of the Civil War, I'm sorry, but you're wrong again. In another *Times* interview a few days later—which is more interviews than the collective *Times* interviews given to bestselling conservative authors—Ayers clarified his remarks from the 9/11 edition by saying that this country makes him want to "puke."[49] The interview was conducted by a reporter who said her parents were Weathermen.

Mr. and Mrs. *What Ever Happened to Baby Jane?* still attend SDS reunions, such as the one in 2007, where Ayers and Dohrn gave vapid speeches about AmeriKKKa being "the greatest purveyor of violence on this earth." They give dramatic renderings of their days "underground" as if it took derring-do to hide in a country where 12 million illegal aliens stroll about Los Angeles unmolested. These so-called "Weathermen" are more boring than the Weather Channel.

In Ayers's 2001 book about his years as a domestic terrorist, *Revolutionary Days,* he cheerfully recalls, "Everything was absolutely ideal on the day I bombed the Pentagon. The sky was blue. The birds were singing. And the bastards were finally going to get what was coming to them."

He concludes his book with the following paragraph:

Finally, my heart and my hope is with every freedom fighter who is, even now, imprisoned for speaking out fearlessly, for action on a passionate conviction that we might work toward a future of peace and justice: Sundiata Acoli [COP KILLER], Jamil Al-Amin (H. Rap Brown) [COP KILLER], Herman Bell [COP KILLER], Anthony Jalil Bottom [COP KILLER], Kathy Boudin [DROVE GETAWAY CAR FOR COP KILLERS], Marilyn Buck [BROKE COP KILLERS OUT OF JAIL], David Gilbert [DROVE GET-AWAY CAR FOR COP KILLERS], Mumia Abu Jamal [COP KILLER], Raymond Luc Levasseur [COP KILLER], Sekou Odinga [ATTEMPTED COP KILLING], Anthony Ortiz [LOSER REVOLU-TIONARY], Leonard Peltier [COP KILLER], Oscar Lopez Rivera [FALN TERRORIST], Michael Santos [LOSER REVOLUTION-ARY], Carlos Alberto Torres [FALN TERRORIST GROUP BOMB MAKER], and the list goes on and on.

I guess Charles Manson is no longer considered one of the "cool" revolutionaries.

But why should Ayers and Dohrn apologize? They are the cosseted love children of the liberal intelligentsia. Liberal America awards them, fawns over them, the Democratic candidate for president hangs out with them. In the fastest automatic rehabilitation you've ever seen, they were taken in by the establishment and given professorships, where they are subsidized to opinionate all day. If only Timothy McVeigh had said he bombed the building in Oklahoma City to protest American "fascism, imperialism, and racism," he too could be teaching at Northwestern University and sitting on a board with a future U.S. president.

The board that Obama and Ayers served on together, the left-wing Woods Fund, gave a big grant to the infamous Tides Foundation. This type of foundation-to-foundation giving is a notorious form of (legal) "laundering," whereby the initial foundation avoids the stigma of the recipient foundation's subsequent ill-advised grants, even while making them possible. Tides is a monstrous group that has funded virtually every evil in the world, including not only outright terrorist supporters in the Mideast but numerous offensive U.S. groups as well.

Woods also gave money to the Arab American Action Network, an Israel-bashing group of loonies headed up by Obama's friend

Rashid Khalidi, the infamous Columbia "professor." When Khalidi was leaving Chicago for New York in 2003, Obama attended a farewell party for Khalidi, along with Ayers and Dohrn, giving him a warm tribute and saying that Khalidi had begun a conversation that was necessary for "this entire world."[50] At Columbia University, Khalidi holds the Edward Said chair. A devoted admirer of Yasser Arafat, Khalidi was at the center of protests by Jewish professors, alumni, and students over the anti-Semitic tone of the Columbia Middle East Studies program. The United Arab Emirates gave a contribution of $200,000 to fund his professorship. Joel Klein, head of New York City's Department of Education, blocked Khalidi's appointment to an advisory position with the department, saying his harangues against Israel made the appointment inappropriate. The Woods Fund also gave a donation to Trinity Church, presided over by another pal of Obama's: racist and anti-Semitic loon Jeremiah Wright.

But none of this mattered because the media warned the public in advance not to believe any information they heard that did not reflect favorably on the Democratic candidate. That is the point of all their wailing about "smears" from the Republican Attack Machine: Republicans should not be allowed to talk. If Republicans make any argument against a Democrat, they are said to be engaging in personal attacks. If telling voters the facts about Democrats constitutes an "attack," then maybe there is such a thing as a Republican Attack Machine. Most people call it a "tape recorder."

In an aggressive move, the media, in tandem with the Obama campaign, began debunking patently preposterous slurs that no one else had heard. To great applause from the media, for example, the Obama campaign launched a website in June 2008 called "Fight the Smears" in response to this purported deluge of false and defamatory information about him and his wife coming from mysterious Republicans. The imaginary slurs were all thematically related to actual facts about Obama. So by loudly defeating a handful of ridiculous claims about him, the media covered up his undeniable problems. The myth of a Republican Attack Machine victimizing Democrats had once again been used to preempt meaningful debate on real issues.

Needless to say, the only smears debunked on Obama's website had already been thoroughly shredded, day in and day out, throughout the media. In fact, the only way anyone had heard of the alleged smears was by hearing them debunked. In all its glory, the famous Republican Attack Machine had produced a few Internet rumors that, even if untrue, were more fact-based than the things the media routinely say about Republicans.

We were repeatedly told, for example, of right-wing smears that Obama was a Muslim. This was particularly ungrateful, in light of the fact that conservative TV and radio host Sean Hannity had done more than anyone else in America to publicize Obama's "Christian" pastor, Reverend Wright. Moreover, when liberals thought no one else was listening, they boasted of Obama's Muslim background, citing it as a reason to vote for him. In a much-heralded article in the *Atlantic Monthly*,[51] liberal Andrew Sullivan wrote:

The Republicans and independents who are open to an Obama candidacy see his primary advantage in prosecuting the war on Islamist terrorism. *It isn't about his policies as such; it is about his person.* . . .

What does he offer? First and foremost: his face. Think of it as the most effective potential re-branding of the United States since Reagan. Such a re-branding is not trivial—*it's central to an effective war strategy.* . . . There is simply no other candidate with the potential of Obama to do this. Which is where his face comes in.

Consider this hypothetical. It's November 2008. A young Pakistani Muslim is watching television and sees that this man—Barack Hussein Obama—is the new face of America. In one simple image, America's soft power has been ratcheted up not a notch, but a logarithm. *A brown-skinned man whose father was an African, who grew up in Indonesia and Hawaii, who attended a majority-Muslim school as a boy, is now the alleged enemy.* If you wanted the crudest but most effective weapon against the demonization of America that fuels Islamist ideology, Obama's face gets close. It proves them wrong about what America is in ways no words can.

Liberals gleefully cited the fact that Obama "attended a majority-Muslim school as a boy" as a reason to vote for him—it will make our enemies love us! But some Americans didn't want our enemies to love us; they would prefer that our enemies fear us. Why weren't they allowed to cite the very same fact—that, as a boy, Obama attended a majority-Muslim school? It's a peculiar form of political debate that allows the exact same information about a candidate to be used if it is given as a reason to vote for him, but constitutes a hate crime if it is cited as a reason not to vote for him.

Sullivan touted the benefits that would come from a "brown-skinned" president, but when former Democratic vice presidential candidate Geraldine Ferraro, a Hillary supporter, said "if Obama was a white man, he would not be in this position"[52]—she was called a vile racist. Obama said her remarks were "divisive" and "patently absurd."[53] Ferraro was later forced to resign from Hillary's campaign.[54]

Maybe there were also some voters who didn't care one way or another about Obama's Muslim background or that he was half-black, but were starting to notice that he was Muslim when it helped, and not when it didn't; that he was a committed member of the Reverend Wright's flock when it helped, and not when it didn't; that he was black when it helped, and not when it didn't. Even that point couldn't be made. Any facts about Obama were portrayed as vicious smears—unless they were being cited as reasons to vote for him.

IN ANNOUNCING HIS "FIGHT THE SMEARS" WEBSITE, OBAMA said, "There is dirt and lies that are circulated in e-mail. And they pump them out long enough until finally, you, a mainstream reporter, ask me about them. And then that gives legs to the story. If somebody has evidence that myself or Michelle or anybody has said something inappropriate, let them do it." First, I would like to know the name of a mainstream reporter who asked Obama any difficult question, much less a question premised on a lie—other than how he planned to respond to Republican lies. Second, I have evidence that Obama and his wife said something inappropriate!

I don't think he's a Muslim, but I do think he said "I would" to the question "Would you be willing to meet separately, without precondition, during the first year of your administration, in Washington or anywhere else, with the leaders of Iran, Syria, Venezuela, Cuba, and North Korea, in order to bridge the gap that divides our countries?" Obama didn't even hesitate or "do nuance"—as he did in response to pastor Rick Warren's question about when life begins. There is no possible result of such a meeting apart from appeasement and humiliation of the United States. If we are prepared to talk, then we're looking for a deal. What kind of deal do you make with a madman until he is willing to surrender?

Would President Obama listen respectfully as Ahmadinejad says he plans to build nuclear weapons? Would he say he'll get back to Ahmadinejad on removing all U.S. troops from the region? Would he nod his head as Ahmadinejad demands the removal of the Jewish population from the Middle East? Perhaps in the spirit of compromise, would Obama agree to let Iran push only *half* of Israel into the sea? Obama: "As a result of my recent talks with President Ahmadinejad, some see the state of Israel as being half empty. I prefer to see it as half full." Obama said he was prepared to have an open-ended chat with Ahmadinejad, so I guess everything would be on the table. Obama could return and tell Americans that he could no more repudiate Ahmadinejad than he could his own white grandmother.

I don't think Obama's wife Michelle made sneering remarks about "Whitey," but I know for a fact that she said, "For the first time in my adult lifetime, I am really proud of my country." I believe he was born in this country, but I know his friends include racists, anti-Semites, and domestic terrorists, such as Jeremiah Wright, Louis Farrakhan, and Bill Ayers, respectively.

Still, the media wildly cheered Obama for fighting back against the Republican Attack Machine, the mendacity of which they illustrated by shouting the words: "Lee Atwater," "Karl Rove," "Willie Horton," "the Swift Boat Veterans," or any combination thereof. You never get details because the details don't help them. A front-page article in the *New York Times* in 2008 described the work of Floyd Brown, a conservative activist, as specializing in "malicious gossip"— without giving a single example.[55]

MSNBC's Chris Matthews somberly complimented Obama for doing "something John Kerry didn't do," which was to "go after Swift Boats swiftly."[56] Praising Obama for his antismear website, Chrystia Freeland of the *Financial Times* said Obama had learned from "these Swift Boat episodes." She observed that "recent political history is really helpful to Barack Obama. He and his campaign have seen what these sorts of stories, if not confronted right away, can do to a candidate."[57] On ABC's *Good Morning America*, the nonpartisan, totally objective George Stephanopoulos explained that Obama was "colored by the experience of the Michael Dukakis Democratic campaign in 1988, of John Kerry's campaign in 2004. In both of those cases, the Democratic candidates were attacked by unfair and untrue charges, but failed to respond and lost the election."[58]

In mentioning the Dukakis campaign, Stephanopoulos was referring to the Willie Horton ad. "Willie Horton" becomes the leitmotif of the Democrats every presidential election year. The way they carry on, you would think Willie Horton belongs in a pantheon of American heroes along with Rosa Parks. It's getting to the point that liberals are going to start naming streets after Horton.

As I explained at length in my book *Godless*, the Willie Horton ads were fantastic. What happened was not, as National Public Radio said, that George H. W. Bush "beat Michael Dukakis with the help of the racially charged Willie Horton ad that implied Governor Dukakis was soft on crime."[59] It was that Dukakis was so ridiculously soft on crime that as Massachusetts governor he was furloughing first-degree murderers, one of whom was Willie Horton. The media would have you believe that Horton's only crime was being black. In fact, he was in prison for carving up a teenager at a gas station and then stuffing his body into a garbage can. And that wasn't Horton's first offense. He had already been convicted—and released—for attempted murder in South Carolina. While on his Dukakis-granted furlough, Horton raped and tortured a Maryland couple in their home for twelve hours. The Maryland couple flew to Boston to sit down with Dukakis and ask why he thought it was a good idea to furlough murderers. Dukakis refused to meet with them. Instead, he issued a statement reaffirming his strong support for furloughing murderers. So Dukakis did not lose the 1988 election because "he did not adequately respond to Republican attacks," as NPR put it.[60] He lost because of an idiotic furlough program he supported, protected, and staunchly defended.

I'll stop pointing out the facts about Willie Horton as soon as liberals stop lying about the ads. I'm only beginning to point out the facts about liberals' other evidence of Republican dirty tricks, the Swift Boat Veterans for Truth.

Kerry did not lose the 2004 election because he "failed to respond" to "unfair and untrue charges" of the Swift Boat Veterans. Although "swift-boating" has become a synonym for a tactic used by lying scoundrels,[61] it actually referred to a group of highly decorated Vietnam veterans who came forward to question the qualifications of one of their own, John Kerry.

If the media insist on using the phrase "swift-boated," they could at least use it properly. Rush Limbaugh cannot swift-boat Obama. Sean Hannity cannot swift-boat Obama. Karl Rove cannot swift-boat Obama. No matter what they do or say, they can never swift-boat him. They never met the man. But if a few hundred people, both Republicans and Democrats, who have been in some sort of community with Obama came forward and called him a liar, then and only then could he consider himself "swift-boated." If, for example, hundreds of Obama's fellow congregants from the Trinity United Church came forward and said Obama was lying about events at his church, that would be swift-boating.

Ironically, even if it were true that the Swift Boat Veterans were lying—and it isn't—it undercut Kerry's main selling point anyway. Kerry's message was *I'm a veteran! Don't talk to me about war and peace!* An ad by two hundred Swift Boat Veterans who served with Kerry saying that he was unfit to be commander in chief completely destroyed Kerry's presumptive credibility as a veteran, whether you believed the two hundred Swift Boat Veterans or not. Either they were telling the truth, and Kerry wasn't fit to be dogcatcher, or they were not telling the truth, in which case military service isn't much of a trump card. Yes, Kerry had served in Vietnam. But so had they.

In May 2004, a group of Swift Boat Veterans held a press conference in front of an old photo of a bunch of Swift Boat officers, including Kerry, that the Kerry campaign was using to tout his military experience. One by one, the officers stood up, seventeen in all, pointed to their own faces in the campaign photo, and announced that they believed Kerry unfit to be commander in chief. Only one officer in the photo being used by the Kerry campaign supported Kerry for president. The bestselling book by John O'Neill, aptly titled *Unfit for Command*, included five dozen eyewitness accounts of Kerry's service in Vietnam.

Fewer than 10 percent of all Swift Boat Veterans contacted refused to sign a letter saying Kerry was not fit to be president. At the beginning of the campaign, O'Neill had signed up 190 Swiftees to say Kerry was unfit for command. By Election Day, he had 294 in all. Only 14 Swift Boat Veterans sided with Kerry, while 294 sided with O'Neill. Let's see, would it be more difficult to get 14 people to tell the same lie or to get 294 people to tell the same lie? I defer to any registered Democrat on this question.

Also, contrary to the incessantly repeated claim that Kerry had "failed to respond"[62] to the Swift Boat Veterans, Kerry was constantly responding. He responded by issuing retractions—about a retraction a day once the Swift Boat Veterans started talking. Kerry had to backpedal on the circumstances surrounding his first Purple Heart for action on December 2, 1968. On Kerry's website, he said it was his "first intense combat." The Swift Boat Veterans said they came under no enemy fire at all that day and that Kerry's injury was a ricochet from a mortar round that Kerry had fired himself. (This rules out the Purple Heart, but did qualify him for another "Boy, is my face red" citation.)

Indeed, among the eyewitnesses who said Kerry came under no enemy fire on December 2, 1968, was John Kerry himself. According to Douglas Brinkley's book *Tour of Duty*, Kerry wrote in his diary nine days later, on December 11, 1968, "We hadn't been shot at yet." His campaign tried to figure out how to claim that Kerry couldn't have known this because he wasn't even on his own boat at the time, but then settled on the Clintonian technique of denying the meaning of the word "we." A Kerry campaign official explained that when Kerry said "we hadn't been shot at yet," he meant that he had been shot at but others on his boat hadn't been. "We": another two-letter word success-fully parsed by a Democrat! Eventually, Kerry campaign official John Hurley admitted that it was "possible" that Kerry's first Purple Heart came from a self-inflicted wound. It was because of that self-inflicted wound that Kerry ended up with three Purple Hearts allowing him to come home from Vietnam after a mere three and a half months.

Most bizarrely, Kerry was caught telling a big, dirty, stinky lie about being in Cambodia on Christmas Eve, 1968. Over the years, he talked about his alleged 1968 mission to Cambodia repeatedly—in a letter to the *Boston Globe*, in various media interviews, and in eight speeches on the Senate floor.[63] It was a memory that was "seared—seared—in me," as he said in the Senate in 1986. "I remember Christ-mas of 1968," Kerry reminisced, "sitting on a gunboat in Cambodia. I remember what it was like to be shot at by Vietnamese and Khmer Rouge and Cambodians, and have the president of the United States telling the American people that I was not there; the troops were not in Cambodia."

No one, not one person, backed him on that claim. So eventually Kerry was forced to retract this one, too.[64] What kind of adult tells a lie like that? (Answer: The kind who carries a home-movie camera to war in order to reenact combat scenes and tape fake interviews with himself.)

Kerry had long maintained that he did not attend the 1971 meet-ing of Vietnam Veterans Against the War (VVAW) in Kansas City, Mis-souri, where the assassination of U.S. senators was discussed. Kerry campaign spokesman David Wade said, "Kerry was not at the Kansas City meeting." Later, FBI files showed that Kerry was at the meeting. So Kerry had to take back that claim, too. As the *Washington Post* re-ported on August 28, 2004, "Told about the FBI records earlier this year, Kerry said through a spokesman that he now accepted he must have been in Kansas City for the November meeting while continuing to insist that he had 'no personal recollection' of the contentious debate. Many people associated with VVAW find this difficult to believe."[65]

By contrast, the Swift Boat Veterans for Truth weren't forced to re-tract any part of their story. There's a reason it was Kerry—and not the Swift Boat Veterans—who told the *Washington Post*, "I wish they had a delete button on LexisNexis."[66]

With all the talk about the dastardly Swift Boat Veterans, one is left to wonder how precisely they were able to spread their wild calumnies against John Kerry. The Swift Boat Veterans were given no time with Tim Russert, no *Today* show appearances, no fawning *New York Times* editorials or *Vanity Fair* hagiographies. The only way they could have gotten less attention would have been to be interviewed on Air America Radio.

When the *New York Times* could no longer ignore the Swiftees, it had to manufacture a special typewriter key for the Swift Boat Veterans so that any story mentioning them would read: "the unsubstantiated charges of the Swift Boat Veterans." As with many words liberals create new meanings for—"everyone," "constitutional," "is," "we"—the *Times* was apparently using the word "unsubstantiated" to mean "tested repeatedly and proved true." At least sixteen times, the newspaper described the Swiftees' charges as "unsubstantiated." By contrast, not once did the *Times* describe the laughably unsubstantiated charge that Bush went AWOL from his National Guard service as "unsubstantiated" out of eighteen mentions of that allegation.

The *Times* got so desperate that it called on the Federal Election Commission to shut down the ads of the Swift Boat Veterans, bitterly remonstrating in an editorial that the Commission had "done nothing to rein in" the Swiftees' free speech.[67] Similarly, the Democratic National Committee threatened to sue TV stations that ran the Swift Boat Veterans' paid ads. When Democrats are this terrified of a book, it's not because they have a good response. The problem wasn't Kerry's want of alacrity in responding, it was that he didn't have an answer.

Far from not responding, Kerry and the media wing of his campaign responded to the Swift Boat Veterans aggressively and repeatedly. Apart from Fox News and the *Navy Times*, stories about the Swift Boat Veterans generally had titles like these:

"Swift Boats: Bet It's Nice to Have Grassroots Support That Writes $35k Checks"

"Anti-Kerry Veterans' Group Now Political Machine with Big Budget"

"Not Too Swift: Vets Questioning Kerry's Record Discredit
   Themselves"

"Slime Slung by Shameless Surrogates Sticks to Bush Gang"

"Swift Boat Veterans Wouldn't Know Truth"

"Kerry-Loathing Swift Boaters Sinking Facts"

"Swiftly Developing Smears"

"Kerry-Edwards: America's Swift Reaction to Bush Backers'
   Latest 'Ugly' Lying Smear Campaign"

"Vietnam: Just Like the War Itself, This Story's Now a Quagmire"

"Attacks on Kerry's War Record Are Dishonorable and Distract
   from Real Issues"

"Vet Group Doing Bush's Dirty Work, Kerry Says: He Urges
   President to Condemn Ads Critical of His Record"

"Kerry Says Group Is a Front for Bush: Democrat Launches
   Counterattack Ad on Combat Record"

"Kerry Insists Veterans Lie, Blames Bush"

"Kerry-Edwards Campaign Debunks False Swift Boat Attacks:
   Sets the Record Straight with New Ad"

Liberal commentator Lawrence O'Donnell offered the most hilarious reaction to the Swiftees. Appearing on MSNBC's *Scarborough
Country* with John O'Neill, the author of *Unfit for Command,* O'Donnell spent two segments shouting down O'Neill as a "liar," a "creepy
liar," a "lying writer" with a "pack-of-lies book"—and similar varia-
tions. In a nutshell, it went like this:

That's a lie, John O'Neill. Keep lying. It's all you do. . . . Lies. . . .
Which is not in John O'Neill's book, because it's a lie. . . . That's a
lie. It's another lie. That's a lie. . . . Absolutely lie. . . . You lie in
that book. . . . You lie about documents endlessly. His name is not
on the reports. You're just lying about it. . . . And you lied about
Thurlow's Bronze Star. You lied about it as long as you could until
the *New York Times* found the wording of what was on the citation that you, as a lying writer, refused to put in your pack-of-lies
book. . . . Disgusting, lying book. . . . You have no standards, John

O'Neill, as an author. And you know it. It's a pack of lies. You are unfit to publish. . . . Lies. . . . He just lies. He just spews out lies. . . . Point to his name on the report, you liar. Point to his name, you liar. . . . You just spew lies. . . . I just hate the lies of John O'Neill. . . . I hate lies. . . . They're proven lies. . . . O'Neill is a liar. He's been a liar for 35 years about this. And he found other liars. . . . Creepy liar . . . liar who makes things up. . . .

Liberals threw so much mud at the Swiftees that anyone who wasn't willing to devote four hours of research to getting the facts would be left with the impression that the Swiftees had been discredited. As the ombudsman for the *Washington Post* put it—a few weeks before the *Post* would begin printing Kerry's retractions and clarifications, "My sense in reading those stories is that, while they found holes in both sides, the most serious holes were poked in the case made by Swift Boat Veterans for Truth."[68]

It would require the labor of Will and Ariel Durant to document all the attacks on the Swiftees, but two examples will give the flavor of the objections: One of the commanders on the mission leading to Kerry's disputed Bronze Star was Lieutenant Donald Droz. He was the only commander—other than Kerry—not to contradict Kerry's version of what happened but only because he wasn't around to object, having been killed in action. So liberals produced Droz's widow, a San Francisco lawyer and Vietnam War protester, to say that she distinctly remembered her husband telling her what happened that very day. She told the *Boston Globe* that her husband had told her about the March 13 action during a leave a few weeks later, when they met in Hawaii, and . . . it matched exactly what Kerry had said![69] So we could not trust the memories of three commanding officers and eleven crewmen who were part of the action that day, but we could trust the memory of a deceased commanding officer's widow, who was not there but was an antiwar activist and Kerry supporter.

The George Soros–funded group Media Matters for America quickly produced a document titled "The Lies of John O'Neill." Among O'Neill's heinous lies was his claim on CNN's *Crossfire* that he had had "no serious involvement in politics of any kind in over 32 years." To this, Media Matters retorted, "In fact, O'Neill has made more than $14,000 in federal contributions to Republican candidates and causes since 1990; most people would consider giving $14,000 a 'serious' involvement."[70] *LIAR!* While I'm not sure how to fact-check what "most people" think, I doubt whether "most people" would consider political donations of about $1,000 a year proof of "serious political involvement."

While the Swift Boat Veterans went back to their lives after the 2004 election, happy to have defeated the mountebank Kerry, liberals never moved on from defaming the Swiftees and their supporters. They never quit. In 2007, ABC News matter-of-factly referred to 294 Vietnam War veterans as "the slanderous Swift Boat Veterans for Truth."[71] That same year Senate Democrats rejected Bush's nominee to be ambassador to Belgium, Sam Fox, because he had donated to the Swift Boat Veterans for Truth. In the committee hearings, Kerry harangued the nominee, accusing him of contributing "to that very group that is smearing and spreading lies." It's perfectly acceptable for a U.S. president to have donated to Trinity United Church, but not for an ambassador to have donated to 294 military veterans.

A 2008 op-ed in the *New York Times* explained that the reason "it took some weeks for the Swift Boat Veterans for Truth campaign against Senator John Kerry to have an effect on his standing in the polls" was that a "false statement from a noncredible source that is at first not believed can gain credibility during the months it takes to reprocess memories."[72] Note the March Hare tenacity of the American liberal. Four years after the Swift Boat Veterans ran their ads, liberals were still feverishly writing articles for the *Times* that nonchalantly called 294 military veterans a "noncredible source."

On the bright side, after four years of maligning the Swiftees, the *Times* finally coughed up how exactly liberals believed the veterans had been "discredited." On August 13, 2008, a *Times* article said O'Neill's book, *Unfit for Command*, had "included various accusations that were ultimately undermined by news reports pointing out the contradictions." In a parenthetical the *Times* article explained, "Some critics of Mr.

Kerry quoted in the book had earlier praised his bravery in incidents they were now asserting he had fabricated; one had earned a medal for bravery in a gun battle he accused Mr. Kerry of concocting."[73]

That was pretty thin gruel after years of hysterical denunciations of the Swiftees. First of all, even if we accept the dubious assumption that "news reports" are more accurate than 294 Swift Boat Veterans, a "contradiction" is not proof of error; it's proof of a contradiction. Second, the *Times*'s objections were noticeably limited to claims in the book and had nothing to do with the four television advertisements run by the Swift Boat Veterans for Truth. But most important, the fact that some Swiftees had once praised Kerry and one had received a Bronze Star for the same action that Kerry did reflected only the fact that Kerry had written his own vainglorious After Action Reports. It was only when Kerry began running for president based on his undaunted military valor that the facts about his service came under scrutiny.

Larry Thurlow was the Swiftee who, according to the *Times*'s account, "earned a medal for bravery in a gun battle he accused Mr. Kerry of concocting."[74] But Thurlow didn't think he had won his medal for coming under enemy fire for the simple reason that there had been no enemy fire. What happened was the first boat in the five-boat convoy, PCF-3, hit a mine that blew up the boat and tossed the sailors into the water. The Swiftees fired on the shore as a precautionary measure, but stopped when they realized there was no return fire. That is according to eleven crew members and three commanders on that mission—or all living commanders, except Kerry.

Thurlow thought he got the Bronze Star for rescuing men from the boat that struck a mine. As he explained between interruptions on *Hardball*, "I felt like I got the award because I saved some people's lives and saved the boat." Kerry had nothing to do with saving the boat that had been hit because—again according to the accounts of all three living commanding officers, except Kerry—Kerry fled on his boat the moment the first boat hit a mine. It wasn't until Kerry was running for president that Thurlow saw the After Action Report and realized Kerry had claimed that the boats had come under enemy fire.

On *Hardball*, Thurlow said he knew Kerry had written the After

Action Report because the report mentioned "none of the action I took about saving the men or the boat," but recounted in glorious detail how Kerry himself had come back and pulled James Rassmann out of the water. Rassmann had apparently fallen off Kerry's boat as a result of the rocking from the mine explosion. Kerry's boat, Thurlow said, "was the central figure in the report. The 3 boat was the one that was mined and badly damaged, but yet the report tells about John Kerry coming back to get Rassmann under intense fire and only casually mentions anything else that even happened that day."[75]

Until Kerry's self-aggrandizing After Action Reports came under scrutiny and were promptly hooted at by eyewitnesses, the only source of information about Kerry's military service were the After Action Reports he wrote himself. In the military, writing After Action Reports is like getting latrine duty. But apparently, Kerry was always the guy saying, "I'll do it!" The reports weren't passed around and checked for accuracy. The sheer number of medals Kerry won during a short three and a half months in Vietnam—one Silver Star, two Bronze Stars, and three Purple Hearts—raises a strong suspicion of chicanery.

Although the media briefly tried disputing that Kerry had written the report testifying to his own valor the day he won the bronze medal, it was soon proved by the DNA evidence of military code that Kerry was the author. The report's author was someone designated: "TE 194.5.4.4/1." The inventer of that military code explained that "194" referred to Admiral Elmo Zumwalt, commander of U.S. naval forces in Vietnam; "5" meant Roy Hoffman's Swift Boat command; the first "4" referred to Adrian Lonsdale's command; the next "4" was Captain George Elliott's Swift Boat base; and the "1" narrowed the sender down to some officer other than the mission commander. A Navy communications expert determined that the report was sent at 11:20 P.M., the night of the mission from the U.S. Coast Guard cutter *Spencer.* The only officer on board the Spencer at 11:20 P.M. was John Kerry.[76]

As for the *Times*'s claim that some "critics of Mr. Kerry quoted in the book had earlier praised his bravery in incidents they were now asserting he had fabricated," that is also explained by knowing just a few facts. The Swiftees who appeared to have changed their minds about

Kerry were his commander, Captain Elliott, and the commander of shoreline operations, retired Coast Guard Captain Lonsdale. Their positive comments about Kerry were made during his 1996 Senate campaign in response to *Boston Globe* columnist David Warsh suggesting that Kerry's Silver Star may have resulted from his committing a war crime.[77]

Elliott, Lonsdale, and other veterans leapt in to defend Kerry from the asinine accusation that it would be a "war crime" to kill a wounded enemy soldier. Even then, Elliott admitted that while he had written the draft of Kerry's Silver Star citation, he had no firsthand knowledge of the action: "The recommendation left over my signature. I was not an eyewitness. . . . I had no reason to question his motives or his actions." Nor was Elliott portraying Kerry as Audie Murphy: "There was a dead guy there and John had a weapon. That's the way it is sometimes. . . . I took the stories down, what I considered to be corroboration . . . There may have been another guy. You try to spread the glory around. It's hard to describe what you try to do with decorations. It's part hype, part leadership."[78]

Only when Kerry ran for president and his After Action Reports came under scrutiny did Elliott realize he had been scammed. Kerry had written in the After Action Report that his own "daring and courageous tactic surprised the enemy and succeeded in routing a score of enemy soldiers."[79] But Kerry's crewmen, including those who supported him, said Kerry had killed only a single, already wounded, enemy troop. Elliott and Lonsdale didn't think Kerry had committed a war crime, but they didn't think he deserved a Silver Star for it either. None of the other Swiftees who had gone ashore that day in the same action and killed many more enemy combatants than Kerry had received Silver Stars. As O'Neill wrote in *Unfit for Command,* "Kerry did follow normal military conduct and displayed ordinary courage, but the incident was nothing out of the ordinary and to most Swift and Vietnam veterans, Kerry's actions would hardly justify any kind of unusual award."[80]

After four years of looking, the best liberals could come up with to discredit the Swiftees were "contradictions" that were not contradic-

tions at all once you knew the details. Ten days after the *Times* finally
gave even this scintilla of specificity to the claim that the Swift Boat
Veterans had been proved to be liars, the paper went back to simply
asserting that the advertisements of the Swift Boat Veterans for Truth
included "allegations since discredited."[81] The legends of Willie Horton and the Swift Boat Veterans prove only that liberals will never, ever
concede the most thoroughly proved facts. Soon liberals will be refusing to communicate in the English language.

THE VERY REASON THAT SHOCKING FACTS ARE LIKELY TO COME
out about Democrats, but not Republicans, during a presidential campaign is that the Media Attack Machine has inevitably given the
Democrat a free ride for his entire political career, while a Republican
can't run for town clerk without reporters poring through his divorce
records and youthful high jinks.

Everything changes when a Democrat becomes a candidate for
president. Media bias alone can no longer censor inconvenient facts
about the media's pet politicians—especially with the existence of the
new alternative media. This is precisely why, in 2008, Democrats
chose a presidential candidate with a thin record. A presidential campaign prompts people to do research and they will start to notice little
things like a history of calling U.S. troops war criminals or a candidate's foaming-at-the-mouth spiritual adviser.

But until a Democrat runs for president, there is no adversary
press to call them on problem issues, and these liberal Walter Mittys
get wilder and wilder. For years, the press had uncritically repeated
every fantasy John Kerry told them. Members of the fourth estate were
so awed by the jaw-dropping fact that one of their own had actually
served in Vietnam, it didn't strike them as odd that Kerry had brought
movie cameras to a war. The media spent months going through pay
stubs for Bush's National Guard service in Alabama during the waning
days of the Vietnam War, but if Kerry told them cockamamie stories of
covert missions to Cambodia ordered by Richard Nixon, they couldn't
be bothered to check if Nixon was president in December 1968.

By coddling the Democrats, the media have turned them into a bunch of crybabies. If hundreds of veterans who were in POW camps with John McCain questioned his story, I promise you, Republicans would question his story. They wouldn't stomp their feet, cover their ears, and complain about a Democratic Attack Machine. But when nearly three hundred veterans who served with Kerry said he was lying about his war record and unfit to be president, Democrats, backed up by the behemoth media, attacked the veterans as lying partisans and wailed that Kerry was a victim of the Republican Attack Machine.

It's getting a little old for the media to pretend Republicans have reached an all-new low every time Republicans quote a Democrat. As John Geer shows in his book *In Defense of Negativity: Attack Ads in Presidential Campaigns,* negative ads tend to contain far more facts than positive ads. Politicians want to make broad promises and issue meaningless bromides—*I will fight for you!*—without anyone looking at their records. "Negative advertising" is really just comparative advertising that, of necessity, includes actual information, such as: *My opponent voted for X.* Unless they're idiots, when people complain about "negative ads" what they really mean is "unfair attacks"— claims that are either untrue or irrelevant. Genuine attack ads provide hard facts that highlight relevant distinctions between the candidates, which is obviously far more valuable than vague claims that they will fight for you. But actual information about the candidates is exactly what liberals do not want.

It is simply treated as axiomatic that any fact Republicans adduce about Democrats—including Dukakis's furlough program, Kerry's Swift Boat career, or Obama's radical associates—is a "smear."

Isn't it a "smear" to call your opponent a liar? As the *New York Times* noted, one tradition presidential candidates had long observed was to never accuse their opponents of lying. John Kerry, for example, complained that Bush "had not been candid" or had "misled" voters, and John McCain's spokesmen said Obama was being "misleading" or "deceitful." But every variation of the L-word—lie, lying, liar—was off-limits. Guess who was the first presidential candidate to break this tradition and call his opponent a liar? That's right: the Hope and Change campaign of Barack Obama. "Rarely does a day go by," the

Times said in the fall of 2008, "when aides to the Democratic nominee, Barack Obama, do not accuse the Republican ticket—John McCain, Sarah Palin, or both—of lies and lying." One example was an Obama spokesman referring to "another flat-out lie from a dishonorable campaign." But instead of marking the end of this gentlemanly custom with regret, the *Times* was tickled pink by the refreshing honesty of the Obama campaign. The article was titled: "Let's Call a Lie a Lie . . . Finally."[82]

In contradistinction to Obama's invigorating candor, the *Times* was deeply disappointed in McCain merely for criticizing his opponent. In a classic more-in-sorrow-than-in-anger line, *Times* columnist Maureen Dowd wrote that "if McCain loses, he will have contributed to his own downfall by failing to live up to his personal standard of honor."[83] Her one and only example of something McCain had said that shocked her conscience was "What has this man ever actually accomplished in government? What does he plan for America? In short: Who is the real Barack Obama?" If that was dishonorable, what could McCain say about his opponent? When McCain merely referred to Obama as "that one" in the second presidential debate, there was such a rending of garments in the establishment press you would think McCain had called him a "nappy-headed ho."

The most amazing thing liberals have done is create the myth of a compliant right-wing media with Republicans badgering baffled reporters into attacking Democrats. It's so mad, it's brilliant. It's one kind of lie to say the Holocaust was when the Swedes killed the Jews. But it's another kind of lie entirely to say the Holocaust was when the Jews killed the Nazis. Liberals have actually neutralized the incredible press orchestration of left-wing propaganda by acting as if they are the victims of the all-powerful Republican National Committee. By obsessively prattling about the "Republican Attack Machine," the media convey their view of conservatives as absolutely evil, masters of the dark arts of character assassination and dirty campaigning. Meanwhile, an examination of the historical record suggests that it is those who pretend to believe in the Republican Attack Machine who are the most vicious attack dogs of all.

4

WITLESS WITNESSES
TO HISTORY

I f the "Republican Attack Machine" is such a fearsome beast, why is it that the media have such an astounding record at luring erstwhile Republicans into denouncing their party? Despite the awesome power of our Attack Machine, actual humans don't seem to fear it that much. It is always Republicans writing backstabbing books about their bosses and being feted in the media. Meanwhile, the famed Republican Attack Machine has a pretty lousy record of luring Democrats into writing kiss-and-tell books about sitting Democratic presidents. Clearly, that's not where the glory is.

When former Bush press secretary Scott McClellan released his book in the spring of 2008 resurrecting all the rote liberal attacks on Bush, the media were ablaze with warnings about incoming missiles from the Republican Attack Machine. Back on earth, McClellan was at more risk from a unicorn attack during a global warming–induced hurricane. The only "attacks" consisted of Republicans trying to defend themselves from the scurrilous charges in McClellan's book. Oh what a hideous beast! When attacked, it responds![1]

White House staffers in Republican administrations write spiteful tell-all books for literally the same reason Willie Sutton robbed banks: because that's where the money is. If Republicans were the ones pulling the strings, a little worm like McClellan would be going for the easy glory by attacking Obama rather than endorsing him. Even stupid people—come to think of it, especially stupid people—will always take the path of least resistance. The young, the stupid, and the weak are invariably impressed with authority figures. College students in Weimar Germany emulated their Nazi-sympathizing professors just as college students in modern America emulate their America-hating professors and the stupid and weak in society at large emulate the liberal establishment.

When Democrats become Republicans—and lots do—it's always a lonely philosophical conversion driven by a substantive disagreement with their party, not petty personal grievances. Zell Miller, Ron Silver, and Dennis Miller moved to the right after 9/11 because they were more hawkish on terrorism than the Democrats. A related phenomenon is that an intellectual in modern America is a liberal who, through years of study and cogitation, finally reaches some small point obvious to any ten-year-old conservative, but which is damnably impenetrable to liberals. By slowly explaining the manifestly obvious to their fellow liberals, the late Daniel Patrick Moynihan, Michael Kinsley, Thomas Friedman, and Malcolm Gladwell are deemed the Aristotles of our day.

Even when Democrats only split with their party on one big issue—say, Bill Clinton's impeachment or the war in Iraq—they say they are holding firm to their liberal beliefs. Tammy Bruce, former head of the Los Angeles branch of the National Organization for Women, thought she was just being a good liberal when she assailed O.J. and Bill Clinton for their treatment of women, but her sisters promptly demanded that she be kicked out of NOW. Christopher Hitchens claimed to be a truer liberal than other Democrats when he supported Clinton's impeachment and the

Iraq War. Pat Caddell still calls himself a Democrat, despite disagreeing with his party on Clinton's impeachment, the Florida recount, and a number of other issues. Joe Lieberman would still be a Democrat if he hadn't lost his party's primary—indeed, he still votes with the Democrats on all but the foreign policy issues.

If anything, liberal converts try to bring their former comrades along with them—they don't try to alienate them by telling tales out of school. But the point is, their arguments are open to everyone; they don't storm out on the Democrats and announce that they overheard a secret conversation in which prominent liberals admitted they hate black people.

By contrast, when Republicans flip, it's almost never the smart ones and it's never for intellectual reasons. Useless conservatives seek fame and fortune by vilifying their former colleagues, that are always suspiciously similar to Democratic

an claimed to have overheard Bush telling someone t maybe he had done cocaine after all! Richard se counsel John Dean wrote a book claiming that he on suggesting he had framed Soviet spy Alger Hiss. Part of David Brock's purported reason for becoming a liberal was his claim that conservatives were mean to him because he was gay. Low-level White House employee David Kuo became disgusted with the Republican Party based on private conversations that proved Karl Rove secretly hated Christians. At least nine insider accounts of the Bush administration attacked Bush for invading Iraq—all at the precise moment the war became unpopular with most Americans! (Why didn't any of them tell us that before we invaded?)

Our incompetent press secretaries go bad, theirs never do. The weakest of the Republican-appointed Supreme Court justices always go bad; Democratic-appointed justices never do. Our soporific pundits go bad; theirs appear regularly on *Larry King Live*. Our unsuccessful conservative writers go bad rather than suffer poverty and disrespect; their loser writers never suffer, but the rest of us suffer when they're hired by

Newsweek, Time, the *New York Times*, or, if they are completely illiterate, *Rolling Stone* magazine. As the expression goes, when a Republican becomes a Democrat, the average IQ increases on both sides of the aisle.

On the bright side, look at how low the mainstream media have had to stoop lately to find their Republican heretics. The most famous "former Republican" is Kevin Phillips, who attended the Bronx High School of Science, Colgate University, the University of Edinburgh, and Harvard Law School. Even John Dean was at least a practicing lawyer. The 2008 version is Kathleen Parker, who went to Converse College and the University of San Francisco. The educational attainments of Republican turncoats may change, but curiously, their gender always remains the same. They are women, not limited to the biological sense.

Meteoric rises are available to any Republican who claims to be disgusted with the Republican Party for one or another reason. The heretofore unknown Kathleen Parker was the media's favorite Republican in 2008, after she called on Sarah Palin to withdraw from the campaign on the grounds that: She "filibusters. She repeats words, filling space with deadwood."[2] This might not have been manifestly insane if Palin's Democratic counterpart had been anyone other than Joe Biden— who filibusters, repeats words, and achieves a personal coup every time he merely fills space with "deadwood," rather than one of his usual deranged pronouncements.

But Parker had attacked Palin, so suddenly a conservative writer no conservative had ever heard of was being quoted as if she were Milton Friedman. Parker was far from the first Republican woman to acquire what Tom Bethell calls the media's "strange new respect." Back in the 1980s, Tanya Melich had been toiling away in obscurity for years, putting up streamers for National Women's Education Fund parties and hanging out her shingle as a "political consultant." Melich first tasted mini-media stardom by denouncing the Republican platform on abortion in 1988, bringing her hundreds of mentions in an admiring press, which called her a "Republican analyst" and "Republican consultant." Melich was a complete unknown to Republicans—but she was on the speed dial of political reporters throughout the land.

When she wrote a book titled *The Republican War Against Women*, Melich really hit the jackpot. Without further ado, Melich became the very definition of the Republican Party—because when you think of the Republican Party, who does not think of "Tanya Melich"? The erstwhile unsung Melich was soon being described in news bulletins as a "lifelong Republican,"[3] a "hot-blooded Republican,"[4] and—most preposterously—an "unlikely critic of the Grand Old Party."[5] Touting her Republican credentials, *New York Times* columnist Frank Rich noted that she had been a Bush delegate from New York in 1992. And that's not all! She began her book: "I cannot remember a time when the Republican Party was not part of my life."[6] It doesn't get much more Republican than that, kids.

If conservative scribblers and streamer-hangers who turn on the Republican Party from the left can expect instant stardom, imagine the enticements that await any of the thousands of employees of a Republican president who are prepared to trash-talk him. It's the same thing every time. The establishment media give the monkey a banana for throwing feces at a Republican and there's always a monkey who wants the banana. The identical carnival sideshow is treated like some shocking new development every time it happens.

LIBERALS' BIGGEST PROBLEM WITH SCOTT MCCLELLAN, GIVEN the way these transactions are generally handled, was how Hollywood doyennes were going to get this butterball laid. Their second-biggest problem was how they were going to treat McClellan like he was Diogenes' One Honest Man after spending years mercilessly (and accurately) ridiculing him as an idiot when he was Bush's press secretary.

One imagines washed-up Republican functionaries like McClellan showing up in a basement office at NBC and announcing they want to be rewarded for snitching on a Republican.

WASHED-UP REPUBLICAN FUNCTIONARY SCOTT MCCLELLAN:
I am here to offer to turn on all my friends and cohorts in a Republican administration.
RECEPTIONIST: *(pointing)* Line's over there. *(Rings bell)* Next!

MAN: Okay, Moonface, what are you selling?

SCOTT: I was Bush's White House press secretary and I would like to write a book attacking him.

MAN: I'm sorry, but there's room for only one oily homosexual apostate in the Republican Party and that position is currently held by David Brock. Move on, young man. You've had your fifteen minutes. Well said! Move on.

SCOTT: Wait—but I overheard President Bush on the phone admitting he didn't even know whether he had ever used cocaine!

MAN: You're not exactly saving abortion here, Scott. Don't expect to get "The Justice Souter" with that.

SCOTT: What's "The Justice Souter"?

MAN: You get a hagiographic profile in the *New York Times Magazine* telling "the rich story of a humble yet utterly self-confident man" with "both exceptional intelligence and a warm circle of friends." Also, no one talks about how strange it is that you're an unmarried man who lives with his mother.

SCOTT: I'm not gay! I just look that way. I'm a married man.

MAN: You're married to a woman?

SCOTT: Yes!

MAN: And she's a heterosexual?

SCOTT: Yes!

MAN: Then you won't be getting "the Arianna Huffington."

SCOTT: She was married to a gay guy? Wait—she was a Republican?

MAN: Are you kidding? She was Newt's best friend. She wrote a book titled *On Becoming Fearless* because she will marry a man *without finding out his sexuality*! You want fearless? That's fearless. It had absolutely nothing to do with Michael Huffington's billions of dollars. Why, she was as surprised that he was rich as that he was gay! She couldn't have cared less—

SCOTT: Could we get back to my problem, sir. I'm going to need protection from the Republican Attack Machine.

MAN: Boy, they weren't kidding—you are dumb.

SCOTT: What do I need to say to get the undying respect of the establishment media—and maybe a teaching position?

MAN: Now you're talking about "the Anita Hill." Again, Scott, you're not saving abortion on demand. All you are offering is to endorse the conspiracy theories of Keith Olbermann.

SCOTT: Well, what can I get for that?

MAN: We might be able to do a modified "Joe Wilson" for you.

SCOTT: He wasn't an insider!

MAN: Yes, but he bravely titled his book *The Politics of Truth.* We had to buy the copyright on that title from Janeane Garofalo.

SCOTT: So I'll get a Hollywood movie? A *Vanity Fair* photo spread? A hotter wife?

MAN: I'm afraid not. Let's face it, Scott, air-brushing is a limited art.

SCOTT: But I'm a real insider! And I'm willing to call Bush a liar!

MAN: Okay, I know I'm going to regret this, but I'm prepared to offer you what we gave David Kuo.

SCOTT: Who?

MAN: You remember that guy—Christian, deputy assistant director in some "Faith" office at the White House, said the Bush White House secretly hated Christians, yada, yada, yada.

SCOTT: What ever happened to that guy?

MAN: We got him massive media coverage to call Bush a phony Christian. And we can do the same for you!

SCOTT: But now no one remembers him . . .

MAN: Remembers who? I can get you—Scott McClellan—a twenty-minute interview with Meredith Vieira on *The Today Show.* The pope doesn't get twenty minutes with those gals.

SCOTT: I'm listening . . .

MAN: I can't get you a prime-time interview on a real network, but I can get Keith Olbermann to praise you for your courage for a full hour.

SCOTT: Yeah, but that's Keith Olbermann. You said yourself—

MAN: I'll have you know, Scott, that Keith Olbermann got 800 million e-mail requests to replay his blistering "Special Comment" demanding that Bush resign.

SCOTT: He did not.

MAN: There's a rumor that children all over America are memorizing it. It is soon to be a staple of the historic events all Americans know. Young couples are reciting it at their weddings.

SCOTT: C'mon, cut it out—I'm not that stupid. What else can I get?

MAN: Look at yourself, Scott. You're a man of limited faculties. You don't have a lot of options here.

SCOTT: How about a review in the *New York Times Book Review*?

MAN: Naturally. That goes without saying . . .

SCOTT: Done.

The media accuse Republicans of playing dirty pool, but they turn to the retarded press secretary for an attack on his former boss.

Liberals control the rewards because they control the media. Journalists love to flagellate themselves for how brutal they were to President Clinton over the Monica Lewinsky scandal in order to scoff at the "myth" of a liberal media. They neglect to mention that these Clinton bootlickers had to be dragged kicking and screaming by the Drudge Report to cover that rather humongous story.

Before reviewing the history of presidential kiss-and-tell books, let's take a peek at these guardians of our liberties in the fourth estate— back before the alternative media started scooping them all the time. This will be a preview of the aggressive watchdog media approach to the Obama administration.

The reason it took thirty years to begin learning the truth about

President John F. Kennedy is that a slavish press corps covered up his failings, rewriting history even as it happened. Prominent White House journalists of the day, such as *Newsweek* Washington Bureau chief Ben Bradlee and *Chattanooga Times* Washington Bureau chief Charles Bartlett sent their articles to Kennedy for his approval before publication.[7] Bartlett and Stewart Alsop, a columnist with the *Saturday Evening Post,* allowed Kennedy to edit their story on one of the biggest disasters of Kennedy's presidency, the Cuban missile crisis. Try to imagine, say, *New York Times* correspondent Elisabeth Bumiller extending such a privilege to President Bush. Okay, now stop or you'll have to start hitting your head against a wall.

Another complete fiasco of Kennedy's short presidency willfully covered up by the press was his calamitous meeting with Khrushchev in Vienna in June 1961—a meeting that led to "the most dangerous crisis of the nuclear age," as a 2008 op-ed in the *New York Times* put it.[8] For two days, Khrushchev used Kennedy as a punching bag, leaving Kennedy's own advisers white-faced and nauseated. By contrast, Khrushchev was ecstatic to discover that the U.S. president was "weak"[9] and that he seemed to be leading a country that was "too liberal to fight."[10] The meeting was so traumatic for Kennedy, there are rumors he swore off prostitutes for a full week.

But at the time, obsequious reporters helped Kennedy prevent the public from finding out about the disastrous meeting. *New York Times* reporter James Reston had an exclusive interview with a shaken Kennedy immediately after he had been shredded to pieces by Khrushchev. Although Kennedy did not hide his mortification from Reston, all that *Times* readers would learn about the meeting was that it was "more cordial than had been expected" and that there were "no ultimatums and few bitter or menacing exchanges."[11]

It was exactly the opposite of the truth—which I believe at the time was the above-the-masthead motto of the *New York Times.* Reston's account of the Kennedy/Khrushchev meeting was so at odds with reality that Reston was seriously considered for a Pulitzer Prize. Even when every Washington journalist was offering to perform exotic fetishes on

Kennedy, we were told he was the victim of an unforgiving press corps. In September 1962, Reston ruefully remarked that Kennedy was more popular in the rest of America than he was in Washington.[12]

Reston was there to cover up another Kennedy family misadventure seven years later. If you've ever wondered how it is that, in a country with an open press, Mary Jo Kopechne's death at Chappaquiddick could remain a mystery, here's your answer! Vacationing in Martha's Vineyard when Senator Teddy Kennedy drove Mary Jo Kopechne off the Chappaquiddick bridge, Reston dictated his story over the phone to the *Times* offices in New York. His first sentence was: "Tragedy has again struck the Kennedy family." He finally got around to mentioning the name of the dead girl in the fourth paragraph. Even the *Times*'s editors recognized that the "tragedy" might have been a little greater for the Kopechne family than the Kennedy family and rewrote Reston's story. A different reporter was immediately dispatched to cover the incident. That evening, Reston announced to the new reporter: "The story is over."[13]

Throughout John F. Kennedy's presidency and beyond, reporters notoriously hid the fact that JFK was a venereal-disease-ridden sexual profligate and drug addict.[14] The courtier press was too busy manufacturing a nonsense image of "Camelot," with rugged Kennedy men in an idealized American family out of *Town & Country* magazine playing touch football.

If the hard work of Kennedy-besotted journalists wasn't enough to clean up the Kennedy presidency, there was always the Hollywood whitewashing in movies such as *Thirteen Days*. The producers must have missed the part of Khrushchev's memoirs where he said: "It would have been ridiculous for us to go to war over Cuba—for a country 12,000 miles away. For us, war was unthinkable. We ended up getting exactly what we'd wanted all along, security for Fidel Castro's regime and American missiles removed from Turkey."[15] Good work, JFK! Way to show Obama how it's done!

When Seymour Hersh asked Associated Press reporter James Bacon why he never breathed a word of Kennedy's well-known affair with Marilyn Monroe, Bacon explained that "before Watergate, reporters just didn't go into that sort of thing." Unself-consciously, he added, "There was no pact. It was just a matter of judgment on the part of the reporters." I've never understood why it should be comforting that there is no "pact" when a uniformly liberal press uses its "judgment" to manipulate coverage of politicians for partisan purposes—held individually!—by each and every practicing journalist.

If, as AP reporter Bacon told Hersh, it was "just a matter of judgment on the part of the reporters" whether to report on the president's torrid affair with Marilyn Monroe, his near-daily use of prostitutes, and his "daunting" list of drugs, as the *New York Times* finally admitted, including but not limited to hydrocortisone, testosterone, codeine, methadone, Ritalin, antihistamines, anti-anxiety drugs, barbiturates, and Procaine injections[16]—in whose judgment were those stories uninteresting? Can I meet that person?

Bacon claimed it was the shocking facts of "Watergate" that nudged the press into a more adversarial role: "Before Watergate, reporters just didn't go into that sort of thing." This gets rather circular. There would never have been a "Watergate" if the press hadn't been a teensy bit rougher on President Nixon than it was on President Kennedy. Reporters are compelled by the facts of the stories they report to report them, but they are not compelled to report the stories they don't report because the public remains unaware of the facts of the unreported stories.

In fact, Watergate was a boring story. The sort of skulduggery for which Nixon was crucified was standard practice in modern politics. Presidents Roosevelt, Kennedy, and Johnson had used the FBI and Justice Department to harass their enemies and tap their phones—often with the gleeful connivance of the media.[17] NBC bugged Democratic headquarters in 1968. President Lyndon B. Johnson openly committed voter fraud to win elections in Texas, and he bugged Barry Goldwater in 1964. JFK's arm's-length attorney general Bobby Kennedy asked the FBI for files on steel company executives and sent agents to their homes to harass them.[18] LBJ assistant Bill Moyers, now of PBS News, monitored the FBI's bugs on Martin Luther King's hotel room, distributing the tapes to select members of the Johnson administration as well as the press. Moyers also ordered the FBI to gather information about the sexual proclivities of Goldwater's staff.[19] A decade later, President Jimmy Carter wanted to make Moyers director of the CIA.[20] I guess it was just the press's "judgment" to flip from toadies to a howling lynch mob when Nixon became president.

Or, in Carl Bernstein's telling, Watergate resulted from two courageous reporters breaking from the docile, pro-Nixon pack. Bernstein told Tim Russert that he and Bob Woodward had a "great advantage" in that they "were not part of that national press corps that actually had been taken in by the new Nixon and was writing about the new, gentler, kinder Nixon."[21] The members of the liberal attack machine work in perfectly synchronous action, but individual members of the wolf pack all insist on being hailed for their unique vision. One editor, apparently unaware that he was being "taken in by the new Nixon," was so enraged by Nixon's landslide victory in 1972 that he said, "There's got to be a bloodletting," adding "We've got to make sure nobody even thinks of doing anything like this again."[22]

If reporters like the president's politics, they will use their "judgment" to allow the president to put the entire country at risk with his whoremongering, amphetamine addiction, arrogance, naïveté, and on-the-job training as he manages a nuclear arms race with a godless empire. But if the media don't like the president's politics, they will use their "judgment" to call him a crook, even as he ends the Vietnam War, saves Israel from total destruction in the Yom Kippur War, and throws the Soviet empire back on its haunches.

Reporters will use their "judgment" to portray Ronald Reagan, who brought peace and prosperity and, incidentally, ended a half-century threat of nuclear annihilation by the Soviets, as having brought about a "mess in Central America, neglect of the poor, corruption in government . . . and the worst legacy of all, the budget deficit, the impoverishment of our children"—as *U.S. News & World Report* editor Roger Rosenblatt put it.[23] America's greatest president will be "judged" by expert Lesley Stahl to have presided over an era of the "largest deficits in history, largest debtor nation, can't afford to fix the housing emergency."[24] Even Reagan's reduction of unemployment to its lowest level in a decade will be "judged" a failure because, as Connie Chung put it, "this low unemployment rate is not entirely good news. Fewer people are looking for work."[25] And they called Reagan stupid.

The different treatment of these presidents is not a matter of changing mores in the pressrooms. Three decades after Kennedy's failed presidency, the media's "judgment" was still to fanatically censor any information suggesting that perhaps JFK had not been a smashing success. For revealing the truth about Kennedy long after the fact in his 1997 book *The Dark Side of Camelot*, Seymour Hersh, a liberal Democrat, was venomously attacked in the media. The national press corps was in a blind rage that anyone would print the truth about the only man born without original sin until Barack Obama. As Canadian journalist Andrew Cohen remarked of the vituperation against Hersh's book: "The attacks have been too personal, the denials too practiced, the vengeance too gleeful." No, he said, "there is something else at work here." Hersh's book "desecrates an icon, as it seeks to replace an old truth with a new one. In doing so, it threatens the mythology of a generation."[26]

Absolutely true, but the myth being so ferociously defended is more than the myth of Camelot. It is the myth that there is no such thing as the liberal media, functioning as a protection racket for liberal politicians from JFK to B. Hussein Obama.

A BRIEF HISTORY OF PRESIDENTIAL BIOGRAPHERS ILLUSTRATES which side really has the more fearsome attack machine.

John F. Kennedy's biographers were more blindly worshipful of him than Monica Lewinsky was of her presidential crush, but substantially less dignified than the chubby intern. Among the hagiographic biographies of JFK are *A Thousand Days* by Arthur Schlesinger, *Kennedy* by Theodore Sorensen, *Johnny We Hardly Knew Ye* by Kenneth P. O'Donnell, and *Sweet Jesus, I Wish John F. Kennedy Were Having Sex with Me Right Now!* by Doris Kearns Goodwin. Such books were described by the Pulitzer Prize–winning Hersh as reflecting the authors' "devotion to the man whom each accepted unquestioningly as his leader."[27]

Meanwhile, Kennedy's single greatest achievement between 1961 and 1963 was inviting photographers to the Oval Office to take his picture as he posed with his arms folded charismatically or leaning on a desk as if deep in thought.

John Dean wrote one of the first nearly contemporaneous books of a president, a scathing account of the Nixon White House called *Blind Ambition*. It was published in 1976—which would have been the last year of Nixon's presidency had he not been forced to resign by a press corps that hated Nixon even more than they hate seniors who don't separate their recyclables properly. Dean's book was widely excerpted, reviewed everywhere, and chosen as a Book-of-the-Month Club selection. In short order, Dean's book was made into an eight-hour miniseries on NBC. This from the people who, according to Bernstein, "had been taken in by the new Nixon."

Just as Scott McClellan claimed to have overheard Bush making the shocking admission that he might have done cocaine, Dean said that he once overheard Nixon saying, "The typewriters are always the key. We built one in the Hiss case." This mind-boggling allegation would be proved a bald-faced lie about twenty years later.

The "Hiss case" referred to Alger Hiss, the top FDR adviser and accused Soviet spy, convicted of perjury for denying that he was a Soviet agent. As a young congressman Nixon had exposed Hiss by pursuing the testimony of Hiss's former fellow spy, Whittaker Chambers. The crucial evidence against Hiss consisted of some highly sensitive government documents that Chambers claimed he had received from Hiss when they were both spying for the Soviet Union. Chambers produced the documents from a hollowed-out pumpkin in response to a subpoena from Nixon's congressional committee. Though Hiss denied the documents had come from him, the Pumpkin Papers, as they came to be called, were proved to have been typed on the Hiss family typewriter.

Forced to explain the unexplainable, Hiss expressed amazement on the witness stand, saying he would always "wonder how Whittaker Chambers got into my house to use my typewriter." The jury laughed out loud at Hiss's excuse—and then convicted him of perjury. But Dean's book purported to confirm Hiss's nutty conspiracy theory by claiming he overheard Nixon saying the "typewriters are always the key. We built one in the Hiss case."

Unfortunately for Dean's shocking exposé, decrypted Soviet cables were declassified in 1995, proving that Hiss had been a Soviet spy—

even to the satisfaction of the *New York Times*. Twenty years later, the Dean version of history that had been avidly promoted by the media turned out to be another left-wing hoax.

There were no tell-all books by former employees of the Carter administration, which makes perfect sense, given Carter's masterful execution of his presidential duties.

But Ronald Reagan's administration yielded a bumper crop of kiss-and-tell books. In 1984, Reagan's secretary of state, Alexander Haig, wrote *Caveat: Realism, Reagan, and Foreign Policy*, in which he described the Reagan White House as "ghost ship" where everyone but the president was in charge. Haig cited disagreements over foreign policy as the reason for his resignation. Reagan wrote in his diary that "the only disagreement was over whether I made policy or the Sec. of State did."

Perhaps the most prescient of the Reagan "insider" books was budget director David Stockman's 1986 book *The Triumph of Politics: How the Reagan Revolution Failed*, which beat his second-choice book idea: *The Internet Will Never Take Off*. Stockman warned that "the American economy and government have literally been taken hostage by the awesome stubbornness of the nation's 40th president," making Stockman yet another writer who literally did not know the meaning of the word "literally." Damn that Reagan! What a crafty, mildly retarded, evil-genius, yet senile bad guy he turned out to be!

After being fired as Reagan's chief of staff, Donald Regan published *For the Record: From Wall Street to Washington*, in which he revealed—to the hilarity of the media—that Nancy consulted with astrologers before approving Reagan's schedule. This revelation proved endlessly amusing to reporters, most of whom worked for newspapers that carried a daily astrology column. It turned out that she did so only after Reagan was shot and that Reagan's schedulers viewed it as a harmless good-luck charm like Jimmy Carter's favorite sweater or Bill Clinton's lucky condom. The left-wing attack machine was not so forgiving. An op-ed in the *Chicago Tribune* called the revelations about Nancy's astrology hobby "plain scary."[28] The book was called "shocking," "devastating," "explosive," "spicy," "controversial," and "deadly"—and naturally it became a *New York Times* bestseller.[29]

There were also some mostly admiring books by insiders during Reagan's presidency, such as Press Secretary Larry Speakes's *Speaking Out*, Michael Deaver's *Behind the Scenes*, and Martin Anderson's *Revolution*. The only contretemps to come out of these books was Speakes's admission that he had twice invented quotes and attributed them to the president. But even that confession inured to the president's benefit—frankly, it was a relief to know that Reagan had *not* said of his first meeting with Mikhail Gorbachev, "I believe the world breathes a little easier because we are talking here together."[30]

President George Herbert Walker Bush's administration (remember the good old days when you could mention a president's middle name?) was too acquiescent to liberals to incite the media's rage. One month before Bush betrayed conservatives on his tax pledge, the *New York Times* ran a major frontpage article declaring: "Grudging Public Thinks Tax Rise Now Must Come." Not only did an overwhelming 68 percent of poll respondents expect Bush to raise taxes, so it was no big deal, anyway, but, according to the Times/CBS News poll, "8 of 10 people say they would accept increased levies on beer and liquor and on upper-income taxpayers."[31] The pressure was building for Bush to exercise "strong Presidential leadership" as a *Times* editorial hectored. His irresponsible "Read my lips" pledge had "softened to 'no preconditions'" and the *Times* said the "change is welcome." Finally, Bush was facing up to the "unpleasant fact that real deficit reduction requires tax increases."[32] Having tricked him into raising taxes, thus breaking his famous "no new taxes" pledge, the media didn't need any insiders turning on Bush to help defeat him after one term.

The one administration that should have produced a cornucopia of kiss-and-tell books was Clinton's—assuming that intrigue, lies, sexual high jinks, and executive office crimes would be considered interesting reading. But there was only one true kiss-and-tell book on the Clinton administration, written by retired FBI agent Gary Aldrich, who had worked in the Clinton White House but was not a true "insider." Among other tidbits, such as Hillary's cursing out Secret Service agents, Aldrich revealed that the government investigation of Bill and Hillary Clinton would not have allowed them a security clearance had they not been the president and first lady.[33] The Aldrich book was dutifully squelched by the establishment media, but book buyers still made it a number-one *New York Times* bestseller.

Three other Clinton insiders wrote books during his administration, but none were kiss-and-tell books—at least if you don't count Monica Lewinsky, whose most interesting revelations had already been scooped by the Starr Report. The first insider account was a flattering 1997 book by pollster Dick Morris, *Behind the Oval Office*.[34] Morris called Clinton "a great President and a great man" in his book and even said that Hillary was "warm, decent, sincere and sensitive, a tireless crusader for children and an excellent wife and mother." That's the sort of dirt Democratic presidents have to worry about being dug up on them. According to Clinton groupie Helen Thomas, Morris "was determined to keep his friendship with Clinton." Apparently, it worked: Clinton acknowledged that he was reading the book.[35] This was a long way from John Dean claiming he overheard Nixon admitting he faked the evidence against Alger Hiss or David Stockman writing that Reagan's administration was a failure.

Another insider report on the Clinton administration was *All Too Human*, by George Stephanopoulos.[36] The book was expected to be "reverent" toward Clinton—in Thomas's words again. But while Stephanopoulos was writing the book, Clinton was impeached. By then, even the media had grown tired of his incessant lies. Consequently, Stephanopoulos played to the only attack machine that mattered and included in his book tepid acknowledgments of the obvious. At the exact moment the media were troubled by Clinton's behavior with the ladies, so was Stephanopoulos!

The shocking insider information in Stephanopoulos's book consisted of his admission that his first impression of Clinton was of "an overgrown boy." He also revealed that Clinton's temper was "like a tornado."[37] Helen Thomas had already been bored by accounts of Clinton's temper in Morris's book two years earlier. Recall that Stephanopoulos was the man who had ruthlessly crushed Clinton's "bimbo eruptions" during the 1992 campaign. In the fawning documentary about that campaign, *The War Room*, Stephanopoulos can be heard threatening a man about to go public with another Clinton sex scandal, calling him "scum" and warning that he would never work for a Democrat again. But for a $2.75 million book advance, Stephanopoulos finally came clean and revealed to the world that . . . Clinton had a temper! As one book reviewer put it, Stephanopoulos "does not dish much real dirt."[38]

For a Democratic president, however, anything short of a Hallelujah Chorus is a shocking comeuppance. Judging by the reaction to *All Too Human,* you would think Stephanopoulos had written a scandalous book, maybe accused the president of some grave misconduct, such as attacking Iraq on false pretenses. (Of course, Clinton had a very good reason for bombing Iraq on the day of his scheduled impeachment and, in fact, appeared on the White House lawn a few days later, after his eventual impeachment, to declare, "Mission accomplished.")[39] NBC quoted one former Clinton adviser saying of Stephanopoulos, "Where does he come off ratting on the President?"[40] Stephanopoulos himself wrote in the epilogue that former colleagues had told him that "as far as Clinton was concerned, I was now a non-person—my name was not to be mentioned in his presence."[41] Democrats are so accustomed to rave reviews for everything they do that the most meager criticism provokes tantrums.

The third book by a Clinton insider was not really an insider book at all but rather a policy book. It was Secretary of Labor Robert Reich's *Locked in the Cabinet,* containing his policy prescriptions on issues like the minimum wage. As it was described by *Library Journal* on Amazon, "His diary brims with stories about successful programs for the poor, the rage of displaced workers, and the futility of trying to pass legislation on behalf of the most vulnerable members of society. Reich tried to use his office as 'secretary of little people,' fighting against corporate greed and the growing chasm between rich and poor by advocating retraining and education programs that would let workers remain productive in a global society."

Top that, Deep Throat!

It would take employees of the George W. Bush administration to remind the world what disloyalty to a boss looks like. The resurgence of kiss-and-tell books under Bush was especially impressive when you consider that Bush is a Christian, doesn't drink, and is asleep by 10 P.M. every night. His administration had the fewest scandals of any modern president's, including Reagan's. In fact, the only scandal was that his former employees kept writing books deriding him. While no one can be sure if this is a complete list, there were at least a dozen books written by Bush "insiders" while he was still in office, most of them attack books:

1. DAVID FRUM, former Bush speechwriter: *The Right Man: The Surprise Presidency of George W. Bush* (January 2003)

Frum's book was positive toward Bush—one reporter called it a "love poem"—and disputed many of the nonsense caricatures of Bush. Still, it must be disconcerting for a president to read a self-described "minor player" in the White House giving a comprehensive account of the president's IQ and temperament. Frum wrote, for example, that Bush was a "good man who is not a weak man. He has many faults. He is impatient and quick to anger; sometimes glib, even dogmatic; often uncurious and as a result ill-informed; more conventional in his thinking than a leader probably should be. But outweighing the faults are his virtues: Decency, honesty, rectitude, courage and tenacity."

That's not an unkind description, but David, c'mon, I've spent more time talking to my gardener than a White House speechwriter spends talking to the president and I don't expect my gardener— Wait. He wouldn't, would he? I'd better check on that. . . .

2. RICHARD PERLE, chairman of the Defense Policy Board, and David Frum, former speechwriter: *An End to Evil: How to Win the War on Terror* (December 2003)

This book was far from a kiss-and-tell book—it was more of a policy book, rather like Robert Reich's *Locked Inside the Cabinet*. Except instead of analyzing the fascinating world of minimum-wage laws, it dealt with international Islamofascism. That, in a nutshell, is the difference between liberals and conservatives.

3. RON SUSKIND, writing with the cooperation of Paul O'Neill, Bush treasury secretary: *The Price of Loyalty: George W. Bush, the White House, and the Education of Paul O'Neill* (January 2004)

In the first of the insider hit jobs, Treasury Secretary Paul O'Neill criticized not only Bush's economic policy but his foreign policy as well, claiming that Bush and his advisers wanted to invade Iraq as of January 2001. This widely publicized claim posed no obstacle to liberals' simultaneous claim that Bush thought Saddam hit us on 9/11.

4. RICHARD CLARKE, former counterterrorism adviser to both Clinton and Bush: *Against All Enemies: Inside America's War on Terror* (March 2004)

Clarke was the chief counterterrorism adviser on the U.S. National Security Council under Bill Clinton, was demoted by George W. Bush, and soon wrote a book saying the 9/11 attack was Bush's fault. As he explained during his sappy grandstanding before the 9/11 Commission, Clarke had warned the White House about everything: "I continued to say it was an urgent problem, . . . I wanted a covert action program to aid Afghan factions to fight the Taliban, . . . I suggested that we bomb all of the Taliban and al Qaeda infrastructure . . . I thought cybersecurity was and I still think cybersecurity is an extraordinarily important issue for which this country is very underprepared. . . ."

> **COMMISSIONERS:** Are you almost finished? We were hoping to get out of here before midnight.
>
> **CLARKE:** I warned the White House about a Category 4 hurricane headed for New Orleans, I warned the president not to nominate Harriet Miers, I warned O.J. not to try to bring a gun to get his sports memorabilia back . . .

Clarke was nearly moved to tears by his own compassion.

On Clarke's watch, the World Trade Center was bombed by Muslim terrorists (1993), a U.S. Air Force housing complex in Saudi Arabia was bombed by Muslim terrorists (1996), U.S. embassies in Kenya and Tanzania were bombed by Muslim terrorists (1998), and our warship the USS *Cole* was bombed by Muslim terrorists (2000).

In Bush's first few months in office he asked National Security Adviser Condoleezza Rice to draft a strategy for going after al Qaeda and killing Osama bin Laden, famously remarking that he was tired of "swatting flies." There has been only one major terrorist attack on U.S. sovereign territory on Bush's watch, eight months into his administration on 9/11. Maybe Bush should have gotten rid of Clarke sooner.

5. JOSEPH WILSON, International Man of Mystery: *The Politics of Truth: A Diplomat's Memoir: Inside the Lies That Led to War and Betrayed My Wife's CIA Identity* (April 2004)

As we all now know—thanks to a massive, bipartisan Senate investigation instigated by Wilson's charges—Wilson was not an "insider" of the Bush White House, he was not an employee of the Bush White House, and, indeed, he was not an employee of any sort to anyone, apart from unpaid, make-work jobs dreamed up by his wife. But since Wilson claimed to be an insider and the media believed it, I am including his book on the list.

The main impression left by Wilson's book is the image of Wilson furtively locking his bedroom door every night, closing the shades, lying in bed, and fantasizing about the glorious biographies that would be written about him someday. Joe Wilson: the conscience of his age.

6. JOHN BRADY KIESLING, former Foreign Service officer: *Diplomacy Lessons: Realism for an Unloved Superpower* (August 2006)

Joe Wilson's brief celebrity status must have been galling to other Foreign Service chair-warmers, toiling away in jobs that have been obsolete since the invention of the telephone. One of their own had broken out! He was even being treated like some sort of expert.

So a couple of years after Wilson's book, a low-level functionary from our embassy in Greece, John Brady Kiesling, released his book, announcing that he too was against the war in Iraq! Kiesling's jacket flap boasts that in February 2003, he "publicly resigned his position as political counselor of the US Embassy in Athens to protest the Bush administration's impending invasion of Iraq." Isn't that the guy who prepares name tags for embassy cocktail parties?

By sheer coincidence, also in February 2003, I publicly resigned my position as a Ben & Jerry's "Chunk Spelunker" to protest the ice cream manufacturer's opposition to the impending invasion of Iraq.

If Kiesling's gripping tale of courage doesn't grab you, the jacket flap also advises that his book discusses "what is possible and affordable in a world Americans share with more than six billion other people." Kiesling only made this list because his name turned up by complete accident in a search for a different Bush-bashing book. One can only imagine how many random idiots with petty bureaucratic government jobs have tried to resign in protest to get in on the anti-Bush loot.

7. CHRISTINE TODD WHITMAN, former head of the Bush Environmental Protection Agency: *It's My Party Too: The Battle for the Heart of the GOP and the Future of America* (January 2005)

In this book, Whitman's main point is that the Republican Party should dump the Christians and return to the halcyon days when the Republican Party was composed of silly, elitist Rockefeller Republicans. A perennial demand of liberal women who find the Democratic Party too déclassé to join, Whitman's plan is known as Throwing Out the Baby and Keeping the Bathwater.

8. L. PAUL BREMER, former U.S. civilian protector in Baghdad: *My Year in Iraq: The Struggle to Build a Future of Hope* (January 2006)

Bremer claims that Secretary of Defense Donald Rumsfeld ignored his requests for more U.S. troops. A mistake, but historically perhaps not as big a mistake as Bremer's decision to formally dissolve the Iraqi army and exclude the Iraqis from being involved in governing their own country.

9. DAVID KUO, former deputy assistant director of the Office of Faith-Based and Community Initiatives: *Tempting Faith: An Inside Story of Political Seduction* (October 2006)

Another book by another minor player, claiming to know the heart and soul of George Bush. Kuo's book tour featured photos of him sitting with George W. Bush on Air Force One, but Jim Towey, Kuo's former boss at the White House, explained that he had given his seat to Kuo that one time as a favor to Kuo before he left his job.[42]

The main point of Kuo's book was to tell Christians to get out of politics. (It's a wonder he didn't work out at the Office of Faith-Based and Community Initiatives.) Kuo derisively called Bush the "pastor in chief" and "George W. Jesus," and complained that at the Bush White House "Christians are viewed as simply only another constituency group. They are the most important constituency group in the Republican Party right now, but that's it."[43] The most important constituency in the Republican Party? Sounds good to me! Why do we have to get out of politics? Why don't liberals get out of politics?

10. GEORGE "SLAM DUNK" TENET, former CIA director: *At the Center of the Storm: My Years at the CIA* (April 2007)

Tenet's book weirdly confirms that the CIA had boatloads of intelligence indicating that Saddam Hussein had weapons of mass destruction and might well have nuclear weapons, but complains that Bush was too eager to go to war with Iraq.

According to Tenet, the intelligence showed that:

- The head of al Qaeda in Iraq, Abu Musab al-Zarqawi, was operating a chemical and poison lab in northern Iraq from May 2002 to 2003.
- Al Qaeda planned a cyanide terrorist attack against the New York City subway system for the fall of 2003, but Ayman al-Zawahiri called it off because he wanted "something better."
- "Baghdad has chemical and biological weapons," the CIA had concluded by the fall of 2002.
- It was a "slam dunk" that Iraq had weapons of mass destruction, as Tenet assured the president in December 2002.[44]

Oh, and also—Osama bin Laden was implying that he had what he needed to build a nuclear bomb back in August 2001. So based exclusively on the intelligence Tenet revealed in his book, the only question is not why Bush wanted to attack Iraq but rather why Tenet did not.

11. LAWRENCE B. LINDSEY, former economic adviser to Bush: *What a President Should Know . . . But Most Learn Too Late* (January 2008)

Lindsey complained that the Bush administration wildly underestimated the cost of the Iraq War (the rebuilding of which went on longer than anyone—including Lindsey—expected), saying that Bush's giving "only a best-case scenario without preparing the public for some worse eventuality was the wrong strategy to follow." We're still waiting for the book from an insider to the Lyndon B. Johnson administration noting that Johnson underestimated the cost of the War on Poverty by a kazillion dollars. What's our "exit strategy" for getting out of that quagmire?

12. DAVID IGLESIAS, former U.S. attorney: *In Justice: Inside the Scandal That Rocked the Bush Administration* (May 2008)

If it weren't for Joe Wilson's book, this would be the most moronic book mentioned here. Former U.S. attorney Iglesias wrote an entire book about the nonexistent "scandal" of the Bush administration firing some of its own employees, including Iglesias. With his book, Iglesias joined a long list of prosecutors going after Republicans: CBS, NBC, *ABC Nightly News, 60 Minutes, The Today Show, Good Morning America, Nightline,* CNN, NPR, the *New York Times* . . . Unfortunately for Iglesias, even the media couldn't keep pretending to care about this synthetic scandal long enough for him to write a book about it, and the book bombed. It should have been titled *Useful Idiot.*

13. SCOTT MCCLELLAN, former White House press secretary: *What Happened: Inside the Bush White House and Washington's Culture of Deception* (May 2008)

In this book, McClellan's last gasp at making a living, the specialed butterball called Bush a shallow thinker who has a "lack of inquisitiveness," engages in "self-deception," and "convinces himself to believe what suits his needs at the moment." Just as John Dean gave liberals what they wanted to hear about Nixon and Hiss, McClellan gave them what they wanted on Bush and cocaine.

Once again making Bill O'Reilly look like Mother Teresa, Keith Olbermann hailed McClellan's book, saying, "I think this is a primary document of American history. I'm very impressed with it and I think at some point, people will be teaching history classes based on it." I think Olbermann might be right. American colleges now employ approximately 84 percent of the former leadership of the domestic terrorist group the Weather Underground, assign books that argue that Jews are responsible for slavery (*The Secret Relationship Between Blacks and Jews*—Wellesley College), and offer courses on transgenderism, mail-order brides, whiteness, and adultery and one course at the University of Michigan that is titled "How to Be Gay." Could McClellan's book be far behind?

Perhaps it's not such a mystery why the Bush administration was so "secretive," as it was called one billion times in the *New York Times:* Any Republican administration is chock-full of potential backstabbers, all of whom know that, at any time, if they turn on Republicans, they might start getting invited to cocktail parties. Name the Democrats who flipped and then saw their incomes skyrocket, their press turn adoring, or their movie roles increase. To the contrary, liberals who merely stop being liberal become pariahs.

Republicans flip to cash in, with book deal after book deal. Whether or not the books ever sell, lickspittles turning on a Republican president will be embraced by the establishment media, if only briefly, like the prodigal son coming home. As far as the media are concerned, Republicans are either teacher's pet or prey.

Faced with a lifetime of pummeling, frightened conservatives take the easy path to win the media's admiration: They peddle lies about fellow Republicans. And when the denounced Republicans respond to the lies, the airwaves erupt with dire warnings about the Republican Attack Machine.

5

THEY GOT THE SEX, WE GOT THE SCANDAL

Projection being liberals' number-one human trait, they insist that Republicans are judgmental hypocrites victimizing liberals. Who's victimizing whom?

Immediately after John McCain picked Sarah Palin as his running mate in August 2008, the entire press corps was air-dropped into Alaska to dig up dirt on the governor and her family. Within a week Palin had been accused of faking her last pregnancy, cheating on her husband, firing the town librarian for her refusal to ban books, belonging to an extremist religion ("Christianity"), not knowing that the founding fathers didn't write the Pledge of Allegiance, and lying about opposing the bridge to nowhere—all false and all repeated to one degree or another in mass-media outlets. Palin's family was accused of a variety of iniquities: her Iraq-bound son was said to have been a juvenile delinquent, her husband charged with strong-arming the Alaska public safety commissioner, and her sister portrayed as a bitter divorcee. And, of course, Palin's eighteen-year-old daughter was cheerfully depicted as a trollop for being pregnant and unmarried—naturally, on the grounds that Republicans would say that about a Democrat in the same circumstance.

At about the same time, both the brother and son of Barack Obama's running mate, Joe Biden, were accused by a former business partner of defrauding him out of millions of dollars. Two lawsuits were filed against them in June 2008. That was mentioned on page A-9 of the *Washington Post* in August.[1] By Election Day, the *New York Times* still had not reported the lawsuit.

Yet when Republican congresswoman Mary Fallin of Oklahoma raised the mainstream media's morbid interest in gossip about the Palin family, MSNBC's Chris Matthews—a former Democratic operative— asked in that laid-back way of his, "Don't both parties hire opposition research people all the time? Of course they do. What's wrong with opposition research? . . . Are you saying that your campaign committee has never done opposition research? Are you saying the Republican Congressional Campaign—the national Republican Campaign Committee has never hired opposition research people? Is that what you're saying?"[2]

One big difference is that Republican opposition research doesn't end up in the mainstream media—unless it is to be denounced as an "attack." It also doesn't concern unsubstantiated allegations from ex-spouses' divorce files released from sealed court records. Republican "opposition research" mostly consists of trying to publicize relevant information the press refuses to report, inasmuch as the entire American press corps works tirelessly to unearth the scandals of Republicans, while aggressively suppressing Democratic scandals. The only way scandalous information about a Democrat will ever see the light of day is if some enterprising Republican operative digs it up—which is why the press is forever fretting about "negative campaigning." The media believe they should be the arbiters of what counts as a scandal.

Without Republicans pushing it, for example, when were the mainstream media planning on telling us that Obama's pastor of twenty years was a racist anti-American lunatic who preached that the U.S.

government invented AIDS to kill black people? When would they have told us that John Kerry lied about his service in Vietnam, that Al Gore called for abolishing the internal combustion engine in his best-selling book *Earth in the Balance,* or that Governor Clinton was a serial adulterer? When were they going to tell us about Gwen Ifill's book?

Consider that those are just the stories that Republicans managed to push past the media embargo. What don't we know? Will they ever report that Palin's speech at the Republican National Convention was disrupted by a major Obama fundraiser?

IN 2008, WHEN REPUBLICANS QUOTED MICHELLE OBAMA'S CLAS-sic feel-good bromide "For the first time in my adult lifetime, I'm really proud of my country," Barack Obama leapt to his finally proud wife's defense. "If [the Republicans] think that they're going to try to make Michelle an issue in this campaign," he said, "they should be careful, because that I find unacceptable, the notion that you start attacking my wife or my family."[3]

In full-dress sanctimony, Obama acted as if an ad quoting a remark his wife made in a campaign speech was a personal attack on his family. "People have tried to make [Michelle] a target," he said, announcing that he "would never consider making Cindy McCain a campaign issue, and if I saw people doing that, I would speak out against it."[4]

It was all very well for B. Hussein Obama to decry "attacks" on his wife and swear off attacks on his opponent's family members, but those were just empty words, much like his speeches. He could count on the Liberal Attack Machine to abuse his opponents and their families for him without his ever having to get his hands dirty. For liberals to call for an end to "negative attacks" is like a rapist coming out for gun control.

CNN's Anderson Cooper responded to the Republican Party of Tennessee's Internet ad showing Michelle delivering her "proud" re-mark by saying the ad "ridicules her remarks by asking ordinary peo-ple why they are proud of their country." First of all, if you can ridicule a Democrat simply by asking everyday Americans why they are proud of their country, I think that may say more about the Democrats than about the ad. Second, Cooper also disgustedly said the ad was "attacking Michelle Obama by mocking her."[5] Actually, the word is not "mocking"—it's "quoting." The ad attacked Michelle by *quoting* her. "Mocking" will describe what I'm about to say about Bob Corker.

Showing the raw manliness that makes one wonder how Republicans ever win any elections, Republican Senator Bob Corker of Tennessee denounced the ad as "negative personal campaigning."[6]

We should have let Harold Ford beat that guy. It is neither "negative" nor "personal" to quote a presidential candidate's wife in full, in context, from a speech she gave in the course of campaigning for her husband in front of a large audience, a speech she knew was being recorded, during which she made remarks that a reasonable person would describe as unpatriotic. In fact, it's urgent in the case of the Democrats, 18 million of whom apparently believe that being first lady is a major qualification to be president. Again, by way of example: A "negative personal" attack would be me describing Senator Bob Corker as a swishy, mealymouthed, gutless, sitting-down-while-urinating, spineless girly-girl who only denounced the ad because he was having really bad menstrual cramps.

Corker's chief of staff, Todd Womack, told the *Tennessean* that "Republicans will be in much better shape if we spend our time focused on issues like reducing federal spending, lowering the cost of health care and creating a coherent energy policy."[7] And the Republicans would be in terrific shape if they could get some men as spokesmen. If quoting what a candidate's wife says while campaigning for him is out of bounds, there's not much Republicans can say. How about "the issues" everyone is always champing at the bit to discuss? Let's take the ones Corker's chief of staff suggested as bang-up topics for the Republicans:

1. Reducing federal spending—
   Republicans: FOR
   Democrats: FOR

2. Lowering the cost of health care—
   Republicans: FOR
   Democrats: FOR

3. Creating a coherent energy policy—
   Republicans: FOR
   Democrats: FOR

When Sarah Palin's daughter came under attack soon after Palin was chosen as McCain's vice presidential choice, Obama again magnanimously announced, "I think people's families are off-limits and people's children are especially off-limits."[8] Of course, his media surrogates continued the attacks on Palin's family full bore.

Moreover, if Obama didn't approve of attacks on his opponents' families, that would have been a first for him. The only reason he was in a position to run for president in the first place was that the Media Attack Machine ripped open the sealed court divorce records of his two principal opponents in his Senate race from Illinois—first in the primary and then in the general election. Why did no one know that during the 2008 presidential campaign? The fact that Obama won his Senate seat by rifling through the divorce records of his opponents is surely at least as important as the fact that Palin's teenaged daughter got pregnant out of wedlock.

One month before the 2004 Democratic primary for the U.S. Senate, Obama was down in the polls, about to lose to Blair Hull, a multimillionaire securities trader. But then the *Chicago Tribune* dropped the fact that Hull's second ex-wife, Brenda Sexton, had sought an order of protection against him during their 1998 divorce proceedings—referring to records that were under seal. With the media flogging the story, demands that Hull unseal his divorce records for the media's enjoyment soon reached a fever pitch. "It's not a 'personal matter,'" the *Tribune*'s Eric Zorn wrote, "when questions about the circumstances behind a request for an order of protection hang over the head of a man who is at or near the top of the polls in the race for his party's nomination for the U.S. Senate." (On the other hand, it apparently is still a personal matter when a U.S. president has sex with an intern in the Oval Office and then commits several felonies to cover it up.)

There were strong suggestions that the Obama campaign had tipped off the *Chicago Tribune* to his opponents' divorce files, especially because Obama's campaign manager, David Axelrod, had worked at the *Tribune* for five years, including as its lead political reporter. The *New York Times* reported that "the Tribune reporter who wrote the original piece later acknowledged in print that the Obama camp had 'worked aggressively behind the scenes' to push the story." Some had suggested, the *Times* intriguingly wrote, that Axelrod had "an even more significant role—that he leaked the initial story."[9] It's an interesting philosophical question, but the problem is, it's virtually impossible to distinguish between the media and the Obama campaign—or the campaign of any liberal Democrat.

The media hubbub about Hull's sealed divorce records was so great that Hull and his ex-wife Sexton eventually relented and allowed their sealed divorce records to be unsealed—eighteen days before the primary. By then, both Hull and Sexton had admitted to every embarrassing detail in the divorce records, including a physical altercation during their divorce. Sexton had declined to press charges and the police dropped the matter, having determined that it was a matter of "mutual combat." Both parties said it was a private matter and had nothing to do with Hull's campaign, which Sexton supported.

But the press coverage was relentless. The Chicago chapter of the National Organization for Women denounced Hull. His first ex-wife, his daughters, and Sexton's nanny held a press conference to say Hull had never been violent. Less than two weeks before the primary, Hull was forced to spend four minutes of a debate again detailing the abuse allegation in his divorce files, explaining that Sexton "kicked me in the leg and I hit her shin to try to get her to not continue to kick me."[10]

After having held a substantial lead just a month before the primary, Hull's campaign collapsed with the nonstop chatter about his divorce. Obama sailed to the front of the pack and won the primary. Hull finished third with 10 percent of the vote.

Luckily for Obama, his opponent in the general election had also been divorced! Jack Ryan, Obama's Republican challenger for the Senate, was a dazzling candidate. In addition to actually having the stunning good looks that the media unaccountably ascribe to Obama, Ryan had a résumé that was so impressive it was almost comical. He grew up in a large Catholic family, went to Dartmouth, Harvard Law School, and Harvard Business School, made hundreds of millions of dollars as a partner at Goldman Sachs, and then, in his early forties, left investment banking to teach at an inner-city Catholic school on the South Side of Chicago. Many thought he was a shoo-in even in liberal Illinois: Recall that Ryan and Obama were running for a seat that was being vacated by a Republican, Peter Fitzgerald.

Obviously, Ryan would be a tough nut to crack, but do not under-estimate the Liberal Attack Machine! Five years earlier, Ryan had been divorced from a Hollywood starlet, Jeri Lynn Ryan, the bombshell borg on *Star Trek: Voyager.* The divorce and custody filings were sealed by a California court in accordance with the wishes of both of the di-vorcing parties. Originally, Jeri Ryan had opposed sealing the records, stating that the only reason her ex-husband wanted them sealed was to protect his political career. But she later changed her mind when she acquired a stalker. Only then did Superior Court judge Robert Schnider place the records under seal.

Jack Ryan wanted the records sealed not for his prospective politi-cal career, but to protect the privacy of his son, who is autistic. By the time Ryan faced Obama, he had already released years of tax returns to the media. He even released his sealed divorce papers. Just not the cus-tody records pertaining to his son. That wasn't enough for liberals. As one charmingly argued on the Democratic Underground blog, "The son is reported as autistic and would not even be exposed to the scandal un-less he were suddenly cured."[11.]

In what would become a familiar pattern, Obama announced, "It's going to be up to other people to determine what's appropriate and what's not." Meanwhile, the Democratic Senatorial Campaign Commit-tee (DSCC) was ferociously e-mailing reporters articles about the con-troversial divorce. A DSCC official unsubtly told the *Chicago Sun-Times,* "I don't believe we've engaged in any *on-the-record* com-mentary about his divorce files" (emphasis added).[12] Obama later pi-ously declared, "I can say unequivocally that this is not something that we are going to be focused on in our campaign." But it's an odd coinci-dence that both of Obama's Senate opponents were knocked out by the unsealing of sealed divorce records, rather as if all his political oppo-nents' cars had blown up.

The Democrats didn't need to push hard on the Ryan divorce issue, since a pack of media wolves had soon taken up the chase and were demanding that all of Ryan's divorce records be released. Lawyers for the *Chicago Tribune* and WLS–Channel 7 flew to Los Angeles to request that the custody papers in the Ryan divorce be unsealed. The *Tribune* admitted it had no idea what was in the custody records; it sought to unseal them precisely "because it didn't know what was in them."[13] This is rather like entering a home without a warrant and tossing the place because you never know what you might find.

They didn't have to ask Judge Schnider twice. So with the acquiescence of an unscrupulous judge, the media won the right to peruse the Ryans' sealed child custody records.

If any news organization can open sealed court records by asserting the novel legal argument "it might be interesting," what is the point of sealing the records in the first place? I think it would be interesting to know the names of women who falsely accuse men of rape. It would be interesting to know the race of rape suspects—especially if there has been a string of rapes in my neighborhood and I want to be on the lookout. The gay community might find it interesting to know the names of HIV-positive men in their communities. Most of all, I think it would be interesting to know the occupant, rent, and number of bedrooms in every rent-controlled apartment in Manhattan. In fact, I would be *fascinated*. But in all these cases, the media engage in ferocious self-censorship in the service of some idiotic liberal cause.

Protecting the privacy of a Republican for the sake of his child did not fall into that category. Even Judge Schnider, in ordering the records unsealed, admitted that "the nature of publicity generated will become known to the child and have a deleterious effect on the child."[14] But this was no time to worry about a child—there was an attractive Republican Senate candidate to be stopped!

Amid the 400 pages of filings from the Ryans' divorce case released by Judge Schnider was a claim by Jeri Ryan, in response to Jack Ryan's claim that she had had an affair, that he had taken her to "sex clubs" in Paris and New York and proposed that they have sex in front of other people. It was the sex clubs, she said, that drove her to fall in love with another man. In a Clintonesque I-didn't-inhale-and-I-didn't-like-it claim, Jeri Ryan described the interior of a "sex club" that she said she didn't enter: "One club I refused to go in. It had mattresses in the cubicles."[15]

Jack Ryan forcefully denied the allegations in his response at the time of the divorce, saying, "I should not have to respond to the ridiculous allegations Jeri Lynn makes in these two paragraphs." He unequivocally denied that their romantic getaway weekends included "the type of activities she describes." Rather, he said, "We did go to one avant-garde nightclub in Paris which was more than either one of us felt comfortable with. We left and vowed never to return." Ryan warned that the filings would become public and complained that his wife apparently "did not consider how [their son] Alex will feel about his parents or himself when he learns of this type of smut"—which is exactly what happened years later when the media unsealed the custody records and broadcast them to the world.

Manifestly, Ryan had accurately described the effect those allegations would have on a nine-year-old child. There were also plenty of reasons to believe he had accurately described the veracity of his ex-wife's allegations. For starters, a case could be made that it is implausible on its face that Jeri Ryan could have had sex in public in the spring of 1998 without setting the gossip pages on fire. As busy as Jack Ryan must have been with investment banking and raising their son in Chicago while his wife was shooting *Star Trek Voyager* in Hollywood,[16] he had to know that she had attained the level of celebrity that does not allow one to have sex in public.

In addition to earlier smaller roles in shows like *Who's the Boss?*, *Melrose Place*, *Matlock*, *The Sentinel*, and *Co-Ed Call Girl* (she was the head call girl), Jeri Ryan had become a well-recognized sexpot since joining *Star Trek: Voyager* in 1997. By the spring of 1998, she had been in hundreds of newspapers, dozens of photos, nine issues of *Entertainment Weekly* (which described her as "a bracing mix of steely sexuality and undiluted aggression wrapped in spandex so tight it'd make ol' Jim Kirk blush"), two issues of *People* magazine, and one issue of *Newsweek*, which purports to be a newsmagazine but also publishes Jonathan Alter. The previous December, TV Guide Entertainment Network had chosen her as TV's "sexiest star."[17] In her spare time, she attended Star Trek conventions around the country.

Moreover, by her own winsome account, Jeri Ryan seems less offended by the public leering of her coworkers than the public leering of her own husband. In a 2006 interview with *FHM* magazine, accompanying a photo spread of her posed in underwear, Ryan said:

> It's a good thing that I'm not one of those prissy girls. Within 30 seconds of meeting Jimmy [Woods], he began commenting on "The Girls," as I refer to my boobs. In fact, The Girls have become a constant topic of conversation on the set. . . . The Girls are very appreciative. . . . Every once in a while, The Girls have got to come out and play. . . . I can't blame a guy: When I talk to a girl like that, I talk to her chest too. I just say, "Oh, nice rack."

Even the laddie magazine interviewer moved on from Ryan's fascination with her own breasts, asking her if she ever talked to fellow *Boston Public* actor William Shatner about *Star Trek*. Ryan replied, "Not really. He mainly talked about The Girls."[18]

So Jeri Ryan wasn't exactly Princess Grace of Monaco. She posed for men's magazines in her underwear and bored an interviewer with endless prattle about her "boobs," but her husband takes her to a New York club "with cages, whips and other apparatus hanging from the ceiling" and she needed smelling salts?

In addition, there's a reason you never hear the expression "As true as claims made by an ex-spouse in divorce papers." Despite the plotline of every movie on Lifetime Television, false allegations of domestic abuse in divorce cases are, to put it mildly, not uncommon—especially in two kinds of cases: child-custody disputes and cases involving a lot of money. Indeed, legislatures around the country are constantly trying to find ways to reduce the incidence of false allegations, from punishing the guilty to inducing the parties to settle out of court.[19]

But punishing false allegations is not the function of divorce court. Long before Obama needed an opponent destroyed in the 2004 Senate race, California's family court—which was responsible for the Ryans' divorce case—was described in a California newspaper as "a place where discovering the truth and punishing the guilty are not the highest priorities." One superior court judge said although judges are well aware that people in divorce proceedings "exaggerate or embellish stories," the family courts simply have no capacity to determine who is telling the truth or to punish liars.[20]

Even the *Chicago Tribune* eventually reported on the unreliability of divorce filings—but only after Jack Ryan had safely been driven out of the race. Legal experts told the *Tribune* that the worst cases were custody battles like the Ryans', where "passions run highest." Divorce attorney James Feldman said, "People are desperate to prevail and are often willing to say almost anything." Another divorce attorney, Lee Howard, said, "People become so hateful, they lose sight of morality, they lose sight of ethics, they even lose sight of protecting the children they love." He estimated that there were false allegations in about 80 percent of custody disputes.[21]

Even assuming for the sake of argument that the questionable allegations against Jack Ryan in a bitter custody battle involving a lot of money were true, it is the least scandalous scandal I've ever heard of. His alleged ignominious act was wanting to have sex with his wife, albeit under somewhat tawdry circumstances. Ryan wasn't accused of having sex with an intern or a male congressional page—indeed, he wasn't accused of having sex at all. This may be the first sex scandal in history in which there was no sex. Jack Ryan was accused of asking his wife to have sex with him and taking "no" for an answer. If being turned down for sex is a disqualification for public office, how did Henry Waxman get elected?

Still, the media were aflame with indignation about Ryan. The scandal was covered on *Entertainment Tonight*—because if there's one thing Hollywood can't tolerate, it's a sex scandal! Although Jeri Ryan had opposed releasing the records to the *Chicago Tribune*, once they were unsealed, she immediately had her publicist shoot out a press release saying she stood by her racy allegations.

The sex club allegations also made *NBC Nightly News*, ABC's *Good Morning America*, *The Tonight Show with Jay Leno*, and NBC's *Today*

Show. International papers were ablaze with the story—the same newspapers that were supposed to be so bored with old-fashioned American sexual mores during the Clinton administration. The *Daily Telegraph* (London) billboarded, "Republican Took Actress Wife to 'Kinky Sex Clubs.'" Newspapers across Illinois, naturally, were demanding Ryan's scalp.

It took gutless Republicans about thirty seconds to dump Ryan as their candidate. You'd have thought Ryan had been caught attending Jeremiah Wright's church the way Republicans shunned him. Four days after Judge Schnider unsealed the Ryans' divorce records, Jack Ryan dropped out of the race.

Republicans tossed aside a spectacular candidate because of uncorroborated allegations in sealed child-custody records so that Republicans could prove that they weren't just picking on Clinton, who had molested an intern in the Oval Office, was credibly accused of raping Juanita Broaddrick, asked Paula Jones to "kiss it," and committed a slew of felonies to cover it all up.

Illinois Republicans used the excuse that Ryan had "lied" when he assured them there was nothing to worry about in his divorce files. A "lie" is one explanation. Another explanation is that Ryan believed that implausible, not particularly scandalous, allegations in divorce files were not, in fact, anything to worry about. In a world of sane people, they wouldn't have been. Did she claim he beat her? Did she claim he molested their child? Did she claim he hired prostitutes? Did she claim he cheated on her? Did she claim he was friends with William Ayers? No, no, no, no, and no. In a he-said-she-said dispute in a nasty custody fight involving a lot of money, Jeri Ryan accused her husband of propositioning her in a nightclub.

And that's how we got Barack Obama, boys and girls. In the Senate race that gave him a national platform, first his Democratic primary opponent and then his Republican opponent were dispatched by the media's digging up dubious claims from sealed divorce records. Obama's Republican opponent was replaced by Alan Keyes, a man of great integrity with zero aptitude as a political candidate, and— surprise!—Obama won. This was a feat roughly equivalent to my beating Elizabeth Taylor in the hundred-yard dash, then demanding that everyone call me "the world's fastest human."

In the few days before Ryan dropped out of the race, Obama nobly proclaimed that voters were more interested in the issues than in Ryan's divorce—though his comments were negated, to some degree, by the plastic "Mr. Spock" ears he was wearing at the time. "And so," Obama said, "it's just not something that we've emphasized or we're planning to comment on." It's easy to be magnanimous when the media vanquish your opponents for you.

Now fast-forward to the summer of 2008, when Sarah Palin appeared out of nowhere and posed the first serious political threat Obama had faced in his life—that is, other than his 2000 campaign for Congress, which he lost. Obama was running for office, so, according to schedule, someone's divorce records would have to be unearthed. This was the third attack on an Obama opponent that involved digging up divorce records. Instead of announcing that he would meet with Iranian president Mahmoud Ahmadinejad without preconditions, Obama should have admitted his secret plan: *First, we find out if Mahmoud has ever been divorced. . . .*

The divorce records in this case were not Palin's; she was not divorced. Reporters were instead poring through the divorce records of Scott Richter, a former business partner of Palin's husband, for evidence that Sarah Palin had had an affair with him, as alleged in the *National Enquirer.*[22]

As a friend of the Palins, Richter tried to seal the divorce records after Palin was chosen as McCain's running mate, correctly anticipating that reporters would be descending on Alaska looking for dirt on Palin and her associates. (Would that Tony Rezko had been as nervous!) The court denied his request to seal the divorce records and the media pounced on them. Sadly for the press jackals—and Obama—there was no mention of Palin in the Richter divorce records. Not only that, but Richter's ex-wife, Debbie Bitney, told *Us Weekly,* "I can tell you this with 1,000 percent certainty, Sarah Palin never had an affair."[23]

Poor Obama. No messy allegations from a divorce file would help him this time.

Moreover, contrary to the Palin "enemy" quoted in the *Enquirer,* who said that Todd had discovered the affair and ended his relationship with Richter, the divorce records showed the Palins still shared a vacation property with Scott Richter. It turned out Mr. Richter was the wronged spouse—Sarah Palin's only involvement in the affair was to fire the man having an affair with Richter's wife. To his credit, the fired adulterer defended Palin's decision, telling the *Wall Street Journal,* "I understand why I had to go. I accept that. I was in the governor's office and a trusted adviser. I betrayed that trust by not being forthcoming about what was going on in my personal life."[24] In Alaska, even the sinners are saints.

In a major profile of Palin, the *New York Times*'s entire summary of this incident was to say that Palin "fired [the man] after learning that he had fallen in love with another longtime friend." There was absolutely no mention in the Newspaper of Record that this glorious love story stomped on by Ebenezer Palin involved a couple who were both married to other people at the time.[25] He fell in love, so the mean governor fired him. There are lies, damn lies, and the *New York Times.*

Lying by omission is not the only way the establishment press slanders Republicans. In a form of respectability-laundering, the *New York Times* has energetically promoted all the left-wing websites that were gustily retailing the demonstrably false Palin affair story. *Salon, Gawker,* and Pam's House Blend, for example, were all hot on the trail of the *Enquirer*'s (false) story about the Palin affair[26]—some noting that "in fact the *Enquirer* is surprisingly good at reporting on these kinds of stories, and it has a decent track record with them," as an article in *Salon* put it.[27]

The establishment media treat these liberal websites like their mistresses, lending them credibility on their lunch hour, but claiming not to know them on the holidays when they publish outrageous lies about conservatives. Pam's House Blend, a "news site for the gay, lesbian, bisexual and transgender community," gets about thirty-eight visitors a month, but merited a front-page story in the *Times*'s Sunday Style section.[28] The *Times* has cited liberal website *Salon* hundreds of times and *Gawker* more than a hundred times. At least those sites get between 1 and 2 million visitors a week—in part thanks to the *Times*'s incessant flacking. But so does the conservative website FreeRepublic, which has received fewer than two dozen mentions in the *Times*—all of them identifying FreeRepublic as a conservative website. With more than twice as many visitors as either *Salon* or *Gawker*, even the Drudge Report has received only as many mentions as they.

So while the Old Gray Lady kept its hands clean from the most scurrilous slanders about Sarah Palin, it used the left-wing nut websites as its cutouts to do the dirty work. True, no one can say the *Times* printed accusations that Palin had had an affair. But websites avidly promoted by the *Times* did.

Contrary to the *Salon* article hailing the renowned accuracy of the *National Enquirer*, the *Enquirer*'s track record varies depending on whether the target is a liberal or a conservative. The *Enquirer* has acquired undeserved credibility for its scandal stories on conservatives because its scandal stories on Democrats usually are true—such as Gary Hart's affair with Donna Rice, Clinton's affair with Gennifer Flowers, and John Edwards's affair with Rielle Hunter.

By contrast, the *Enquirer* is constantly running preposterous stories about conservatives, such as the Sarah Palin affair story, the banner reports about Palin's son vandalizing school buses—proved false before the juicy *Enquirer* story even hit the newsstands[29]—the David Schippers affair story, the story of Rush Limbaugh's impending marriage to Daryn Kagan, as well as every detail of the Limbaugh prescription drug story, including the lurid tales of Rush skulking around parking lots to buy drugs and even which painkiller he was taking. Many people are under the impression that the *National Enquirer* is accurate but tasteless. When it comes to its stories on conservatives, it's just tasteless. I wonder if that has anything to do with the fact that a "key owner" of the *Enquirer* is prominent Democrat Roger Altman.[30]

THE SAME YEAR THAT THE ESTABLISHMENT MEDIA WERE BUSY opening sealed court records of Obama's electoral opponents, Democratic presidential candidate Howard Dean refused to release even sealed gubernatorial records—you know, documents plausibly relevant to assessing his governing abilities. Dean said he'd prefer to "end the campaign than let the world see everything."[31] The media went ballistic when it was discovered in March 2008 that State Department contractors had glanced at Obama's passport file. There were banner headlines, breaking news reports on the cable networks, and even an ABC *Nightline* special on this shocking breach of privacy. The matter was quietly dropped when it turned out the passport files of John McCain had been breached, too. The media consider a passport file the very soul of privacy when a Democrat is the target, but the sealed divorce records of a Republican are fair game.

At least both Obama and McCain were running for president. When Ohio plumber Joe Wurzelbacher asked Obama the Redeemer a question, prompting Obama to casually reveal that he was a Marxist whose plan was to "spread the wealth," state employees working for Democratic governor Ted Strickland set to work examining government files protected by law to find dirt on "Joe the Plumber." At the direction of Obama supporter Helen Jones-Kelley, director of the Ohio Department of Job and Family Services, they searched tax records, child support files, and business license records for embarrassing information about a private citizen.

Soon government busybodies were jubilantly announcing that Joe the Plumber didn't have a plumber's license! This was shocking to people who are unaware that plumbers don't need licenses, owners of plumbing companies do. But that's not all: Joe the Plumber's name wasn't even Joe!!! His given first name was Samuel. *People just called him Joe as a nickname!* Clearly, this "Joe" character was one of those con artists who goes around taking advantage of decent people by impersonating a plumber.

And yet none of that changed the fact that Obama had still said he wanted to "spread the wealth."

I think most people would rather have the government listening to their phone calls to see if they are terrorists than have the government designate them as "enemy combatants" for asking Obama a question. Government employees searched state databases for the specific purpose of destroying one citizen. If this sort of scrutiny were directed at a Pakistani immigrant training to be a crop duster pilot, everyone involved in the investigation would be fired and publicly humiliated. But Governor Strickland, also an Obama supporter, took no action against Jones-Kelley. To the contrary, he enthusiastically defended her.[32]

If it's open season on random American citizens, how about reporters? *Washington Post* reporter Dana Priest has revealed boatloads of classified national defense information over the years that has been extremely damaging to the War on Terror. For endangering all Americans, she won a Pulitzer Prize. I think it would be "interesting" to see the medical records of Dana Priest to find out if she's ever had an abortion. Can I get a peek?

The concept of "privacy" is respected solely to protect liberals. While President John F. Kennedy carried on an affair with a mob boss's mistress, Judith Exner, fed his mind-boggling drug addictions supplied by his own "Dr. Feelgood," and brought whores to the White House to satisfy a dangerous sex addiction, the media aggressively covered it up, on the grounds that it was private. CBS's Dan Rather explained why most of the mainstream media buried Juanita Broaddrick's claim that Bill Clinton had raped her, saying, "When the charge has something to do with somebody's private sex life, I would prefer not to run any of it."[33] But Joe the Plumber, Jack Ryan, and Rush Limbaugh might as well be living in a police state for all their privacy is respected.

Oddly, the media never used their innovative "it might be interesting" argument to unseal the divorce records of John Kerry (Democrat), Joe Lieberman (Democrat), or Teddy Kennedy (Democrat). I'm not sure about the first two, but *Ted Kennedy's divorce records not interesting?* I'm surprised they haven't been optioned by a major Hollywood film studio. With a string of drunk-driving offenses, adulteries, a night of boozing with his younger relations on Good Friday leading to a rape accusation against nephew William Kennedy Smith, and one dead girl to his credit, if anyone's personal life ever deserved looking into, it is surely the Fredo of the Kennedy family. But as far as the media were concerned, it was America's responsibility to deal with the Kennedy self-esteem problem. Kennedy's divorce was not deemed sufficiently "interesting."

You know when Teddy Kennedy's divorce records would have been really interesting? In 1994, when he faced Mitt Romney in a tough battle for the U.S. Senate. During that very campaign, Joan Kennedy filed sealed papers to reopen her divorce from Ted.[34] That would have set reporters' hair on fire if Kennedy were a Republican.

Filing in a Boston courthouse, Mrs. Kennedy specifically stated that their divorce papers had been originally filed in Hyannisport simply to avoid "public scrutiny and publicity," because "Mr. Kennedy was fearful the press would learn of the divorce and the provisions of our separation agreement, which incorporated our financial settlement."[35] *Hello? Watchdog media? Anything "interesting" there? Or were you still trying to reinterview the same three people claiming that Newt Gingrich was a beast to his first wife?*

In September 1994, Romney led Kennedy 43 percent to 42 percent in polls.[36] But on election day, Kennedy clobbered Romney 58 percent to 42 percent. What happened in the interim?

In innumerable newspaper articles and TV reports, Romney was portrayed as an uncaring robber baron who had laid off hundreds, thousands, maybe millions of hardworking blue-collar workers. The specific charge involved a strike at a paper plant in Indiana that had been acquired by a company named Ampad, which in turn was owned by the company Romney founded, Bain Capital. As was later admitted in the *Boston Globe*—after the election—Romney had absolutely nothing to do with the Indiana paper mill even using the crazy corporate-connection logic of liberals. Ampad bought the Indiana paper plant six months *after* Romney had left Bain. To put this in perspective, it would be like blaming a guy who sold Kennedy a car six months before July 19, 1969, for Mary Jo Kopechne's death.

But as the *Globe* would ruefully remark after the damage was done, "politics is about emotion, not logic."[37] Who creates that emotion? Could it have anything to do with the 8 billion news stories the *Globe* ran smearing Romney as a ruthless corporate raider?

The first of the literally two dozen stories in the *Globe* pursuing the story of "Mitt Romney: Robber Baron" featured heartrending tidbits like these:

- A union official said the paper company's problems "are evidence that Romney is insensitive to workers." *Then the union official got back into a Lincoln town car and had his driver take him back to his country estate.*

- The union official added that "Romney is just another robber baron." *You'd think Romney had amassed a great family fortune through unscrupulous business ventures, like bootlegging liquor during Prohibition.*

- He added that Romney's firm "destroyed 10 jobs for every job they have allegedly created"—*whereas the union rarely destroyed more than 5 jobs for each job it created.*

- Among those laid off at the paper plant "were two pregnant women."[38] *By contrast, Kennedy was so compassionate he would have immediately offered both women free abortions.*

In its postelection analysis, the *Globe* said the Kennedy campaign had cleverly coordinated with union officials to concoct a major media scandal out of a strike at a paper plant acquired by a company that was bought by a private equity firm six months after Romney left the private equity firm. The *Globe* acted as if it were merely an unwitting accomplice in this ridiculous slander.

WHILE THE MEDIA WERE UNABLE TO STOP THEMSELVES FROM spreading unsubstantiated rumors about Romney's business, they were an impenetrable firewall for rumors swirling around presidential candidate John Edwards in 2007.

During the 2008 Democratic primaries, it was generally assumed that John Edwards's presence hurt Hillary more than it hurt Obama, by peeling off some of her blue-collar voters. The same mainstream media that were mad to produce Jack Ryan's sealed divorce records when he was running for the Senate obstinately refused to report on Edwards's extramarital affair. Perhaps they were still working on that Chappaquiddick exposé that hadn't been ready for publication for forty years.

In 2007, the *National Enquirer* began reporting on Edwards's affair with New Age divorcée Rielle Hunter, formerly Lisa Druck. The establishment media completely ignored the story and Edwards continued with his campaign for president. Even when the *Enquirer* reported that Hunter was pregnant with Edwards's love child, the media ignored the story.

The Edwards campaign denied the affair, pawning it off on an apparently very loyal Edwards campaign official, Andrew Young. Like Edwards, Young was married with children, but also like Edwards, Young was a Democrat, so it was possible. Except that, not only did Young's wife not leave him, she was perfectly agreeable to having her husband's mistress move into their gated community for the duration of the pregnancy, and even join her, Andrew, and the kids for dinner. This did not pique the media's interest.

The campaign videos Hunter had been hired to make for Edwards were stripped from the campaign website. The mainstream media remained uninterested.

Finally, in the summer of 2008, the *Enquirer*, still the lone news outlet covering the affair, staked out the Beverly Hilton in Los Angeles after receiving a tip that Edwards would be there to visit Hunter and the love child, who reportedly has her mother's eyes and her father's dramatic flair in front of a jury. Edwards fled from the reporters and blockaded himself in a hotel bathroom until hotel security came to rescue him. Even more suspicious, while Edwards was barricaded in the bathroom, no one reported hearing sounds of a blow dryer. If only Republican Larry Craig had been in that bathroom, NBC might have covered it!

A memo from an *L.A. Times* editor to his bloggers was leaked to *Slate* blogger Mickey Kaus soon after the *Enquirer*'s hotel stakeout, firmly instructing the *Times*'s bloggers not to mention the brewing Edwards scandal. This would suggest that there was some interest in the topic. The memo said:

From: "Pierce, Tony"
Date: July 24, 2008 10:54:41 AM PDT
Subject: John Edwards

Hey bloggers,
There has been a little buzz surrounding John Edwards and his alleged affair. Because the only source has been the National Enquirer *we have decided not to cover the rumors or salacious specu-*

lations. So I am asking you all not to blog about this topic until further notified.

If you have any questions or are ever in need of story ideas that would best fit your blog, please don't hesitate to ask.

Keep rockin,
Tony

A *Washington Post* reporter defended the total media blackout on the story, telling the *Times* of London, "Edwards is no longer an elected official and he is not running for office now. Don't expect wall-to-wall coverage."[39] But Edwards wasn't some no-name congressman: He was the Democrats' most recent vice presidential candidate, he had been a candidate for president just months earlier, and he was being talked about for cabinet positions in any Democratic administration.

Say, what sort of "elected official" was Ted Haggard again? He was the Christian minister no one outside of his own parish had ever heard of until he was caught in a gay sex scandal the previous year. Then he suddenly became the Pope of the Protestants. And yet, despite the fact that Haggard was not an "elected official," the *Post* gave that story wall-to-wall coverage. And what office was Bill Bennett running for when he was caught gambling in Las Vegas? What office was Rush Limbaugh running for when the media was saturated with coverage of his unused bottle of Viagra?

The non-American press was not so demure about the Edwards scandal. Here is a sampling of some of the foreign headlines within a couple of weeks of the *National Enquirer* bathroom stakeout: "Sleaze Scuppers Democrat Golden Boy" (*Sunday Times*—London), "Scandal Sinks Edwards's VP Hopes" *(The Australian)*, "VP Dreams End in Rielle Nightmare" (*Sunday Independent*—Ireland), "The 'Scoop' the US Papers Ignored" (British *Independent Media Weekly*—Britain), "Edwards' 'Love Child' Silence Fuels the Gossip Mills" *(Toronto Star)*, "It's Enough to Make You Veep Down a Rich US Path" (*Canberra Times*—Australia). There was also this evocative line from an article in the Canadian *Hamilton Spectator:* "I was sweating like John Edwards looking at the *National Enquirer.*"

Why do liberals always want us to be more like foreigners when it comes to "tolerating" the sex scandals of Democrats, but not when it comes to reporting the sex scandals of Democrats? To paraphrase Michelle Obama, after reading those foreign headlines, for the first time in my adult lifetime, I'm proud to be a European American!

Isn't there some level of coverage between "wall-to-wall" and "double-secret probation, delta-force level total news blackout" when it comes to a sex scandal involving a Democrat?

Apparently not. The only way consumers of the establishment media might have ascertained that Edwards was embroiled in some sort of scandal was that, after the incident in the hotel, his name was summarily dropped from discussions of possible vice presidential candidates. The Democrats' most recent vice presidential candidate was suddenly getting less coverage than Ron Paul. It was reminiscent of the Soviet press. His name had simply been completely whitewashed out of the news. *Say, why isn't anyone talking about John Edwards for vice president anymore? No, seriously— Hey! Why are we going to a commercial break?*

It was not until Edwards himself confessed to the affair that the media had dispensation to report the story. Edwards copped to the sexual relationship, but said the child he was visiting in the hotel wasn't his, and he also gallantly added that he had never loved his mistress anyway. He said he was being "99 percent honest" when he had denied the affair. Apparently if you simply removed the words "not" and "false" from his denials—which is about 1 percent of what he said— the rest was true. He also boasted that he only cheated on his wife when the cancer was in remission—I guess by regularly checking her red blood cell count. I wish I had a nickel for every time a married guy in a bar said to me, "My wife just doesn't understand me—and her cancer is in remission!" Needless to say, the love child landed Edwards in hot water with the feminists, who were hopping mad that Hunter had decided not to abort the baby.

Edwards had no explanation for why his national finance chair, Texas trial lawyer Fred Baron, was paying his mistress—allegedly about $15,000 a month—and was also paying Andrew Young, the Edwards aide who bravely claimed to be the father of the love child. Finally, Edwards said the affair was over before he announced he was running for president, but that claim collapsed almost immediately, after photos were released showing Edwards and Hunter together after he had announced. For his next story, I recommend: Yes, the child is mine—but she looks nothing like me.

Forced by Edwards's admission to report this blockbuster story, the establishment media decided to cover it on . . . the opening night of the Olympics. That seemed really weird, because for weeks the media had been talking about how no one would be paying attention to politics during the Olympics. On CNN, John King said the Olympic Games were "expected to push politics off the center stage for most of August." The Associated Press referred to "the August summertime lull when attention is focused not on politics but on the Olympics." And an article in the *Wall Street Journal* said, "With the opening ceremonies of the Beijing Olympics just days away and hordes of voters on vacation, the American public's attention span for politics is minimal at best."

If you were paranoid about media bias, you might think that the networks got together to figure out how to report the Edwards story so that it would have the least conceivable impact. Through months of increasingly dramatic coverage in the *Enquirer*, the mainstream media had played Soviet Commissars, refusing to mention Edwards's shocking sex scandal. And then the media waited until the opening night of the Olympics to finally break the story. Evidently, ABC got the short straw, and it had to broadcast Edwards's admission. As planned, the Edwards interview got abominable ratings. In two years, liberals will be boasting about ABC's airing of Edwards's confession—forgetting to mention it was on the opening night of the Olympics—as proof that there is no liberal media bias.

Say, do you think the *Enquirer*'s "love child" story would have attracted media attention if it had involved Mitt Romney? His presidential campaign ended one week after Edwards's did. But I'm fairly certain the press would be able to manufacture an all-new rule to justify nonstop coverage of any lurid sex scandal in Romney's life. They'd bring Ted Koppel out of retirement to cover that. Katie Couric, Brian Williams, and Charles Gibson would be anchoring the evening news from Romney's front yard. They might even get Dan Rather to produce some forged documents for the occasion! But with a Democratic sex scandal, major media outlets compete for the Pulitzer for Best Suppressed Story.

The media never display skittishness about purported sex scandals involving Republicans. In 1992, when President George H. W. Bush was running against the draft-dodging, pot-smoking horny hick from Arkansas, the establishment media gamely produced a long-ago-disproved charge that Bush had had an affair with an aide named Jennifer Fitzgerald. The rumor had been hotly pursued in the 1980s by a variety of news organizations, but they all came up dry. Ann Devroy, who was working for the *Washington Post* when the affair rumor first surfaced, said, "I spent two solid months looking into this in the early 1980s and I never found any evidence of it."[40]

But in the middle of the 1992 presidential campaign, with a well-known philanderer running for president on the Democratic ticket, the very same mainstream media that was busy sneering at Gennifer Flowers's claim that she had had a long-term affair with Clinton—backed up with tape-recorded telephone conversations—suddenly was hot on the trail of Bush's already-disproved "affair."

The only "evidence" was a quote from former ambassador Louis Fields that came out in a book published that year, although Fields had died six years earlier. Fields allegedly claimed he had arranged for Bush and the putative mistress Fitzgerald to use his guesthouse when they were traveling on official business. One of the dead man's "corroborating witnesses" confirmed that Fields said they had used the guesthouse, but denied that Fields had ever suspected they were having an affair.[41] Nonetheless, the Democrats blast-faxed this tidbit from the book to a compliant media.

The resurrected, but still unsubstantiated, rumor was published in thousands of news reports during the campaign, including major front-page coverage in the *Baltimore Sun*, *USA Today*, the *New York Post*, the *New York Daily News*, and the *Boston Herald*, and a full-page story in the *Philadephia Daily News*. New York University professor Mark Crispin Miller wrote in the *Baltimore Sun,* "The press is obliged to pursue the story because of the way it pursued Clinton. To do otherwise would be unfair."[42] If the press covered Bush's nonexistent affair the way it covered Clinton's actual affair—as Clinton eventually admitted— editorials would be denouncing anyone who mentioned it.

A week before the false Bush affair story was relaunched by the media, the *New York Times* had issued a blistering editorial lambasting a "snarling press release" from Bush's deputy campaign manager, Mary Matalin, calling it "raw innuendo," a "broadside," "surrogate sleaze"— and claiming that the press release "embarrassed President Bush." What was this foul excrement? Matalin's press release had mentioned Clinton's "bimbo eruptions"—a term coined by Betsey Wright, Clinton's own deputy campaign chairman. The *Times* went on to praise Bush for being "politically shrewd" when he had attacked an independent ad against Clinton that dared mention Gennifer Flowers.[43] "Politically shrewd" is *Times*-speak for "a Republican who is about to lose."

CNN reporter Mary Tillotson sprang a question about the alleged affair on President Bush during a presidential press conference with Israeli prime minister Yitzhak Rabin. Bush was asked about it again in an Oval Office interview with Stone Phillips for NBC's *Dateline.*[44] Bush angrily denied the claimed affair and reporters, who would have loved nothing more than to prove a Bush affair, found nothing to substantiate it.

But for voters without the time or inclination to investigate the details, the story was set: Both Bush and Clinton had been accused of having affairs and both had denied it. The ersatz symmetry was captured in a *USA Today* editorial titled: "Jennifer, Gennifer." John Harwood summarized the situation in the *Wall Street Journal,* saying, "The allegations against both candidates are suspect. Ms. Flowers was paid by a supermarket tabloid to publicize her allegations." As for President Bush, Harwood said, "the purported source of the allegation against Mr. Bush is dead." Also, even if he were alive, his evidence was that Bush and his aide had stayed in his guesthouse. Flowers was a somewhat more direct eyewitness to her own affair with Clinton, and she had tapes. But for Harwood, the evidence of both affairs was equally scanty.[45] With the benefit of hindsight, does it appear that the press was giving the voters an accurate picture of the two candidates' alleged affairs?

Clinton was an absolute prince about the rumored Bush affair—while also linking his affair to Bush's—saying, "I didn't like it when it was done to me. And I don't like it when it's done to him. I felt for him. I like him on a personal level."[46] A mere sixteen years later, in 2008, Kurt Andersen told us what Clinton's real reaction was to the press coverage of Bush's alleged affair. (It's great how people like Andersen and Todd Purdum waited until 2008—when Hillary Clinton was challenging the angel Obama—to tell us the truth about Bill Clinton.)

Andersen said Clinton was introduced to a reporter from *Spy* magazine during the 1992 Democratic National Convention at a New York restaurant. *Spy* had just run a cover story with the bold headline "1,000 Reasons Not to Vote for George Bush—No. 1: He Cheats on His Wife," written by rabid Clinton defender Joe Conason, or as liberal Mickey Kaus dubs him, "distinguished chronicler of George H. W. Bush's alleged marital infidelity."[47] Andersen reports, "The future president smiled, popped to his feet, and ushered the reporter off for a private chat. . . . 'I want to thank you guys,' Clinton told the man from *Spy*, 'for leveling the playing field with that piece you did on Bush's girlfriends.' *But were there more women?* he asked repeatedly in the course of a several-minutes-long chat."[48]

It's always the same with Democrats: The candidate gallantly forswears "negative campaigning," while the press does all the dirty work for him, generating phony scandals for Republicans while burying real scandals of the Democrats.

But they are the victims of Karl Rove.

THE MEDIA'S FAVORITE EXCUSE FOR COVERING THE PRIVATE lives of conservatives is "hypocrisy," a one-way ratchet that apparently demands constant vigilance over the personal foibles of conservatives and a total blackout on much worse behavior by liberals. By peremptorily disavowing personal principles, liberals can never be accused of hypocrisy for not living up to the principles they cheerfully reject. Admittedly, everyone knows liberals have no moral scruples, but that's not what Democrats say when they are posing for the voters. President Clinton walked to and from church every Sunday carrying a ten-pound Bible for the cameras—and then returned from church on Palm Sunday 1996 to use a cigar as a sexual aid on Monica Lewinsky.

Why didn't this raise an issue of hypocrisy for the media about the Bible-toting churchgoer? How about his flashing Paula Jones when he was the governor of Arkansas? Former Arkansas state employee Jones held a press conference in 1994 claiming that, in 1991, Governor Clinton had pulled a smooth Cary Grant move on her, dropping his pants and asking her to "kiss it." The establishment media ignored her for more than two years. If Clinton were not a pro-"choice" liberal, I think that would have qualified as "hypocrisy." The Stalinist self-censorship only began to lift when legal reporter Stuart Taylor wrote a cover story for the November 1996 *American Lawyer* magazine, which took Jones's claims seriously and chastised the press for ignoring her.

How about John Edwards's hypocrisy? His entire political life was based on saccharine stories about seeing the light flickering while his old man learned math by watching TV.[49] People had to take showers after watching Edwards deliver one of his hokey speeches about being the son of a mill worker. I can't imagine anyone watching him speak and not retching. Then in 2008, he based his entire presidential campaign on his selfless dedication to a cancer-stricken wife. Meanwhile, in order to pass the time between giving $50,000 speeches on poverty, Edwards was cheating on the cancer-stricken wife. No practicing journalist with the establishment media would be able to pinpoint the hypocrisy in that.

But as soon as pro-life, pro-gun, pro-drilling American woman Sarah Palin materialized on the Republican ticket, the press suddenly took a keen interest in hypocrisy again. Or at least their version of "hypocrisy," by which liberals mean they have spotted a conservative— or better, a Christian.

In an essay posted on the "On Faith" website hosted jointly by *Newsweek* and the *Washington Post*, University of Chicago divinity professor Wendy Doniger (O'Flaherty) said Palin's "greatest hypocrisy is in her pretense that she is a woman." Doniger (O'Flaherty) also accused Palin of "hypocrisy" for "outing her pregnant daughter in front of millions of people."[50]

Claiming that the Republican Party said Palin "speaks for all women" because she "has a womb and makes lots and lots of babies," Doniger (O'Flaherty) proclaimed that Palin "does not speak for women; she has no sympathy for the problems of other women, particularly working class women." I gather Doniger (O'Flaherty) speaks for women— especially working-class women—from her perch at the University of Chicago Divinity School, where she spells "God" with a small *g* and her university bio describes her "interests" as focusing on "two basic areas, Hinduism and mythology." By way of comparison, Palin's husband is in the United Steel Workers union, her sister and brother-in-law own a gas station, she married her high school sweetheart, and she has five children. Doniger (O'Flaherty)'s classes, the bio continues, cover "cross-cultural expanses" including gender, psychology, dreams, evil, horses, sex, and women.[51] At *Newsweek* and the *Washington Post, that's* working-class.

TO: Wendy Doniger (O'Flaherty)
FROM: Newsweek Fact-Checking Dept.
RE: Palin hypocrisy article

(1) Confirm Sarah Palin is female despite being anti-choice.
(2) Confirm G.O.P. ever said Palin "speaks for all women."
(3) Five babies not usually considered "lots and lots?"; better to use "lots."
(4) "Womyn" is misspelled "women."

No other errors noted.

Katha Pollitt of the all-American *Nation* magazine blamed Palin for tricking the media into spreading ugly rumors about her children, giving Palin an opening to triumphantly announce her daughter's embarrassing pregnancy to the world. Just as Doniger (O'Flaherty) had said Palin was hypocritical for "outing her pregnant daughter in front of millions of people," Pollitt said, "It takes chutzpah for a mother to thrust her pregnant teen into the world's harshest spotlight and then demand the world respect the girl's privacy."[52]

What were liberals saying Palin should have done to shield her daughter's pregnancy from the press short of turning down McCain's offer to be his running mate? Oh, wait—now I see! Liberals think Palin should have refused the vice presidential nomination for the good of her family, which would have had the incidental effect of eliminating a great campaign asset for McCain. Once again, the Obama plan for victory was to force the other side to scratch.

Pretending they are doing something other than furthering the left-wing agenda, the media make up new rules for each case as they go along. If Palin was to blame for "outing her pregnant daughter in front of millions of people," then was Bill Clinton to blame for outing his sex toy, Monica Lewinsky, in front of millions of people? No. Again, establishment journalists would be stumped at the comparison. The rules keep changing to accommodate new circumstances. The one constant is that only conservatives will have their personal affairs paraded before the public by an indignant media claiming to expose conservative "hypocrisy."

Palin was a "hypocrite" because she was a Christian.

Love, The Mainstream Media.

Conservatives are adjudged guilty for sending inappropriate e-mails or foot-tapping in bathroom stalls. Those acts of base sexual perversion are enough to be driven from civilized society by the media if you're a conservative. Contrarily, Democrats are as pure as the driven snow—unless they sign a written confession. As long as Clinton said he did not have sex with "that woman," there were only tawdry allegations from tacky people. Until John Edwards appeared on TV to announce that he had been cheating on his wife, his assignations with a former campaign staffer were off limits. Even when the evidence is overwhelming, headlines about a Democrat's scandal will announce, "Records Prove Accusations False, Aides Say."

Winning the Quote of the Year Award from the Media Research Center, the *Chicago Tribune* ran the following correction on September 5, 1996—long after Gennifer Flowers, the Arkansas state troopers, and

Paula Jones had given detailed accounts of Bill Clinton's legion infidelities (and the more honorable Dick Morris had already resigned over his infidelity): "In her Wednesday Commentary page column, Linda Bowles stated that President Clinton and the former campaign adviser Dick Morris both were 'guilty of callous unfaithfulness to their wives and children.' Neither man has admitted to being or been proven to have been unfaithful. The *Tribune* regrets the error."[53]

THE 2006 SENATE RACE BETWEEN REPUBLICAN SENATOR GEORGE Allen and his Democratic opponent, James Webb, produced a potpourri of both alleged and actual ethnic slights, but you've only heard about the one from the Republican.

At one of his campaign speeches, Allen jokingly introduced a "tracker" from the campaign of his Democratic opponent, Jim Webb, to the audience. Trackers are little Nazi block-watchers, who follow a candidate around, recording everything he says—and everything his audience says—so the selectively edited videos can be posted online for ridicule. Democrats think they are living in Nazi Germany if the government monitors phone calls from this country to al Qaeda training camps in Pakistan, but they have no problem with liberals constantly intruding on peoples' enjoyment of public events with intimidating video surveillance.

Needless to say, it can be kind of a buzz-kill at a campaign event to have some sulking kid in the crowd filming everything. Allen also probably wanted to alert audience members that they were being filmed by a hostile cameraman and that if they asked a stupid question, they might end up as YouTube jokes. So Allen cheerfully introduced the Nazi block-watcher to the audience, getting in some swipes at Webb for being at a Hollywood fundraiser at the same time.

Allen said:

My friends, we're going to run this campaign on positive, instructive ideas and it's important that we motivate and inspire people for something.

This fella here, over here with the yellow shirt, macaca or

whatever his name is, he's with my opponent, he's following us around everywhere.

And it's just great. We're going to places all over Virginia and he's having it on film and it's great to have you here, and you show it to [my] opponent. Because he's never been there and probably will never come.

So it's good to have you here, rather than living inside the Beltway or—his opponent actually, right now, is with a bunch of Hollywood movie moguls. We care about fact, not fiction.

So welcome. Let's give a welcome to macaca here. Welcome to America, and the real world of Virginia.

Now my friends, we're in the midst of a war on terror. . . .

On the basis of that, the Nazi block-watcher, S. R. Sidarth, claimed to be a victim of a hate crime. As he told the *Washington Post*, "I think [Senator Allen] was doing it because he could, and I was the only person of color there, and it was useful for him in inciting his audience,"[54] adding that he was "disgusted" that Allen "would use my race in a political context."[55] (Using race is only appropriate in a college-application/affirmative action context.)

How self-absorbed do you have to be to think that you were singled out for being a "person of color" when you also happened to be the only person in the audience doing opposition research for the rival candidate? The son of a wealthy banker, Sidarth had grown up in an affluent Fairfax suburb, where he attended good schools and at the time was a student at the prestigious University of Virginia. The Allen event was in Breaks, Virginia, a town on the Kentucky border with a median household income of $23,431.[56]

Sidarth was probably the wealthiest person in the audience—the audience that he was there to humiliate. At least when the Cossacks rode in to rape and pillage, they didn't simultaneously cry that they were the ones being victimized. Today's privileged elites go to distant rural towns to ridicule ordinary Americans and then run back to the *Washington Post* to whimper that they have been mortally offended.

In the first of more than one hundred articles in the *Post* about the victimhood of Sidarth, Senator Allen told the *Post*, "I would never want to demean him as an individual. I do apologize if he's offended by that. That was no way the point."[57] In a world in which the media were not doing PR for the Democratic Party, that would have been the end of it. But Allen was a Republican and Sidarth was of Indian descent—not black, but good enough—so the *Post* kept flogging the story right up until election day. The media triumphantly reported that a macaca is a type of monkey in Gibraltar! And Allen's mother had grown up in Tunisia! The evidence was in: Allen had called the liberal pill a "monkey" in a foreign language, which no one in his audience would have understood—whether or not Allen did. It was as if Bull Connor had returned from the grave and set rabid dogs on Sidarth.

Notwithstanding reporters' obsessive interest in Allen's "macaca" line, I note that the NAACP could not have cared less about the matter. When Allen spoke to the NAACP a few weeks before the election, he didn't get a single question about the "macaca" remark burning up the pages of the *Post*. Allen was, however, invited to become a lifetime member of the NAACP, which he did.[58]

Allen made his "macaca" remark on August 11, 2006—or two months after Democratic senator Joe Biden told a questioner of Indian descent at a town hall in New Hampshire, "You cannot go into a 7-Eleven or a Dunkin' Donuts unless you have a slight Indian accent. I'm not joking." Biden's line was treated, as it should have been, as a buffoonish comment from a harmless fool. Indeed, Biden's repeated gaffes didn't even prevent him from being chosen as Barack Obama's running mate in 2008. Remarks that would be political death for a Republican are said to demonstrate "authenticity" in a Democrat, as an article in the *New York Times* put it. Biden's idiocies proved he "doesn't take himself too seriously."[59]

So one can well imagine George Allen's surprise when his "macaca" line was not cited as evidence that he "doesn't take himself too seriously" but rather as proof that we were dealing with an incipient Adolf Hitler. In a somber, deadly serious editorial, the *Times* described "macaca" as a "discouraging word," and accused Allen of playing "the race card." Compared with the *Washington Post*, the *Times* was the soul of reason: The *Post* mentioned "macaca" 109 times in the two months before the 2006 election.

In a career of talking, anyone will make mistakes and this was Allen's. Not the "macaca" line, which was amusing enough. His mistake was to grovel to phony race-baiters pretending to be offended. When did rich college kids harassing rural voters become a new protected category that must be shielded from words that are insults *in other languages*? How did Sidarth become a specially anointed victim? What did we ever do to India?

In short order, Allen was issuing "repeated apologies," explaining over and over again that if he had "had any idea that in some parts of the world or some cultures that this would be an insult, I would never have used that word because that's not who I am." He went on, "It's not how I was raised. It's not what I believe in."[60] If Allen had treated the media's self-righteous-athon with the derision it deserved, we'd have one more Republican in the Senate and one fewer illegal gun. (In March 2007, Senator Webb's executive assistant was arrested for trying to walk into a Senate office building carrying a loaded gun and ammunition, which he said belonged to Webb, a staunch advocate of gun control.[61] Charges were later dropped when it was proved that the aide had never used the word "macaca.")

The people who were the real victims of the "macaca" incident were the legions of young white males who aspire to be Democratic Nazi block-watchers themselves someday. What would the media have done without Sidarth's beige skin, certifying his victim status? No reliving the Jim Crow era if Sidarth had been a privileged white male instead of a privileged Indian American male. I guess it's lucky for the Democrats: They'd have a hard time finding a white man in their party these days, anyway—going from winning a majority of white men with John F. Kennedy, to only about a third of white men in the past twenty years.[62] As long as their political snitches remain upper-middle-class "people of color," the Democrats have ready-made fake victims as they actually victimize ordinary Americans.

James Webb was Allen's Democratic opponent in that race. One didn't have to search for words in foreign languages to get the point of

Webb's ethnically insensitive remarks about his primary opponent, Harris Miller. One flyer produced by Webb's campaign called Harris, who is Jewish, the "anti-Christ of outsourcing" and "killer"—the latter cleverly disguised in one use as "*job*-killer." Resembling something out of Al Jazeera comics, the cartoon on the flyer depicted Miller in grotesque caricature as a hook-nosed Jew with money bulging out of his pockets.

In the cartoon's first panel, a bespectacled, hook-nosed Miller is saying, "Let them eat cake." In the second panel, the again hook-nosed Miller is standing in front of a framed dollar sign, saying, "Costs are down and profits are up! U.S. workers will just have to get used to lower wages." In the third panel, with only the money in his pocket showing, Miller says, "Now, get those jobs overseas *now*! Blame it on technology while I count my money!" The fourth panel shows a muscular, Aryan-looking Jim Webb, saying, "Shut your mouth, Killer! I'm gonna fight to keep those jobs here and to bring the others home! The last thing we need in DC is another lobbyist!"[63] The flyer promised, "There is a solution."

Not only was the Webb campaign flyer more obviously offensive than Allen's one-time use of the nonsense word "macaca," it wasn't an extemporaneous remark made about one specific jerk at a campaign rally. This was a printed flyer, approved by Webb and distributed by the official "Webb for Senate" campaign. The *Washington Post*'s entire coverage of this blindingly anti-Semitic flyer consisted of three very brief mentions of the flyer near the bottom of articles on other topics. The fullest, most graphic discussion of the anti-Semitic flyer appeared in a *Post* article modestly titled "Webb, Miller Spar on Spending":

> *Post* columnist Marc Fisher, [a panelist at a Webb/Allen debate], grilled Webb on a flyer from his campaign that some have criticized as anti-Semitic. The ad shows Miller as a cartoonish figure with a hook nose. Miller called it "despicable."
>
> Webb said he did not think the ad was anti-Semitic but added that "if anyone views in any way that ad as being anti-Semitic, they certainly have my apologies, because that was certainly not my intent."[64]

Each of the three brief mentions of the flier in the *Post* included a conclusory announcement from the Webb campaign that the flyer was not anti-Semitic. And that was the end of it. The *Post* published more than a hundred articles citing Allen's offhand use of a word no native English speaker would recognize as a slur, but barely mentioned an unmistakably anti-Semitic flyer distributed by a man who is now a United States senator. Amazingly, there was so little press about Webb's anti-Semitic flyer that in June 2008 he felt free to complain to the *New York Times* about the "Karl Rove" techniques that had been used against *him* during the 2006 Senate campaign. Claiming his Senate campaign was "one of the most brutal things I've ever been through," Webb said, "It's more than the name-calling. It's the whole attempt to destroy your personal credibility. That's the Karl Rove approach. Until you've been through that, you don't really know what it's like."[65]

Anti-Semite James Webb: victim of imaginary forces.

After Webb won his primary against the apparently money-loving "anti-Christ of outsourcing," a left-wing Jewish magazine helped Webb continue with his anti-Semitic attacks during the general election campaign by outing George Allen as part Jewish. The *Forward* looked into Allen's ancestry and excitedly revealed that his mother's maiden name was the same as that of a prominent Jewish family that settled in Italy in the fifteenth century. Allen asked his mother about the article and found out, for the first time, that his maternal grandfather, Felix Lumbroso, was Jewish. It was a fortuitous discovery, allowing Webb's campaign front office—the media—to Jew-bait Webb's second opponent in the Senate race.

At a September 18, 2006, Allen-Webb debate, WUSA-TV's Peggy Fox popped Allen with the Jewish ancestry question completely out of the blue. Fox said, "It has been reported that your grandfather Felix, whom you were given your middle name for, was Jewish. Could you please tell us whether your forebears include Jews and, if so, at which point Jewish identity might have ended?"

Stunned by the question, and with his supporters in the audience booing the vulgar inquiry, Allen said, "To be getting into what religion my mother is, I don't think is relevant. Why is that relevant—my religion, Jim's religion or the religious beliefs of anyone out there?"[66]

The same *Washington Post* that had shown not the slightest interest in Webb's anti-Semitic flyers suddenly felt the cruel lash of anti-Semitism! Not in the question about Allen's Jewish grandfather, of course, but in Allen's response. The *Post*'s Dana Milbank speculated that Allen's anger at the question may have reflected his concern "that Jewish roots wouldn't play well in parts of Virginia."[67] What did Webb's flyers indicate about how he thought Jewishness would play in parts of Virginia?

Soon other Democrats were merrily baiting Allen both for using the recently banned word "macaca" (newly ethnically offensive) and for being Jewish (newly permitted as a line of attack). A staffer for Democratic congressional candidate Al Weed of Virginia was forced to resign after sending a mass e-mail encouraging liberals to protest a Republican rally for "George 'Macacawitz' Allen."[68]

Admittedly, I am in no position to judge, not finding the word "macaca" offensive in the first place. But if you think "macaca" is a "racial slur"—the equivalent of the N-word—then isn't "Macacawitz" twice as offensive? According to my Liberal-to-English dictionary, a Democrat had called Allen, "George Niggerwitz Allen."

Far from being outraged, liberals claimed the double-whammy, N-word/Jew-baiting combo platter was just a "bit of funning"—as James Wolcott put it in *Vanity Fair*.[69] The *Post* ran one short item on the "Macacawitz" incident. How can the same word be political death if a Republican says it but a "bit of funning" if a Democrat says it? There is no clearer proof that liberal victimology has nothing to do with being sensitive to people's feelings and everything to do with beating up their political opponents.

Allen didn't end his campaign by using an offensive word. Manifestly, "macaca" isn't offensive and no one seriously believed it was—least of all liberals who instantly began calling Allen "Macacawitz." Allen ended his campaign by capitulating to media bullies and apologizing for a completely media-generated scandal. Allen's apology tour lasted so long, he ended up apologizing for Senator Biden's claiming you had to be Indian to work at a 7-Eleven and Hillary Clinton's saying Mahatma Gandhi "ran a gas station down in St. Louis."

Democrats apologize for nothing, even when an apology is deserved. Senator Webb didn't apologize for his anti-Semitic flyer—except in the enraging nonapology/apology of the politician: "If anyone views in any way that ad as being anti-Semitic," then I apologize. So for anyone who misinterpreted a flyer with a hook-nosed caricature of a Jewish candidate that repeatedly called him the "anti-Christ of outsourcing" and "killer"—to those crazy people, Webb apologized. I'd like to meet the person who wouldn't find Webb's flyer anti-Semitic.

Webb never apologized for his shockingly rude behavior to President Bush at a White House reception for new members of Congress. First, Webb refused to go through the receiving line to shake Bush's hand. Then, when Bush later approached him and asked, "How's your boy?" referring to Webb's son in Iraq, who had been the centerpiece of Webb's Senate campaign, Webb said, "I'd like to get them out of Iraq, Mr. President." Bush said, "I didn't ask you that, I asked how's your boy?" Webb snottily replied, "That's between me and my boy." Is that an honorable way to treat the president of the civilization he defended?

On the *Times* op-ed page, they nearly fainted in admiration of Webb's churlish behavior. Paul Krugman wrote, "Good for him. We need people in Washington who are willing to stand up to the bully in chief."[70] Frank Rich said, "You can understand why Jim Webb, the Virginia senator-elect with a son in Iraq, was tempted to slug the president at a White House reception."[71] Democrats treat antiwar military veterans as if they're just another special-interest victim group, like welfare recipients or public school teachers. Any liberal who has worn the uniform has carte blanche to be a boor and a cad. Webb was a victim—he fought, Bush didn't. Meanwhile, two positions Webb did retract were positions he shouldn't have apologized for: his opposition to women in combat in a 1979 *Washingtonian* article titled "Women Can't Fight" and his reference to the Tailhook investigation as a "witch hunt."

The media were aquiver with indignation when someone attending a John McCain rally in the 2008 campaign called Obama an "Arab."

The dark underbelly of the GOP had at last been exposed! (I thought they liked Arabs.) Even assuming the random person attending the McCain rally was not a liberal plant, how about we compare that with what elected Democrats and other Democratic officials—even Obama himself—had said about Republican vice presidential nominee Sarah Palin?

On the House floor Democratic representative Steve Cohen of Tennessee compared Palin to Pontius Pilate—and Obama to Jesus: "Barack Obama was a community organizer like Jesus, who our minister prayed about. Pontius Pilate was a governor."[72] Cohen might want to stay away from the New Testament: There are no parables about Jesus lobbying the Romans for less restrictive workfare rules or filing for grants under the Community Redevelopment Act. *Sorry—I'll have to get back to you on that soul-saving business after I get Fannie Mae to ease off those lending standards.*

The head of the South Carolina Democratic Party, Carol Fowler, said Palin's "primary qualification seems to be that she hasn't had an abortion."[73] By contrast, Democrats believe that having had an abortion is the primary qualification for higher office.

The very week that liberals were launching these venomous attacks on Palin, an article in *Slate* magazine—owned by the *Washington Post*—ran an article bitterly complaining that Democrats weren't fighting hard enough. "Team Obama needs to break out the knives and start rolling in the mud, too," Terence Samuel wrote. "Once again," he complained, "we have Democratic dignity on display. They are taking the high road, constantly acknowledging John McCain's honorable service to the nation and saying that Sarah Palin is a tough and talented politician."[74] Short of an actual assassination, it's hard to imagine how Obama and his media helpers could have fought any dirtier.

Obama himself compared Palin to a pig and then denied doing so. Palin's speech at the Republican National Convention was the most famous political speech in at least two decades. This was Palin's first introduction to the nation, delivered less than a week after most people had first heard her name.

And the most famous line in the most famous speech was a joke that ended with the word "lipstick": "What's the difference between a pit bull and a hockey mom?" Palin asked. Pointing to her own lips, she answered, "Lipstick."

Within days of Palin's convention speech, Obama criticized the McCain-Palin ticket saying you can put "lipstick on pig, but it's still a pig." His audience clearly grasped a reference to Palin, hooting in appreciation, but Obama pleaded innocence, explaining on the *David Letterman Show* that "it's a common expression in at least Illinois."[75] Yeah, we're familiar with the expression. That's why it's called "an expression." Here are some more expressions: "Monkey see, monkey do," and "I'm just calling a spade a spade." You think anyone would have noticed if McCain had used those about Obama? He'd have to drop out of the race, resign from the Senate, and leave the country.

But in a familiar pattern, Obama's insulting Palin became the Republicans' scandal. How dare Republicans suggest that the cherub Obama was referring to Palin! Why, it never crossed his mind! Obama accused Republicans of "Swift-boat politics" and the media indignantly defended Obama's honor.

It was not the expression, but the context. There's also nothing wrong with mentioning "Dallas," but shortly before the movie *Dr. Strangelove* was released, JFK was assassinated in Dallas and the word "Dallas" was changed to "Vegas" in Slim Pickens's commentary on the military survival kit: "A fella could have a pretty good weekend in Dallas with all that stuff." If only the producers had thought to explain, in exasperation, "'Dallas' is a common name for a city in Texas, at least in Illinois,"[76] they wouldn't have had to change a thing.

Liberals angrily demanded that no one draw any conclusions from the fact that Obama's audience laughed and hollered when he mentioned "lipstick on a pig," which I guess was just the idiosyncratic reaction of one particular crowd. But I seem to recall a headline or two regarding Sarah Palin and lipstick in the days before Obama made his lipstick-on-a-pig remark.

"Sarah Steps Out: Republican Candidate a Pit Bull with Lipstick" —*Salt Lake Tribune*, September 3, 2008

"Pitbull in Lipstick: Palin Rips Obama" —*Daily News* (New York), September 4, 2008

"Putting Lipstick on a Pit Bull" —*Hotline,* September 4, 2008

"She's a 'Pit Bull with Lipstick'"—Palin Wows 'Em by Pounding DC Snobs" —*New York Post,* September 4, 2008

"The 'Pit Bull in Lipstick' Savages the Opposition" —*Belfast Telegraph,* September 4, 2008

"A Pit Bull with Lipstick" —*Salon,* September 4, 2008

"At Stake in '08; It's About the Lipstick, Stupid" —*News & Record* (Greensboro, NC), September 5, 2008

"Mrs. Smith (In Lipstick) Goes to Washington" —*Record* (Bergen County, NJ), September 5, 2008

"Hunting Season: 'Feisty' Palin Takes Aim at Obama: Pitbull with Lipstick" —*Advertiser* (Australia), September 5, 2008

"The 'Pitbull in Lipstick' Bites Back" —*Belfast Telegraph,* September 5, 2008

"'Pit Bull in Lipstick' Savages Obama and Wows Delegates" —*Birmingham Post,* September 5, 2008

"'Lipstick' Pit Bull Bares Her Teeth" —*Courier Mail* (Australia), September 5, 2008

"Happy Families? Or Did the Lipstick Pitbull Cheat?" —*Daily Mail* (London), September 5, 2008

"What's the Difference Between a Hockey Mom and a Pitbull? Lipstick! McCain Running Mate's Rallying Cry" —*Daily Record* (Glasgow, Scotland), September 5, 2008

"Sarah Palin: A Pit Bull with Lipstick" —*Fresno Bee* (California), September 5, 2008

"Enter the Pit Bull with Lipstick" —Media General Washington Bureau, September 5, 2008

"Sarah Barracuda: Pitbull in Lipstick" —*Democratic Daily,* September 6, 2008

"The Difference Between Palin and Bush? Lipstick" —*Moderate Voice,* September 6, 2008

"Pitbull in Lipstick: Palin Rips Obama" —*Daily News* (New York), September 4, 2008

"Putting Lipstick on a Pit Bull" —*Hotline*, September 4, 2008
"Gloss May Wear Off Republicans' 'Lipstick-on-a-Pitbull'
    Moment" —*Times* (London), September 6, 2008

So there did seem to be some vague connection between Sarah
Palin and lipstick in the public consciousness when Obama made his
remarks on September 9. When *Washington Post* columnist Howard
Kurtz sneered: "Does anyone seriously believe that Barack Obama was
calling Sarah Palin a pig?"—perhaps he should have addressed that
question to his fellow journalists writing endless headlines about Palin
and lipstick.

Using the "lipstick on a pig" line just days after Palin's "lipstick"
joke would be like using the hoary expression "that dog don't hunt,"
about Vice President Dick Cheney days after he shot his friend in a
hunting accident or coyly accusing John Edwards of "throwing the
baby out with the bathwater" after the *National Enquirer* broke the
"love child" story. *What? What'd I say?* Or, to use an actual example
from the Democratic primaries: In 2008, Jesse Jackson *did* win the
South Carolina primary in 1988, but when Bill Clinton appeared to
minimize Obama's primary win by saying Jackson won South Carolina
too, no one bought Clinton's explanation that he was just "talking about
South Carolina political history."[77]

While the mainstream media feigned outrage that anyone would
suggest that Saint Obama was referring to Palin with his lipstick crack,
apparently not every liberal got the memo. On *Salon*, which I wouldn't
consider a serious publication except that the *New York Times* is constantly citing it so warmly, University of Michigan professor Juan Cole
wrote a column titled "What's the Difference Between Palin and Muslim Fundamentalists? Lipstick."[78] The author of the *Slate* magazine
article demanding that Obama hit Palin harder, which ran two days
after Obama's "lipstick on a pig" line, titled his article: "Slaughter the
Pig."[79]

George Allen apologized for "macaca," but Obama wouldn't apologize for calling Palin a "pig." Quite the opposite; Obama claimed to
be a victim of Republican "lies and phony outrage."

I no longer care about Republicans' policies, flip-flops, or personal lives. I just want a Republican who is not constantly apologizing to liberals. I promise, apologizing won't make them like you. Apologies have precisely the same effect on liberals as they do on Muslims: It just fuels their rage. The pope apologized to rioting Muslims for quoting Byzantine emperor Manuel II Palaeologus: "Show me just what Mohammed brought that was new, and there you will find things only evil and inhuman, such as his command to spread by the sword the faith he preached." Muslims accepted the pope's apology by spelling out the words "apology accepted" in burning cars.

President George W. Bush apologized for his statement in the 2003 State of the Union Address that "the British government has learned that Saddam Hussein recently sought significant quantities of uranium from Africa." Endless investigations, here and in Britain, proved that Bush's claim was irrefutably true. What was Bush apologizing for? Telling the truth? I don't even think Hallmark has a card for that. Incomprehensibly, Bush also apologized for firing his own political appointees.

Despite this constant string of apologies, Bush was accused of dividing the country. After the 2004 election, columnist E. J. Dionne announced that he was "disgusted" by Bush's "effort consciously designed to divide the country."[80] In full anaphylactic shock, Dionne proclaimed, "We are aghast at the success of a campaign based on vicious personal attacks, the exploitation of strong religious feelings and an effort to create the appearance of strong leadership that would do Hollywood proud. We are alarmed that so many of our fellow citizens could look the other way and not hold Bush accountable for utter incompetence in Iraq and for untruths spoken in defense of the war."

Apparently the country could only be united if John Kerry had won just a tiny bit more of the vote in Ohio that year. Only then would the nation be able to come together in peace and harmony.

Why do Republicans never learn? They will never get credit for apologizing to the endless stream of fake liberal victims. Instead, everyone sees that Republicans are milquetoast sops. Republicans have turned themselves into such doormats that a major Obama fundraiser felt free to sneak into the Republican National Convention to disrupt Sarah Palin's speech—and then portray herself as a victim of the Republicans for being asked to leave.

The storm troopers at the Republican National Convention were Jodie Evans, a major Obama fundraiser, and her fellow outside agitator, Medea Benjamin.[81] Evans is the founder of the "grassroots" anti-American group "Code Pink," which is funded with the multiple millions of dollars she got in her divorce from billionaire Max Palevsky. Evans supports Fidel Castro, Hugo Chávez—and Barack Obama—having pledged to bundle more than $50,000 for the Obama campaign.[82] This major Obama contributor once proclaimed, "Why is being a communist anti-American?"—which narrowly lost out to "Change We Can Believe In" as the Obama campaign motto.

As Palin was giving her inaugural address to the nation, Evans and Benjamin stood up in their Code Pink outfits—dresses spray-painted with the words "Palin is not a woman's choice"—and began shrieking at Palin.

However much Max Palevsky paid to divorce Evans, he got a bargain.

What are the odds that if a major campaign donor to McCain disrupted Obama's convention speech, only two newspapers would report it? But the fact that an Obama contributor rushed the stage as Sarah Palin accepted the vice presidential nomination at the Republican convention was reported in only two newspapers: the *Post Register* (Idaho Falls) and the *Pioneer Press* (Twin Cities).

Newspapers didn't even have to pull reporters off the Palin scandal watch to write the story themselves; they only had to run the Associated Press story about Evans's disruption of Palin's speech. But not one newspaper picked up the wire story. Newspaper editors must have been saving space in case any of Palin's enemies in Alaska started making more unsubstantiated claims about affairs, false pregnancies, or the juvenile delinquency of her children.

The privileged protesters later admitted that they had been given illegal credentials to get into the convention by people in the media—which may explain why Palin's cracks about the media were such a hit with the convention delegates. No one will ever know who gave the disrupters access, because there was no investigation. There was no out-cry. There was certainly no violent pummeling of these howling harridans. The protesters at Palin's speech weren't arrested or even issued a citation.

Indeed, it was *they* who were indignant at their "harsh" treatment in not being allowed to prevent Palin from speaking. These poor put-upon billionaires were shocked that they were removed from the convention hall, rather being permitted to scream throughout Palin's speech and perhaps to storm the stage. Male chivalry is evidently the last refuge of female barbarians. "Hello?" Evans said. "Why do you have to drag two women out?"[83]—not the first time "drag" had been used in reference to Democratic activists.

This wasn't a free-speech issue. Interrupting speeches at a private event is the equivalent of sneaking into the *New York Times*'s typesetting room and inserting your own op-eds over theirs. A political party's national convention costs more' than $100 million and takes nearly two years to plan.[84] The people who pay for it don't owe space to people who want to shout down their speakers. Disrupting a convention is like disrupting someone's wedding. It is a feral attack on civilized society. If they can do it at a Republican convention, why not at a presidential debate? Why not during a live TV show or an NFL football game?

Pro-lifers can't stand on a public sidewalk within 36 feet of an abortion clinic, but liberals think they have a divine right to disrupt speeches at the Republican National Convention.

And Republicans fall for fake victims every time. Blake Hall, one of the Republican delegates who removed the screaming banshees, sent an e-mail to the *Idaho Falls Post Register* contritely explaining that the protesters had "violated convention rules by being in a place not permitted by their guest passes." He continued defensively, "They were asked to cease and they refused." And—as Palin continued to try to speak over the disrupters—they "continued their disorderly behavior at which point I was requested by the Sergeant at Arms and other deputies to assist in their removal."[85] Not exactly Ronald Reagan saying, "I'm paying for this microphone!" Republicans are apologetic about not supinely turning over their convention to satanic dervishes.

How about a sock to their yaps? In numerous photos of the melee, the screaming shrews can be seen with arms flailing and mouths agape while able-bodied men stand right next to them doing nothing. So-called men stood slack-jawed while the Republican warrior in heels attempted to deliver her speech. And Republicans wonder why they needed a woman to be their vice presidential candidate.

On MSNBC, host Rachel Maddow was appalled at the rude way hecklers were treated at the Republican National Convention. Describing a protester who sneaked into the Republican convention and started screaming and waving a sign that said, "McCain votes against vets" during McCain's speech, Maddow said, "To have one of the two [vets from Iraq or Afghanistan] getting to speak at the Republican National Convention, having to speak essentially from the rafters while getting dragged out of the room. That says something."[86] How dare the Republicans not let the heckler finish his heckle!

THE MEDIA ARE INSTANTLY PANIC-STRICKEN ABOUT EVERY REpublican scandal, no matter how petty, while aggressively burying all Democrats' scandals, from President Kennedy's pathological whoring to Edwards's affair with Rielle Hunter. Battered wife–syndrome Republicans are so obsessed with trying to prove to the media that they are not being mean that they immediately abandon even legitimate attacks on Democrats, such as Michelle Obama's "proud" comment or Obama's deranged associates and thuggish campaign tactics. And to prove they are not hypocrites, Republicans hold members of their own party to much higher standards than they ever would hold a Democrat. Consider that Republicans Jack Ryan, Larry Craig, and Mark Foley were all forced to withdraw from politics for sex scandals that did not involve anyone actually having sex. If any Democrat is ever hounded out of a race for propositioning his own wife—I don't care if it's in the middle of Madison Square Garden—I will stop writing about politics for a full year.

But Republicans give the bum's rush to any colleagues who have made the slightest verbal gaffe, like Trent Lott, or been accused, however implausibly, of the most ridiculous malfeasance, like George

Allen or Jack Ryan. They naively cling to the belief that their own uni-lateral surrender will so impress liberals that someday liberals will play fair. Republicans have been trying this strategy for fifty years and so far it hasn't worked. They never get credit for these ecumenical at-tacks on their fellow Republicans. What they got was Barack Obama, who won his Senate seat after knocking out his two opponents by por-ing through their sealed divorce records, and John McCain, who chas-tised any Republicans who mentioned Jeremiah Wright or Obama's middle name.

Let's count. George Allen is gone (said "macaca"). Jack Ryan is gone (allegedly propositioned his wife). Mark Foley is gone (sent inap-propriate e-mails to pages). Tom DeLay is gone (raised campaign money legally). Needless to say, any Republicans who broke actual laws are gone, gone, gone.

Meanwhile, Democrats are utterly unabashed about Senator Teddy Kennedy (killed a girl), Bill Clinton (flashed an employee, molested an intern, and perjured himself about both incidents), William "Refriger-ator" Jefferson (had $90,000 in bribe money hidden in his freezer), Sandy Berger (stole and then destroyed classified national security documents relevant to 9/11), Barney Frank (homosexual prostitute ran a call-boy ring from Frank's house), John Edwards (cheated on cancer-stricken wife), and Joe Biden (made comments about Indians one thou-sand times more offensive than Allen's nonsense word).

At least the Edwards sex scandal proved him right about one thing: There really are two Americas. There's one for right-wingers, where every jaywalking offense will be covered like the O.J. murder trial, and one for left-wingers, where they can do anything and blithely count on a total media cover-up. In an article about the rich and fa-mous arranging to have their divorce records sealed apropos of the Jack Ryan debacle, *USA Today* quoted Paul McMasters of the left-wing First Amendment Center indignantly asking, "Do we have one system of justice for one group of people and another system of justice for an-other group of people?"[87] Yes, of course we do. There is one system of justice for liberals and another for conservatives.

6

WHEN 95 PERCENT
WORLD DOMINATION
JUST ISN'T ENOUGH . . .

ainstream media journalists are so desperate to be victims that they've had to leap beyond their torment at the hands of Fox News to start claiming they're victims of . . . the mainstream media! After decades of patiently explaining to conservatives that before becoming journalists they had their opinions "surgically removed," as CBS's *60 Minutes* correspondent Lesley Stahl told Fox News's Bill O'Reilly back in 2000,[1] suddenly liberals can't stop complaining about how biased the media are—against liberals. The media flagellate themselves for not being tough enough on Republican administrations. They complain about issues not being covered sufficiently by the media and issues that are being covered too much. They complain about what's front-page news and what isn't. The media are victims of the media!

Whenever the establishment media is complaining about "the deluge of the media's coverage"[2]—as the *New York Times* did about coverage of 9/11 on the very first anniversary—you know they are chafing at having to pretend to care about something that plainly bores them. By the sixth anniversary of 9/11, the *Times* was running a front-page article proposing we shelve the 9/11 commemorations altogether. "Each year," the *Times* reported, "murmuring about September 11 fatigue arises" and "many people feel that the collective commemorations, publicly staged, are excessive and vacant, even annoying."[3]

Who are those "many people"? Do any of them live outside of the Upper West Side? Liberals are not merely bored with 9/11, they fear that reminders of 9/11 will anger Americans and reawaken the fighting spirit.

Admittedly, the terrorist attack of 9/11 might not be deserving of the prodigious coverage devoted to the Augusta National Golf Club's discriminatory membership policies against women. But some continued recognition of the deadliest terrorist attack in U.S. history would be nice. In fact, I think it should be mentioned at the start of each school day, like the Pledge of Allegiance. Congress should show video of the towers coming down before each session. Everybody's screen saver should be a photo of the towers in flames. On every anniversary we should have wall-to-wall TV coverage of the savage attack lest anyone, ever, anywhere, forget what those animals did to us. Again, not as extensive as the *New York Times* coverage of the Augusta National Golf Club, but something.

Or here's a proposal: Maybe we could cancel just one major motion picture, prime-time special, PBS documentary, play, dramatization, rally, parade, staged reading, Broadway musical, evening of interpretive dance, opera, feature film, or seminar about the Jim Crow era each week and replace it with one about 9/11. In 2007, the year the *Times* was complaining about having to commemorate a terrorist attack on U.S. soil that happened only six years earlier, the *Times* reminded its readers of the 1965 Civil Rights March in Selma more than a dozen times and Jim Crow five dozen times. Even the liberal Kausfiles blog noted a new feature at NPR in 2007: "Pointless Stories from the Civil Rights Era."[4] Mind you, we 9/11 hobbyists want only one substitution per week. Would that be a fair compromise? Or, even better, maybe they could keep all the Jim Crow remembrance specials and give us a substitution for one Hollywood blacklist movie per week.

The only other subject the media were ever this irritated about having to cover was the Monica Lewinsky scandal. Two weeks after the Lewinsky story broke, before the evidence on the blue dress was even dry, *Times* columnist Frank Rich huffily reported that "75 percent of the public tells ABC pollsters that there's too much media coverage of the scandal."[5] That was the same public that produced record-breaking Nielsen ratings for TV shows covering the Monica Lewinsky scandal for the rest of the year.

A decade later, *Times* columnists were still complaining that the Clinton scandals had gotten too much attention. Paul Krugman attributed the hype to "the right-wing noise machine."[6] Is that the "noise machine" that controls the *New York Times*, the *Washington Post*, the *Los Angeles Times*, and indeed nearly every newspaper in America, every major news network, CNN, MSNBC, *Saturday Night Live, Vanity Fair, Glamour, Time, Newsweek, Good Housekeeping, Rolling Stone, Vibe*, the entire movie industry, the Oscars, and the Emmys? That right-wing noise machine? Or is it the right-wing noise machine that's limited to niche outlets on the radio, the Internet, and a few hours a day on Fox News, between Greta Van Susteren, Shep Smith, and Geraldo Rivera?

Krugman dismissed the Clinton scandals as "pseudoscandal[s]" and bitterly remonstrated about the "headlines, air time and finger-wagging from the talking heads" over nothingness. And yet he claimed that the "eventual discovery in each case that there was no there there, if reported at all, received far less attention." Fully determined to earn his presidential knee pads, Krugman said, "The effect was to make an administration that was, in fact, pretty honest and well run—especially compared with its successor—seem mired in scandal."[7]

According to Krugman, the "fake scandals" from the Clinton years were "Whitewater, Troopergate, Travelgate, Filegate, Christmas-card-gate. At the end, there were false claims that Clinton staff members trashed the White House on their way out." Each one of these was not only a far more serious scandal than anything the media ever managed to produce against the Bush administration, but none could be described as having received overwhelming media attention.

The "pseudoscandal" of Whitewater, for example, produced more

GUILTY

GUILTY 185
governor of Arkansas, Jim Guy Tucker; former Arkansas municipal
judge David Hale; Clinton's associate attorney general, Webster L.
Hubbell; and Clinton's former business partners Susan McDougal and
the late Jim McDougal.[8] Not bad for a "pseudoscandal."

In eight years, with several thousand political employees circulating in and out of the executive branch, only five felonies came out of
the entire Bush administration. That's a crime rate at least 1,000 percent less than in the population at large.[9]

Lewis Libby was the only perpetrator Bush likely had ever met and
is certainly the only one the public had ever heard of. The others were
obscure employees in the far reaches of the executive branch, such as a
homeland security deputy press secretary and a chief of staff of the General Services Administration. But just among Clinton's friends and associates from Arkansas, the Whitewater investigation produced more than
a dozen felony convictions. Ken Starr had a more significant effect on reducing crime in the 1990s than Clinton's crime bill.

Krugman would no doubt argue that the true scandal of the Bush
administration was that "Mr. Bush has no empathy for people less fortunate than himself"—actually, he did write that.[10] Although Bush had
nothing to do with it, many people did lose their homes and life's sav-
ings in dirty deals. One company offered homes for "sale," the pur-
chase price to be paid in installments. But if a purchaser defaulted on
a single monthly payment, there would be no foreclosure proceeding or
short sale: The purchaser would automatically lose everything he had
invested in the property—the house, the equity, and all prior payments. The small print of the contract said that if a monthly payment
was not made within thirty days, all prior "payments made by the purchaser shall be considered as rent for the use of the premises"—not a
mortgage payment, not a down payment on a house.

This is what happened to some of the people who fell behind on
their payments:

Clyde Soapes was a grain-elevator operator from Texas who heard
about the lots in early 1980 and jumped at the chance to invest. He

put $3,000 down and began making payments of $244.69 per month. He made thirty-five payments in all—totaling $11,564.15, just short of the $14,000 price for the lot. Then he suddenly fell ill with diabetes and missed a payment, then two. The [corporation] informed him that he had lost the land and all of his money. There was no court proceeding or compensation. Months later they resold his property to a couple from Nevada for $16,500. After they too missed a payment, the [corporation] resold it yet again.

Soapes and the couple from Nevada were not alone. More than half of the people who bought lots [in the development]—teachers, farmers, laborers, and retirees—made payments, missed one or two, and then lost their land without getting a dime of their equity back. According to records, at least sixteen different buyers paid more than $50,000 and never received a property deed.[11]

Who were these unscrupulous businessmen? Jack Abramoff? No, Abramoff went to prison for scamming rich Indian tribes. Vietnam ace and former Republican congressman Randy "Duke" Cunningham? No, he sits in prison for taking bribes from well-heeled defense contractors. Indeed, when has a Republican ever been accused of ripping off the less fortunate?

The business plan described above was, of course, the Clintons' Whitewater Development Corporation. And that was the legal part. Although many states made such contracts illegal on the sensible grounds that it involves scamming the poor and gullible, Arkansas was not among them. I'm sure the technical legality of Whitewater provided great consolation to all the people who lost their homes when Hillary Clinton enforced the small print.

The Clintons always loudly boasted that they didn't put any money into Whitewater, as if that fact proved they had clean hands. But Hillary Clinton created the Whitewater Development Corporation, wrote the fine print, and ran it out of the Rose Law Firm, with purchasers' checks sent to: Whitewater Corporation, c/o Hillary Clinton at the Rose Law Firm. As Peter Schweizer says, "Hillary herself sold a home to Hillman Logan, who went bankrupt and then died. She took possession of the home and resold it to another buyer for $20,000. No one was compensated (and she didn't report the sale on her tax return)."[12] The Clintons' involvement with Whitewater continued right up until the 1992 election.

Forget the multiple felony convictions growing out of Krugman's "pseudoscandal." Would even the legal aspects of Whitewater constitute a scandal if George Bush had done it? How about Mitt Romney or Cindy McCain? But for Paul Krugman, liberal troubadour of the poor, a barely legal scheme to rip off the least fortunate Americans—which also happened to yield a dozen felony convictions, taking down the sitting governor of Arkansas—is a "fake scandal."

"Troopergate" led to the Paula Jones lawsuit, which in turn led to the Monica Lewinsky scandal when Jones's attorneys subpoenaed Lewinsky. Unable to avoid answering Jones's charges in court, Clinton eventually was forced to pay her $800,000 to settle the case. What Krugman called a "pseudoscandal" created many new legal rulings, including the Supreme Court's august decision holding that a sitting president *can* be sued for flashing a female employee when he was a governor.

The "pseudoscandal" of Travelgate consisted of the Clintons' using the full resources of the federal government in an attempt to destroy career employees of the White House, in order to turn over operation of the White House travel office to a Clinton contributor out of Hollywood. To make the travel office firings look like something other than rank cronyism, the Clinton White House publicly accused the fired employees of criminal acts and ordered the FBI and IRS to investigate. Unfortunately for the Clintons, the travel office employees were innocent of any wrongdoing.

Travel Office Director Billy Dale was criminally investigated by the FBI for two years, but the jury took less than two hours to acquit him of the embezzlement and conversion charges. The end result of the IRS investigation was that the IRS owed the head of the travel office's partner airline about $5,000.

Admittedly, a president's misuse of the IRS and the FBI to harass American citizens whose jobs he wants for Hollywood friends may not constitute a "scandal" on the order of cutting the capital gains tax in Paul Krugman's book. But for most people, that's a scandal.

Filegate was the discovery that the Clinton White House had

collected more than 900 secret FBI files on individual American citizens, including hundreds and hundreds of files of Republicans who had worked in the Reagan and Bush administrations. Luckily for Clinton, he was only caught perusing classified FBI files of his enemies and not Muslim terrorists. Who knows what the ACLU would have done had the White House been caught with files on Mohammed Atta or Khalid Sheikh Mohammed! Even the Clinton administration gave up trying to defend its possession of the files, eventually simply denying any knowledge of who hired the White House employee who was pawing through them—former bar bouncer Craig Livingstone.

If that's a pseudoscandal, someone owes Nixon aide Charles Colson three years of his life back. The *New York Times* article on Charles Colson's guilty plea for possessing a single FBI file in the Nixon White House was languorously reported under a headline spanning several columns on the front page:

COLSON PLEADS GUILTY TO CHARGE IN ELLSBERG CASE AND IS EXPECTED TO AID JAWORSKI AND RODINO PANEL MOVE IS SURPRISE
Watergate Prosecutor to Seek Dismissal of Other Counts[13]

When Clinton White House employee Livingstone was caught with 900 confidential FBI files the *New York Times* headline was rather more low-key: "White House Announces Leave for Official Who Collected Files."[14] This would be like an article on American Airlines Flight 11 crashing into the Pentagon headlined: "California-Bound Plane Fails to Reach Destination."

When Senator Bob Dole merely mentioned the White House's collection of 900 confidential FBI files, NBC anchor Brian Williams virtually accused him of committing a hate crime: "The politics of Campaign '96 are getting very ugly, very early. Today Bob Dole accused the White House of using the FBI to wage war against its political enemies, and if that sounds like another political scandal, that's the point."[15] Williams must be part of the "right-wing noise machine" that overreacted to the "pseudoscandal" of Filegate.

I gather that by "Christmas-card-gate," Krugman is referring to a sleazy excuse the Clinton administration used for its violation of the campaign finance laws—heretofore considered by the *Times* to be the most sacred laws of the republic. It appears to be the only scandal involving Christmas cards. When Clinton was caught doling out Lincoln bedroom sleepovers, White House coffees, and dinners to big campaign contributors based on lists of political donors on file at the Democratic National Committee,[16] the Clinton White House denied that the database was being used for campaign purposes, explaining that it was the president's Christmas card list. It was an odd Christmas card list, inasmuch as it included notations recording the amount each donor had contributed.

In any event, the Christmas cards weren't part of the accusation, they were the Clintonian justification for a violation of the campaign finance laws more serious than anything Tom DeLay has even been accused of. To describe this scandal as "Christmas-card-gate" would be like calling the O.J. Simpson murder trial "ugly-ass-shoe-gate" because O.J. denied that his shoes left bloody footprints at the scene of the crime by claiming that he would never wear "ugly-ass" Bruno Magli shoes. (The O.J. Simpson case provides many helpful parallels to the Clinton White House.)

As for Krugman's final accusation that "there were false claims that Clinton staff members trashed the White House on their way out," those claims were not false. Apparently, like the Willie Horton ad, we're going to have to keep citing the facts on this incident until liberals stop lying about it. Although there was never any formal complaint from the Bush White House, the story broke in the first days of the Bush administration, when anonymous Republican White House staffers were quoted in news reports accusing Clinton administration staff of doing "a lot more vandalism to the White House and other offices than just yanking 'Ws' off typewriters," mostly in the vice president's offices, including "cut cables, phone lines and electric cords, plus a mess of rubbish."[17]

Practicing a "new kind of politics" before a new kind of politics was cool, President Bush dismissed the rumors, saying, "There might have been a prank or two. Maybe somebody put a cartoon on the wall, but that's O.K."[18] So here you had a situation where the official White House position was to deny any vandalism and refuse to produce an official accounting of the damage, even as White House staffers were telling reporters what they had seen with their own eyes. For the first time in world history, the establishment media believed the official White House line from a Republican president.

With the White House refusing to produce records of the damage, the General Accountability Office (GAO) concluded that no damage had been done.[19] The GAO didn't issue an official report; it merely provided a one-page letter reflecting the fact that the administration refused to produce records of the damage, noting that "White House repair records do not contain information on the causes of damage being repaired."[20]

Suspiciously, White House spokesman Ari Fleischer refused to comment one way or another on any damage, saying, "The White House is going to continue to be gracious in its approach to the matter." He added, "I think all parties are best served by letting this matter and what was done become a part of history."[21] In what was to become a pattern, Bush left his fellow Republicans twisting in the wind, accused of being liars, while he tried fruitlessly to appease Democrats.

Seeing that the White House was refusing to cooperate with an investigation into the Clinton staffers' vandalism, Democrats got on their high horses, claiming to be offended, outraged, shocked, and appalled by the original reports of vandalism from anonymous staffers. The howling hyenas wailed that they were victims of Republican smears. Democratic congressman Anthony Weiner delivered a letter to the White House—and more important, the press—signed by thirty-five members of the Clinton administration demanding an official apology. Mark Shields expressed the prevailing dudgeon about the vandalism story, saying, "The whole story was a fabrication and, to be blunt, a lie. It was a deception carefully cultivated by the Bush White House and then fed to friendly conservative journalists who were duped into perpetrating this fraud upon their readers and their listeners."[22]

The headlines blared the news that the vandalism was a "lie" and a "hoax":

"'Vandalism' Looks a Lot Like a White House Lie"
　　—*Deseret News* (Salt Lake City), June 12, 2001

"White House Vandalism an Exploited Lie?"
   —*Grand Rapid Press* (Michigan), June 11, 2001
"Hoax Adds to Readers' Skepticism"
   —*Seattle Post-Intelligencer,* June 4, 2001
"No Apologies for Lies About Clinton"
   —*Sun-Sentinel* (Fort Lauderdale, Florida), May 24, 2001

Finally, exasperated House Republicans demanded that the GAO actually investigate, enraged that Republicans were being called liars on the basis of Bush's gallantry.

Forced to investigate something the Bush White House didn't want investigated, the GAO eventually concluded—as described in the *New York Times,* June 12, 2002:

> The General Accounting Office, an investigative arm of Congress, said today that "damage, theft, vandalism and pranks did occur in the White House complex" in the presidential transition from Bill Clinton to George W. Bush.
>
> The agency put the cost at $13,000 to $14,000, including $4,850 to replace computer keyboards, many with damaged or missing W keys.
>
> Some of the damage, it said, was clearly intentional. Glue was smeared on desk drawers. Messages disparaging President Bush were left on signs and in telephone voice mail. A few of the messages used profane or obscene language.
>
> "A Secret Service report documented the theft of a presidential seal that was 12 inches in diameter from the Eisenhower Executive Office Building," next to the White House, on Jan. 19, 2001, the accounting office said.

So I guess it was Krugman's own newspaper that put out the "false claims that Clinton staff members trashed the White House on their way out"—by quoting the official GAO report. Foiled by the conservative bias of the *New York Times* again! This is how liberals rewrite history: No matter how many times we correct them, they just keep repeating provable lies. Over and over again, conservatives are forced to keep reminding people:

- The Willie Horton ads were the most magnificent campaign ads in political history.
- At the conclusion of the Anita Hill hearings, only 24 percent of Americans believed Hill, while nearly 60 percent of Americans believed Clarence Thomas,[23] and the ratio was closer to 20 to 1 among those who worked with Thomas and Hill.[24]
- Pat Buchanan's speech at the 1992 Republican National Convention was a barn burner, not only with the delighted delegates but also with liberal commentators, who gave the speech rave reviews, such as NBC's John Chancellor ("an excellent speech") and ABC's David Brinkley ("an outstandingly good political speech"),[25] Hal Bruno ("I've never seen a better first night"), and Ted Koppel ("[The delegates] walked out of here tonight enthusiastic, [with] a sense of optimism"). Apparently the viewers at home liked it too, giving Bush a 10-point leap in the polls, his biggest one-day bump in the entire campaign.[26]
- The Bush campaign did not spread rumors that John McCain had a black illegitimate child during the 2000 GOP primary.[27]
- Liberals behaved so abominably at Senator Paul Wellstone's memorial service, showering Republican senators "with boos and catcalls from the crowd," that a disgusted Jesse Ventura stormed out. That's according to former Democratic senator Tom Daschle, who also said that the audience's behavior was so "inappropriate and wrong" that on the plane back to Washington that night, he and his fellow Democratic senators Chris Dodd and Byron Dorgan agreed "we were going to pay a price for what had just happened."[28]

And . . .

- The GAO investigation concluded that Clinton's staff trashed the White House on the way out.

Interestingly, Krugman dropped from his list of "pseudoscandals" the Monica Lewinsky scandal, which might strike some as a slight oversight. This is on the order of not mentioning Watergate in a list of Nixon administration scandals. How about the scandal that led to only the second presidential impeachment in U.S. history, which came out of what Krugman called the "pretty honest" Clinton administration?

But according to Krugman the "pretty honest" Clinton administration was victimized by unfair news coverage. The only living human who might agree with that assessment is Bill Clinton, who derisively referred to *Newsweek* magazine as "the house organ of Paula Jones"[29]—an unfortunate use of "Paula Jones" and "organ" in the same sentence.

Yes, he was referring to the magazine that refused to report Paula Jones's accusations against Clinton for months, described Jones as a "dogpatch Madonna," killed Michael Isikoff's exclusive on the Monica Lewinsky scandal, and unaccountably employs braying left-wing slattern Eleanor Clift, who named Clinton the "Biggest Winner of the Year" for being a "a colossus on the world stage" in 1999—the very year Clinton was impeached and the entire Supreme Court boycotted his State of the Union Address.[30]

This is the magazine that Clinton accuses of victimizing him.

WHILE MAINSTREAM JOURNALISTS COMPLAIN THAT THE SCANDAL that led to the only presidential impeachment of the twentieth century got too much media coverage, they are always bitterly complaining that their synthetic little scandals aren't getting enough media coverage. Hitler blamed the Reichstag fire on the Communists to consolidate power—but at least there really was a fire. America's establishment media just go about creating fake news stories and then demanding that the rest of us take them seriously. "No one is covering X" is mainstream media code meaning there has been nonstop coverage, the subject has been exhausted, the zone has been flooded—but, alas, the public doesn't care.

Thus, Paul Krugman claimed that the media allowed themselves to be manipulated by Bush into ignoring the Harken Energy and

Halliburton scandals. Which is why, to this day, no one in America has ever heard the word "Halliburton."

According to Krugman, the administration was on the ropes in "the spring of 2002, after the big revelations of corporate fraud." Democrats were confident of a big win in the midterm elections, but "suddenly," Krugman says, "it was all Iraq, all the time, and Harken Energy and Halliburton vanished from the headlines."[31]

I'm not sure what Krugman means by "the spring of 2002," but if he means anytime before July of that year, the news coverage of Halliburton and Harken was not overwhelming. Harken Energy was mentioned only once in the *New York Times* in the first half of the year (January 1 to June 30), compared with 40 times in the second half of the year (from July 1, 2002, to the end of the year), when it allegedly "vanished from the headlines"—no doubt on orders from the Bush administration to throw a midterm election. Similarly, Halliburton was mentioned twice as many times in the second half of 2002 (86 times)—as the election drew closer—as in the first half (43). And that was just in Krugman's own increasingly unread newspaper. Thousands and thousands of news organizations were howling about Halliburton throughout the 2002 election campaign and beyond. Rarely are people as self-righteous as Paul Krugman when they make up facts.

The only topics the *Times* ever covered with greater urgency than Halliburton and Harken Energy were prisoner abuse at Abu Ghraib and the Augusta National Golf Club's refusal to admit women members. If the *Times* had ever discovered a terrorist being tortured *at* Augusta, it would have had to cease operations and turn itself into "The Augusta Torture Hotline Formerly Known as 'the *New York Times*.'"

I believe the reason the Harken Energy and Halliburton scandals never interested normal people was that there was absolutely no wrongdoing involving anyone at the White House. The only scandal was how much energy the mainstream media devoted to covering boring nonstories.

The corpus delicti of these media-hallucinated scandals was that George W. Bush used to work for Harken and Dick Cheney used to work for Halliburton. It's not illegal to work for a living rather than be a "community organizer." Paul Krugman, for example, used to work for

Enron and currently works for the nation's leading clearinghouse for left-wing conspiracy theories. But Harken and Halliburton are corporations and as such are subject to reams of regulations and laws, which always gives liberals endless opportunities for overwrought stories with baseless accusations.

Even Krugman's fellow hysteric on the op-ed page, Frank Rich, admitted there was no suggestion of "any criminality" in Bush's dealings with Harken Energy or Cheney's with Halliburton. When America's leading drama queen thinks you're overreacting, you might be a few tweaks away from cool dispassion. Nonetheless, Rich said we still needed to know every little detail about Bush's and Cheney's employment with these companies because "of what they may add to our knowledge of the ethics, policies and personnel of a secretive administration to which we've entrusted both our domestic and economic security."[32] Would that liberals had used that standard to examine Barack Obama's dealings with Tony Rezko, William Ayers, and Jeremiah Wright!

After a year of Abu Ghraib–level coverage of Bush's and Cheney's dealings with Harken Energy and Halliburton, what we learned was: They had both behaved completely honorably. The Securities and Exchange Commission said so. Thank you, *New York Times*, for wasting months of our lives on that.

The phony Harken scandal was that Bush sold his stock in Harken in 1990 to pay off a loan used to buy the Texas Rangers. A few months after Bush sold his stock, the stock price dipped slightly. Then it went back up, until, just a year later, it was worth twice what Bush had sold it for. It's not illegal to own or sell stock, even if the price later declines. It's illegal to sell stock based on insider information. Because of the stock's subsequent price decline, Bush's sale of stock was exhaustively investigated by the Securities and Exchange Commission in the early nineties. The SEC found that Bush had done nothing wrong. That is, if you don't include selling stock for half of what he could have gotten for it a year later.

As CNN's Brooks Jackson explained, "Internal SEC memos show that the career staff at the SEC concluded they couldn't come close to making a case against Bush."[33] The SEC's investigation of the sale concluded before Bush ever announced his first run for governor way back in 1993,[34] but the media resurrected the sale as a major potential scandal during Bush's presidency—*Questions Remain; Unresolved Issues Exist; Doubts Linger!* No questions ever linger around Democratic scandals because no questions are ever asked.

The Clinton White House's illegal possession of 900 FBI files on American citizens, Krugman called piffle. But a twenty-year-old investigation, which resulted in Bush's complete vindication by the SEC and which requires a bottle of NoDoz to follow—that was a major scandal.

The phony Halliburton scandal was that Cheney was Halliburton's chief executive from 1995 to 2000, which at the time was not considered a crime. But on May 22, 2002, the *New York Times* published a frantic story accusing Vice President Cheney of dark conspiracies involving minor accounting changes made at Halliburton back in 1998. In response to the article, the SEC launched an investigation.[35]

NOTE TO READERS: SKIP THE FOLLOWING PARAGRAPH IF YOU ARE OPERATING HEAVY MACHINERY, DRIVING, OR IF YOU ARE NOT PRESENTLY TAKING AMPHETAMINES: The accounting change concerned the fascinating issue of how Halliburton recorded cost overruns on long-term construction projects. Because of disputes with customers over the cost overruns, the expense might not ever be fully recouped . . . zzzzzzzzzzzzzz. Oops, sorry! How long was I out? Anyway, following the practice used by most publicly traded construction companies, Halliburton claimed as income money that it expected to receive based on an estimate of how the cost-overrun disputes would be resolved, but which it had not yet received.

After a two-year investigation, the SEC concluded that the accounting change was fine but Halliburton erred in not telling investors about the change sooner. Halliburton settled the case for $7.5 million, a piddling amount of money for both the multibillion-dollar corporation and for the SEC, which settled another case that week for $150 million. Business columnists called it a "wrist slap."[36]

The SEC found absolutely no wrongdoing by Cheney and promptly issued a statement saying Cheney had cooperated "willingly and fully."[37] But the indisputable proof that Cheney had been completely exonerated was that Paul Krugman never mentioned the settlement. He just waited a few months, hoping no one had seen the news, before renewing his demand that Cheney be "confront[ed] over Halliburton."[38]

In another column, Krugman complained that the press was refusing to report the problems with Iraq and Afghanistan and the Bush tax cuts—allowing the president to revel in media glory! Only Bush's "initial triumphs," Krugman said, "get all the headlines." At this point, you could knock me over with a feather: I had no idea liberals had any complaints with the Iraq War or Bush's tax cuts!

A lonely voice in the wilderness, Krugman attacked the menace of tax cuts, saying, "I could demonstrate [their] irrelevance by going through an economic analysis"—but he decided against it. So in that case, Krugman was victimized by his own shoddy reporting.[39]

The truth was, Americans supported the president's policies, so Krugman concluded the media weren't doing their job. For Krugman, there were only two possibilities—either (1) Americans wanted to burn Bush at the stake or (2) the press wasn't doing its job. How about the third, most obvious, possibility? Maybe people grasped the facts but weren't indignant?

Krugman also detected pro-Bush media bias in the media's coverage of Alan Greenspan's testimony on the Bush tax cuts and Social Security privatization plan. Despite the total blackout from the pro-Bush media, Krugman said, Greenspan had offered "caveats and cautions" about Bush tax cuts in 2001. And yet, Krugman harrumphed, "the headlines trumpeted Mr. Greenspan's support." Then when the Fed chairman expressed general support for privatizing Social Security in 2005, Krugman noted that he also "went on to concede that the opponents of privatization" also had some points. But again, liberals were screwed over by the pro-Bush media: "The headlines didn't emphasize his concession that crucial critiques of the Bush plan are right."[40]

Liberals are like people with stale breath who keep talking to your face at a party making the same boring point. You try to back away, maybe offer them an Altoid, but then they start whimpering and claim you're being mean to them. If *New York Times* columnists think they can't get their message out because of media bias, it might be time to consider whether the problem is that no one is buying the message.

Some will say it's unfair to attack a columnist with only nine readers (two if you don't count those identified by ACORN). Fair enough. But someone has to speak up on behalf of wasted Internet space used to post Krugman's column—maybe two columns—that run over and over and over again under different headlines. Moreover, Krugman must be promoting his theory of liberal media bias around the newsroom, because there's an epidemic of liberal journalists attacking the media for covering up Republican scandals. Perhaps it's not just an epidemic. It could be a pandemic. Ask anyone if the media is biased in favor of Republicans—and by "anyone," I mean Dennis Kucinich.

Another story that the mainstream media denounced the mainstream media for ignoring was the Jeff Gannon mystery scandal. It was a mystery scandal because it was a mystery why it was a scandal. In 2005, Frank Rich bitterly complained that the "'Jeff Gannon' story was getting less attention than another media frenzy—that set off by the veteran news executive Eason Jordan."[41]

Rich, who became qualified to comment on U.S. foreign policy, national security, and presidential politics after spending a childhood dancing his favorite numbers from *Oklahoma!* in his mother's panties and then spending twelve years reviewing theater for the *New York Times,* attacked Gannon for not being a "real newsman." Not only that, but, Rich breathlessly reported, there were "embarrassing blogosphere revelations linking [Gannon] to sites like hotmilitarystud.com and to an apparently promising career as an X-rated $200-per-hour 'escort.'"[42] In Rich's estimation, $200 an hour was way too much to pay a male escort who wasn't Latino. Now, if there's anybody in this world who knows what a real man is, it's Frank Rich. But as for knowing what a real newsman is, that's another story.

Since he brought it up, let's compare the Jeff Gannon and Eason Jordan scandals in terms of newsworthiness. The big contretemps with Gannon was that he had supposedly operated a gay escort service, thereby cutting into the business of the *Village Voice.* Also—and this was the crux of the matter—Gannon was a Republican. Liberals think gay men should be Boy Scout troop leaders but are outraged that a gay man could be a Republican.

Apart from the media's lurid obsession with outing gay Republicans, this was a tough one to turn into a really big scandal inasmuch as, until liberals started attacking him, no one had heard of Jeff Gannon. But showing the industry and determination that gave us the famed reportage of Jayson Blair, the mainstream media claimed that Gannon was a White House plant. *Times* columnist Maureen Dowd, for example, griped that she had been rejected for a White House press pass "but someone with an alias, a tax evasion problem and Internet pictures where he posed like the 'Barberini Faun' is credentialed."

If there's one thing Democrats are sticklers about, it's who gets into the White House. During the Clinton years, for example, you had to show press credentials, government-issued photo ID, or a thong. No exceptions!

The truth was, Dowd had been turned down for a permanent press pass. Gannon only had a daily pass, which virtually anyone can get, even *New York Times* fantasists. A daily pass and a permanent pass are altogether different animals. Editors at the Talon News Service probably would have caught an error like that.

The media's other excuse for leering over Gannon's apparent homosexuality was, as MSNBC's David Shuster put it, "the phony alias" he had used "to play journalist." You can tell Shuster is a crackerjack journalist because he uses phrases like "phony alias."

Democrats in Congress actually demanded an investigation into how Gannon got into White House press conferences while writing under a pseudonym. Next up: Major investigations into the pen names of Wolf Blitzer (Ze'ev Barak), Bill Clinton (Billy Blythe), Geraldo Rivera (Gerald Rivera), Gary Hart (Gary Hartpence), John Kerry (John Kohn), Larry King (Larry Zeigler), George Orwell (Eric Blair), Michael Savage (Michael Weiner), and Randi Rhodes (it must be a doozy!)

Congressional Democrats also called on independent prosecutor Patrick Fitzgerald to investigate Gannon. They claimed he was given access to classified information from sources within the government, which I believe would make Gannon what we used to call "a reporter." As one *New York Times* article on the fake Gannon scandal said, "Two Democrats in Congress are pressing for investigations into how a Washington reporter who used a pseudonym managed to gain access to the White House and had access to classified documents that named Valerie Plame as a C.I.A. operative."

This was a nutty claim circulating on the left-wing blogs, which the *Times* had apparently lifted without one iota of independent investigation.[43] It turned out Gannon's suspect references to classified material came from documents that had been printed in the *Wall Street Journal* weeks earlier. Democrats in Congress were demanding that the independent counsel investigate how Jeff Gannon managed to get his hands on information that millions of people had already read in the *Journal*.[44] We're working on a number of different theories, but the most promising scenario so far is "bought a copy at a newsstand."

Once the smoke had cleared from the media hate campaign against Gannon, Gannon's only remaining offense was that he might be gay. Gannon didn't write about gays. No "hypocrisy" was being unveiled. He wasn't caught in Central Park at 3:40 A.M. with a rope tied from his neck to his genitals and methamphetamine in his pocket, as a certain CNN journalist was in 2008.[45] The entire scandal that Frank Rich complained was not getting enough attention was that Gannon was a gay Republican. (Because if there's one thing Frank Rich can't abide, it's a gay man who's too scared to come out of the closet.)

The episode with Eason Jordan, chief news executive at CNN was arguably a bigger story. On January 27, 2005, in front of an international audience at the World Economic Forum in Davos, Switzerland, Jordan made the astonishing assertion that the U.S. military was targeting journalists for assassination. Jordan's remarks drew gasps from the crowd—and slaps on the back from the anti-American Europeans and Middle Easterners.

This incident, which Rich said sparked a "media frenzy," was not reported at the time by the *New York Times*.

On February 1, 2005, after a number of conservative blogs picked up on the story, CNN issued the following statement, defending Jordan:

Many blogs have taken Mr. Jordan's remarks out of context. Eason Jordan does not believe the U.S. military is trying to kill journalists. Mr. Jordan simply pointed out the facts: While the majority of journalists killed in Iraq have been slain at the hands of insurgents, the Pentagon has also noted that the U.S. military on occasion has killed people who turned out to be journalists. The Pentagon has apologized for those actions.

Mr. Jordan was responding to an assertion by Cong. Frank that all 63 journalist victims had been the result of "collateral damage."[46]

The CNN statement did not bestir the *New York Times* to report the burgeoning scandal. In the *Times*'s defense, the newsroom was gearing up for its usual wall-to-wall National Gay Valentines Day coverage at this point.

Jordan issued his own statement, saying, "I have never once in my life thought anyone from the U.S. military tried to kill a journalist. Never meant to suggest that." He added, "Obviously I wasn't as clear as I should have been on that panel."[47]

The *New York Times* still did not report the story. Perhaps *Times* reporters were hot on the story of another all-male golf club somewhere in America.

The statements from both CNN and Jordan quickly became inoperative as various people who were present at the Davos panel gave accounts at odds with Jordan's version.

Liberal Democrat Barney Frank, who was on the panel with Jordan, said he was "agog" at Jordan's remarks[48] suggesting that "it was official military policy to take out journalists."[49] Frank said he had asked Jordan "to basically clarify the remarks. Did he have proof and if so, why hadn't CNN run with the story?"[50] According to Frank, Jordan then "modified" his statement to say that it was only some U.S. soldiers, "maybe knowing they were killing journalists, out of anger."[51]

Jordan had described one particular case in which American troops imprisoned an Al Jazeera reporter, taunting him as "al Jazeera–boy" and forcing him to eat his shoes. A producer for Al Jazeera later denied the story.[52] This is what's known in the news business as a story "unraveling."

When Frank got home from Davos, he called Jordan, asking for more information and offering to hold a congressional investigation if there was any truth to the allegations. Frank said he never heard back from Jordan.[53]

Guess whether the *New York Times* reported the Eason Jordan story yet. No, but this time it was possibly owing to an important break in the Harken Energy scandal that week: *Still No Proof of Bush Wrongdoing*. Folks, a newspaper is only so big. I mean, where is it written that the *Times* has to print all the news?

David Gergen, a longtime friend of Jordan's who had moderated the Davos panel, said he, too, had been "startled" by Jordan's claim and had also immediately asked him to clarify his remarks. Jordan began to speculate, so Gergen decided to shut the panel down because "the military and the government weren't there to defend themselves."[54] Again the *Times* did not run with the story.

Democratic senator Chris Dodd, who had been in the audience, had his office release a statement saying that he, "like panelists Mr. Gergen and Mr. Frank—was outraged by the comments. Senator Dodd is tremendously proud of the sacrifice and service of our American military personnel."[55]

The *New York Times* still did not report the story. Even I will admit, at this point, the *Times*'s silence was starting to look fishy.

On February 11, 2005, Jordan resigned from CNN "to prevent CNN from being unfairly tarnished by the controversy."[56]

At long last, the *New York Times* reported on Eason Jordan's remarks at Davos in a demure Business section article explaining why he was resigning after twenty-three years at CNN. The *Times* was not alone in refusing to sully its pages by mentioning the mushrooming scandal engulfing CNN's chief news executive. A major player in American news had accused the U.S. military of intentionally killing journalists. But apart from opinion columns and enraged letters to the editor, that was considered newsworthy by fewer than a dozen U.S. newspapers.[57]

And yet, a week after the mainstream press finally relented on its censorship of the story in order to report Jordan's resignation, Frank Rich was complaining that the "'Jeff Gannon' story was getting less attention than another media frenzy—that set off by the veteran news executive Eason Jordan."[58] Here's the rundown at that point:

NUMBER OF ARTICLES IN THE *NEW YORK TIMES* ON JEFF GANNON,
GAY: 4

NUMBER OF ARTICLES IN THE *TIMES* ON EASON JORDAN ACCUSING THE
U.S. MILITARY OF ASSASSINATING JOURNALISTS: 2

NUMBER OF WORDS ON JEFF GANNON IN THE *TIMES:* 5,097

NUMBER OF WORDS ON EASON JORDAN IN THE *TIMES:* 2,785

NUMBER OF WORDS ON EASON JORDAN IN THE *TIMES* NOT ATTACKING
BLOGGERS FOR MAKING AN ISSUE OF IT: 938

NUMBER OF TV NEWS PROGRAMS DISCUSSING JEFF GANNON: 45

NUMBER OF TV NEWS PROGRAMS DISCUSSING EASON JORDAN,
EXCLUDING FOX NEWS: 33

As a group, the figures above suggest a "Jeff-Gannon-to-Eason-Jordan-stories" ratio of about 2 to 1. I don't know where Rich falls on the "real newsman" scale, but it seems to me that even an average newsman ought to be able to count.

ANOTHER STORY THE MEDIA HAD KEPT OUT OF THE MEDIA, according to *Times* columnist Paul Krugman, was the Bush U.S. attorneys scandal. After the 2006 midterm elections, Krugman exulted that the new Democratic Congress could finally shed some light on Bush's firings of U.S. attorneys, which he called a "suppressed Bush-era scandal—a huge abuse of power that somehow never became front-page news."[59]

Krugman's complaint that the media had been burying the story was, as usual, completely deranged. By that point, the *Times* alone had made the U.S. attorneys "scandal" the subject of eleven major news stories, including two front-page articles, for a total of more than 9,000 words. The *Times* had also published six overwrought editorials, three op-ed pieces, and one indignant letter to the editor on the subject. The topic was featured in seven news summaries. The only way the U.S. attorneys story could have gotten more press is if one of the U.S. attorneys had been caught on the greens of the Augusta National Golf Club.

The wall-to-wall coverage was especially impressive since it had never before been a scandal for a president to fire his own political appointees, such as U.S. attorneys.[60] U.S. attorneys serve at the pleasure of the president. The president may fire them for no reason or any reason at all, including but not limited to: not implementing the president's policy about criminal prosecutions or being in the way of a patronage appointment. Why wasn't a fuss made when Bush fired Donald Rumsfeld? U.S. attorneys are political appointees, just as much as the secretary of defense is. Bush should have said, "We did it, it was political, and there's nothing you can do about it." Instead, the administration stupidly apologized for firing its own employees, thereby embroiling itself in the most ridiculous nonscandal scandal in human history. We had gone from "Watergate" to "Troopergate" to "Gategate."

If Bush's firing of U.S. attorneys he had appointed himself was a scandal, then what was President Clinton's unprecedented firing of virtually all U.S. attorneys appointed by his predecessor? This wholesale dismissal in March 1993 was a complete break with tradition. Historically, incoming presidents would gradually replace U.S attorneys from the opposing party as the president found replacements and the prosecutors wrapped up major cases and resigned. A total switchover to the president's appointees would generally take a few years. The Clinton administration requested that all U.S. attorneys submit their resignations by the end of the week.

Clinton's audacious move was particularly troubling because one of the U.S. attorneys targeted for dismissal was Jay Stephens, who was in the middle of a massive investigation of criminal wrongdoing in the House Post Office that was pointing to a key Clinton ally in Congress, House Ways and Means chairman Dan Rostenkowski. The prosecutor had already won several guilty pleas and was within thirty days of making a decision on whether to indict the powerful Democrat, when the Clinton administration peremptorily asked for Stephens's resignation.[61]

In that case, the *Times* lightly rapped Attorney General Janet Reno's knuckles, saying that firing all U.S attorneys was "an odd first step in the wrong direction," while quickly admitting, "Nobody questions her right to dismiss every Bush Administration holdover."[62]

For liberals to complain about Bush replacing his own U.S. attorneys after excusing Clinton's firing of all U.S. attorneys, not to mention his purge of the White House travel office employees—who were career civil servants, not political appointees—would be like ignoring Gennifer Flowers's audiotape-backed claims of an affair with Clinton, while running an innuendo-laced front-page article on John McCain's friendship with a female lobbyist. Oh wait . . . bad example. Okay, then, it would be like the breezing over of how John Kerry came into his money via a recent marriage to an heiress five years his senior, while fixating on McCain's marriage to a hot young heiress thirty-eight years earlier with whom he had four children. Oh wait . . . another bad example. How about: It would be like the *Times* defending the "Sensation" exhibit at the Brooklyn Museum of Art, with "art" defacing the Virgin Mary with close-up photos of women's vaginas, while criticizing John McCain's insensitivity to Catholics for receiving an endorsement from the Reverend John Hagee, a minister who had tough words for Catholicism. No, still another bad example.

Indeed, *Times* editorialists complained that the media had not bashed Hagee enough, with Frank Rich grousing that videos of Hagee's sermons "have never had the same circulation on television as [the Reverend Jeremiah] Wright's." When the media are complaining about their own massively left-wing coverage being biased in favor of conservatives, we have gone through the looking glass into the nuthouse.

But through eight years of the Bush presidency, liberals wailed that a docile media was ignoring administration scandals. That's if you don't include the entire liberal establishment relentlessly attacking Bush from the moment he took the oath of office. Consider the arsenic hoax.

In his first months in office, Bush was bedeviled by hundreds of regulations the Clinton administration had issued in its final days. The most famous of the Clinton last-minute rule changes was the new rule lowering the amount of arsenic permissible in drinking water. During eight years of Clinton's presidency, his administration considered 50 parts per billion of arsenic in drinking water an acceptable standard—the standard since 1942. But just days before Clinton left office, the Environmental Protection Agency suddenly issued a new rule that would lower the standard to 10 parts per billion over a five-year period, knowing that it would be madness for the Bush administration to implement the rule.

In order to comply with the new rule, small towns in western states, where arsenic naturally occurs, would be forced to spend hundreds of millions of dollars to buy new water plants. The liberal Brookings Institution and the conservative American Enterprise Institute produced a joint study showing that rather than saving lives, the new standard would actually cost about ten lives annually.[63] Money spent on new water-treatment plants is money that is not being spent on ambulances, cancer research, and healthy food. So obviously this rule was a joke, the equivalent of Clinton staffers removing all the Ws from White House typewriters before leaving. To paraphrase Will Rogers, every time the Clinton administration made a joke, it was a law, and every time they made a law, it was a joke.

But the facts were irrelevant when the word "arsenic" allowed liberals to scream that Bush was poisoning us. In a typical doomsday editorial, the *San Francisco Chronicle* intoned, "Arsenic and Water Don't Mix."[64] Other apocalyptic editorials were titled "A Powerful Poison" (*News and Observer* [Raleigh, NC]), "Serve Up a Tasty Glass of Arsenic (*Detroit Free Press*), and "Arsenic, Ozone and Lead Are Poison, Not Politics" (*South Bend Tribune* [Indiana]).[65] Letters to the editor reached a fever pitch. Noe Coopersmith wrote a letter to the editor of the *Chronicle* saying that Bush "seems determined to poison us all with arsenic in our water."[66] James F. Gerrits wrote to the *Times Herald* (Port Huron, Michigan), "The new administration in Washington seems to be bent upon poisoning the general population."[67] Kurt Weldon wrote to the *Los Angeles Times* that Bush was "getting ready to . . . poison our children with arsenic-laden water."[68]

These letters were impressively panic-stricken. But excited liberals firing off letters to newspapers could not hold a candle to the professional hysterics at the *New York Times*. (There must be something in the water over there.) The *Times* ran three separate editorials and more than a dozen op-ed columns attacking Bush for not immediately adopting the new arsenic standard that was so urgent, it had not been implemented throughout eight years of the Clinton administration. America's most easily fooled journalist, Bob Herbert, raged that "Mr. Bush is presiding over a right-wing juggernaut that has . . . withdrawn new regulations requiring a substantial reduction in the permissible levels of arsenic, a known carcinogen, in drinking water."[69] Paul Krugman wrote, "And about those who thought Mr. Bush meant something kinder and gentler by 'compassionate conservatism,' all I can say is, let them eat cake. And drink arsenic."[70] Guest columnists Paul Begala and James Carville wrote a column saying Bush's "environmental agenda would put more arsenic in the water and more pollutants in the air." I guess that depends on what your definition of the word "more" is. In Carville and Begala's sentence, it meant "the same as it was for the past six decades, including during the Clinton administration."

But the winner of the prestigious Lombardi Award for Best Beating of a Dead Horse was Maureen Dowd, something of a nag herself, with a grand total of seven op-eds denouncing the Bush administration's decision to delay implementation of a new arsenic rule dumped on them by the departing Clinton administration. These columns are believed to contain considerably more than 10 parts per billion of pure b.s., also a known carcinogen. Sample: "As W. and Uncle Dick went about strip-mining the nation, allowing arsenic in the water and turning Alaska into a gas station . . ."[71] (We started drilling for oil in Alaska under Carter, incidentally.)

By August of Bush's first year in office, the Democratic National Committee was running an ad with Senate minority leader Tom Daschle saying, "Under FDR, all we had to fear was fear itself. Now we have to fear arsenic in our drinking water." The late *Washington Post* columnist Michael Kelly ruefully remarked, "The charges are manifestly false and they stick anyway."[72]

In the end, the Bush administration adopted the rule, requiring vast amounts of money that could no longer be spent on other things, like heart disease research, lifesaving vaccines, or . . . I don't know . . . how about shoring up some levees in Louisiana? A stupid regulation was adopted because of a prank pulled by the Clinton administration and then elevated to an emergency lifesaving measure by a ferociously anti-Bush press. Bush didn't even get credit for finally adopting the idiotic rule hysterically demanded by liberals. The article reporting Bush had adopted the new arsenic rule ran on page A18 of the *Times*.[73]

Clinton himself had frozen all midnight regulations promulgated by the first Bush administration. Guess how that was portrayed by the media. If you guessed "heroic," you would be correct. When Clinton did the exact same thing as W., he was depicted as a brave young president protecting the country from Republican dirty tricks. An article in the *Wisconsin State Journal* explained, "President Clinton ordered his Office of Management and Budget to freeze all last-minute rulings by Bush *to make sure Bush wasn't hurting the country through a lot of last-minute favors.*"[74] An Associated Press article began, "The Clinton administration is putting the brakes on scores of regulations pushed in the waning days of President Bush's term, including an alternative-fuels proposal *backed by a big Republican contributor and ethanol maker. . . . 'There were some that were pretty questionable,' White House Press Secretary Dee Dee Myers said Sunday.*"[75] How prescient of Clinton to be opposing alternative fuels as far back as 1992!

It was entirely up to the media which new rules would become permanent and which would be scuttled.

Having dealt with last-minute rule-making himself, George W. Bush directed his agencies to refrain from proposing any new rules after June 1 of his last year in office, to avoid creating similar headaches for his successor.[76] Again, liberals smelled the whiff of fascism. The *New York Times* ran a front-page article quoting "legal specialists" who denounced Bush for his ban on eleventh-hour rules, saying "the policy would ensure that rules the administration wanted to be part of Mr. Bush's legacy would be less subject to being overturned by his successor."[77] First of all: Huh? Second of all: So by not sneaking through eleventh-hour rule changes, the Bush administration was nefariously denying its successor administration the opportunity to revoke those rules?

The *Times* even got an environmentalist, John D. Walke, to attack Bush for trying to "shut down regulation for the remainder of the Bush administration." It is unlikely that Walke would have liked any new rules being issued by the Bush administration, anyway. Not six months earlier, Walke had called the EPA's new rule on coal-fired emission plants "the Bush administration's parting gift to the utility industry."[78] You can't win with these liberals.

If Bush wanted to have fun, just before leaving office he would have signed executive orders reinstating the "wall" between the FBI and the CIA, banning waterboarding, ending terrorist surveillance, prohibiting extraordinary rendition, and shutting down Guantánamo. After he defied all predictions by keeping America terrorist-free for eight years, let's see Obama do it without having to explain to the *New York Times* why he's "tearing up the Constitution."

TO PROVE THAT THEIR OWN MASSIVELY LEFT-WING MEDIA BIAS is actually right-wing media bias, the media cite phony polls showing how overwhelming popular liberal ideas are with the public. It is not insignificant how the media report polls, because liberals consider polls—opinion surveys of the uninformed—more accurate than actual elections.

The biggest story of the 2004 election was the fraudulent Edison/Mitofsky Research exit poll on election day. Early exit polls showed John Kerry the clear winner by mind-boggling margins. The Mitofsky poll had overstated Democratic percentages by about 6 to 8 percent since the 1992 election,[79] but in 2004, the pro-Democratic tilt was absurd. For example, the exit polls had Bush tied with Kerry in Mississippi. Yes, Mississippi, the state where 9 out of 10 white men voted for Ronald Reagan in 1984. The 2004 exit poll results were so implausible that renowned political analyst Michael Barone initially speculated that the sites of exit polling had been leaked to the Democrats, enabling them to flood those precincts with Democratic voters eager to answer the pollsters' questions.

These stunningly inaccurate exit polls began to be released around noon on election day and convinced news anchors, talking heads, and even the campaigns that Kerry would win walking away. Recall that when Jimmy Carter conceded the election to Reagan in 1980 before the polls had closed on the West Coast, Carter was blamed for costing a slew of down-ticket Democrats their elections. In 2004, the entire punditocracy had essentially conceded the election to Kerry. Only at 9 P.M., when the real results began to come in, did the election flip to Bush. It was the first Kerry flip-flop that actually served the national interest.

Had the wildly inaccurate 2004 exit polls turned the election, this would have been the most spectacular October Surprise in history—better than a simple, little "October Surprise," this was an "Election Day surprise." How many voters were discouraged by the leaked exit polls showing Kerry to be the clear winner? In the end, Bush won, so Republicans walked away from this jaw-dropping near-theft of an election without complaint.

After the election, the designer of the exit poll, Warren Mitofsky, frantically examined the results to try to figure out what had gone so horribly wrong. What Mitofsky found was that "the biggest discrepancies between actual precinct votes and the exit pollsters' results occurred in precincts where the exit poll personnel were female graduate students."[80] Barone suggested that Republicans might have been less likely than Democrats to answer the pollsters' questions, "especially when the interviewer is a young woman whose appearance signals she is some kind of Bush hater."[81] Perhaps it was the "Bush = Hitler" buttons that Republicans found off-putting. Next time, how about having Mormon women take the exit polls?

But ludicrous exit polls showing Kerry winning Florida by 110 percent were soon being cited by liberals as proof that Bush stole the election. Contributing to the conspiracy theories was the fact that Mitofsky's exit polls in other countries have always been accurate. But as Mitofsky told Barone, in other countries, such as Mexico and Russia, everyone answers the exit polls. It may even be mandatory in Russia. In the United States, he said, about half of those leaving polling places refused to participate in exit polls.

Those facts, adduced by the exit poll author himself, didn't slow liberals down. Robert F. Kennedy Jr. wrote a major piece for the pretentious and stupid *Rolling Stone* magazine, titled "Was the 2004 Election Stolen?" (I responded in a spellbinding article titled "No.") As his smoking gun, Kennedy noted that "the first indication that something was gravely amiss on November 2nd, 2004, was the inexplicable discrepancies between exit polls and actual vote counts."[82] But the discrepancies weren't "inexplicable"—they were unexplained, soon to be explained by Warren Mitofsky. Kennedy somberly noted that "the exit poll created for the 2004 election was designed to be the most reliable voter survey in history." And the *Titanic* was "designed" to be unsinkable.

University of Pennsylvania professor Steven Freeman also relied on the exit polls for his book, rhetorically titled *Was the 2004 Presidential Election Stolen?* (Look for my follow-up book, tentatively entitled *No.*) Freeman argued that exit polls "should be like measuring precipitation after rain has already fallen."[83] Except, according to the man who designed and oversaw the exit poll, 50 percent of the raindrops refused to participate. As Charles Murray says, it's not an accident that for the last two decades the only really useful public policy ideas that have had an effect on public debate have come from think tanks and not American universities.[84]

There was also conspiracy theorist David Earnhardt's documentary *Uncounted: The New Math of American Elections*, which again took the exit polls as the fact-based control group that proved the actual voting results were a fraud and a hoax. You know what we need? We need a system even more reliable than an exit poll for determining how people want to vote. Maybe if we could get every voter to go into some sort of booth and cast a secret ballot . . .

If liberals will challenge actual election results based on these sacred polls, you can imagine how liberals can twist "public opinion" results with no election to contradict them. Actually, you don't have to imagine. I've looked it up.

After the media have flogged an issue to death, they direct pollsters to ask people whether they are "concerned" about the calamity being broadcast in headlines across the nation. Poll respondents, who seem to think they can get an answer wrong, dutifully agree to be alarmed by these media-generated "crises." Completely phony political issues—such as campaign finance reform, earmarks, bipartisanship, health care, and global warming—suddenly roil national political campaigns as politicians become convinced that the public will lynch them if they don't pass, say, campaign finance reform laws. Proving that media coverage can turn any issue into a crisis, in the midst of the media's overblown coverage of Halliburton, Harken, and Enron—the last of which was connected to Bush by virtue of the fact that both Bush and

Enron were from Texas—the *New York Times* triumphantly produced a *Times*/CBS poll showing, as the headline said: "Poll Finds Concerns That Bush Is Overly Influenced by Business."[85]

One of the most deceptive polls in world history was used to advocate liberals' dearest cause: killing an innocent person. After a Florida state court judge ordered that Terri Schiavo be starved to death on the basis of hazy claims from her adulterous husband that she had once expressed a wish to die after watching a TV show, ABC promptly produced a poll purporting to demonstrate that the vast majority of Americans were rooting for Schiavo's death.

The poll question asked:

Schiavo suffered brain damage and has been on life support for fifteen years. Doctors say she has no consciousness and her condition is irreversible. Her husband and her parents disagree about whether she would have wanted to be kept alive. Florida courts have sided with the husband and her feeding tube was removed on Friday. What's your opinion on this case—do you support or oppose the decision to remove Schiavo's feeding tube?[86]

It was not true that Terri was on "life support"—anymore than a child up to about age four is on "life support" because he needs help to eat. It was not true that Terri had "no consciousness" nor that her condition was "irreversible." That was the position of doctors produced by her adulterous husband; doctors produced by her loving parents disagreed. It is not true that the question at issue was whether Terri should be "kept on" life support inasmuch as she was not *on* life support. It was not even true that Florida "courts" had sided with the husband. One lone judge had sided with the husband; the other courts simply found they did not have authority to overturn the first judge's finding of fact that Terri would have wanted to die.

Not surprisingly, a poll question composed of a series of lies managed to give liberals the answer they wanted: 63 percent supported removing Terri's feeding tube; only 28 percent were opposed.

In a follow-up question, ABC asked whether it was "appropriate or inappropriate for Congress to get involved in this way?" To this question, 70 percent said "inappropriate" and 27 percent said "appropriate." (There was no question about the appropriateness of a state court judge ordering an American citizen's death without the possibility of meaningful review.)

Soon thereafter, a Zogby poll asked a question that—in contradistinction to ABC's poll—actually bore some relation to the facts of the Schiavo case: "If a disabled person is not terminally ill, not in a coma, and not being kept alive on life support, and they have no written directive, should or should they not be denied food and water?"[87]

Without ABC's invented facts driving the question, 79 percent of respondents said the patient should not be denied food and water. Only 9 percent said she should be denied food and water.

Zogby's follow-up question about governmental intervention asked: "When there is conflicting evidence on whether or not a patient would want to be on a feeding tube, should elected officials order that a feeding tube be removed or should they order that it remain in place?" This time only 18 percent said that the feeding tube should be removed. Forty-two percent said elected officials should order that the feeding tube remain in place.

But on the basis of the tendentious ABC poll, the media set to work creating the myth that Americans were furious with Congress for intervening in the Schiavo case to try to save an innocent woman's life.

A *New York Times* article on end-of-life legislation asserted: "Polls indicating broad public opposition to government involvement in the Schiavo case may be giving some politicians second thoughts."[88] In a *Times* article on Senator Rick Santorum, the *Times* reporter incidentally threw in the false fact that in the Schiavo case, "Republicans took positions opposed by most Americans, according to polls."[89] Months later, another *Times* article reported that Congress was held in disfavor by Americans because "Congressional intervention in the medical care of Terri Schiavo, the Florida woman whose feeding tube was removed, is inflicting new damage on the public image of Congress and both parties."[90]

The *Los Angeles Times* waved the bloody shirt in an article defending Democratic filibusters in a majority Republican Congress, saying,

"Democrats are preparing to link the Republican move against fili-busters with Washington's last-minute effort to require additional judi-cial review in the Schiavo case—a step polls showed was opposed by a large majority of Americans."[91] This concocted "fact" generated by a completely dishonest poll was slipped into news articles incessantly over the next two years, driving Republican politicians to flee from the issue of life.

When the numbers are with liberals, you read about it in banner headlines, the case is closed, America has decided, let's all move on. When the numbers are not with liberals, they triumphantly announce: It's not unanimous! Why are they always informing us that opposition only to their opinions is not unanimous? Belief in global warming is far from unanimous, but they are unimpressed by the lack of unanimity on that issue.

The *Times* headline on one of its promotional pieces for Cindy Sheehan was titled "In War Debate, Parents of Fallen Are United Only in Grief."[92] I'm not sure what poll they relied on for that assertion, but it doesn't seem likely. A *Military Times* survey released in September 2004, during an election in which the war in Iraq was the main issue, showed that active-duty military personnel supported President Bush by 73 to 18 percent.[93] So apparently, more than 70 percent of the mili-tary were "united" in at least one respect: They supported the war.

Only a slightly higher percentage of blacks supported Kerry than active-duty military supported Bush. Yet the *Times* described that phe-nomenon in a headline that said, "Energized Black Voters Flock to Polls to Back Kerry."[94] So why not a headline saying, "Active-Duty Military Flock to Polls to Back Bush"?

After 9/11, liberals got the bright idea to commemorate the attack with a "Freedom" museum at Ground Zero that would showcase every-thing the terrorists believed about America. Exhibits were planned on slavery in America and America's "genocide" of the Indians—you know, the first things that usually come to mind when the average American thinks about 9/11. For good measure, the museum was also to include exhibits about the Holocaust and the Gulag, perhaps be-cause those damn lazy Americans didn't liberate victims of the Nazi and Soviet empires fast enough. (Oddly, the planned memorial contained no explicit references to the all-male membership policies of the Augusta National Country Club.) As Columbia professor Eric Foner described the purpose of the museum, "One of the things that most annoys people in other countries is the idea that we have a monopoly on freedom. It will be salutary for the museum to suggest that America has sometimes fallen short of the ideal."[95] Americans can barely save people as fast as people in other countries can kill them—no wonder the rest of the world is testy with us! The fact that Eric Foner was an official adviser to the project told you all you needed to know about it.

Needless to say, normal people erupted with rage at the planned "Great Satan" museum. Even New York's own Great Satan, Senator Hillary Clinton, came out against it.

The *New York Times* reported that among those opposing the Hate America museum were "many—*but not all*—relatives of 9/11 victims."[96] There were 3,000 victims of the 9/11 attack. If every one of them had only three living relatives, surely a low estimate, that's 9,000 "relatives of 9/11 victims." In a group of 9,000 people, there are probably a few who think the world is flat.[97]

In a major front-page article on the abortion "experience" during the confirmation hearings for Chief Justice John Roberts, the *New York Times* said that abortion "cuts across all income levels, religions, races, lifestyles, political parties and marital circumstances."[98] That was on the front page. Seven hundred paragraphs later, deep inside the paper, one would find a graph of data from the pro-abortion Alan Guttmacher Institute showing that at least 78 percent of women who had abortions were unmarried, the abortion rate for blacks was three times that of whites, and the abortion rate for "other races" was 2.2 times that of whites.

So I'm not sure what information the *Times* was trying to convey by saying that the abortion "experience" cuts across "all income levels, religions, races, lifestyles, political parties and marital circumstances." Was it to dispel the ugly rumor that 100 percent of abortions are performed on women of a single race with the same religion, lifestyle, political party, and marital status?

Lopsided percentages that favor the Democrats are not hidden in these technically true but utterly pointless statements. Jews voted for Kerry over Bush by about 80 percent to 20 percent in 2004—in other words, about in the same ratio as unmarried/married women having abortions. But there were no statements along the lines of "Support for Bush cuts across all religious and racial lines" or "Jews united only in religion." That's a voting bloc that's bad for Republicans, so the *Times* isn't shy about mentioning it.

A single *Times* article noted the difficulty Bush would have getting Jewish votes five separate times, referring to (1) "a crucial element of the Democratic base: Jewish voters and donors," (2)"Jewish contributors, long a backbone of the Democratic Party's financial support," (3) "the roughly 20 percent share of the Jewish vote Mr. Bush won in 2000," (4) the "traditional Democratic dominance [of Jewish voters]," and (5) the sense that Bush would probably win "less than the nearly 40 percent [of the Jewish vote] Ronald Reagan received in 1980 when he ran against Mr. Carter, the last time Republicans did especially well among that group."[99]

If liberals are winning—even if it's only among Hispanic single mothers in the Bronx—you will be told about it. Only when they don't want you to know how bad the numbers are for liberals do you get the vitally important information that "it's not unanimous!" One exception to this rule is that the media tend to downplay how well the Democrats do among convicted felons, at least 70 percent of whom vote Democratic,[100] or how well Barack Obama polled in Germany, where 83 percent supported him.[101]

The most comical set of highly specific polls came when Walter Mondale ran against Ronald Reagan in 1984. Reagan won nearly 60 percent of the popular vote that year and claimed the greatest Electoral College vote in history. He won such Democratic bastions as Massachusetts, New York, California, and Hawaii. In fact, he won every state in the union save Mondale's home state of Minnesota—and that was a cliffhanger. Needless to say, Reagan was substantially ahead of Walter Mondale in the polls throughout the year. Thus, the *New York Times* ran hopeful headlines about increasingly narrow demographic groups that favored Mondale:

"Poll Finds Blacks United on Political Views"[102]

   Mondale Abandons Hope of Attracting White Voters

"Chicago Teamsters, In Poll, Prefer Mondale Over Reagan"[103]

   *Chicago Teamster wearing Reagan button found dead (The
   Teamsters as a whole endorsed Reagan.)*

"Sierra Club Breaks Its Tradition and Backs a Candidate:
   Mondale"[104]

   *May Have Thought Mondale Was Endangered
   Species*

"The Elderly May Dump Reagan"[105]

   *Pigs Seen Flying in Des Moines; Weathermen Predict
   Sub-Zero Temps in Hell; Sun to Rise in West Tomorrow,
   Say Experts (All age groups voted 60-to-40 for
   Reagan.)*

"Jersey Poll Says Mondale Cuts Into Reagan's Lead"[106]

   *In a Related Story, Jersey Pollster Wins $20 Bar Bet With
   "Mondale Surge" Hoax*

"New Mondale Support Seen in New York State"[107]

   *Meet Bob Smith, Walter Mondale's New Supporter in New
   York*

"Church-State Issue May Hurt Reagan's Effort to Attract
   Jews"[108]

   Non Sequitur Festival Ends on a High Note

"New Mondale Ads Impress a Skeptic"[109]

   *The "Skeptic" Was Raymond Strother, a Democratic
   Campaign Consultant in D.C.—Who Also Can't Believe
   Rich, Buttery Taste of Margarine*

"Poll in Minnesota Shows Mondale Leads Reagan"[110]

   Reagan Pulls Stomach Muscle Laughing Himself Silly

"Midwest Crowds Applaud Mondale"[111]

   *In a Related Story: Scientists Say Applause Often Motivated
   by Pity*

"Ivy League Poll Gives Mondale a Clear Lead"[112]

   *Among Ivy Leaguers, That Is. Too Bad He's Not Running for
   President of the Ivy League*

Reagan may have been 18 points ahead in the national polls, but Mondale showed surprising strength among uniformly Democratic voting blocs, people who showed up at his rallies, and members of his immediate family.

The *New York Times* also issued repeated reports that Mondale was "gaining" on Reagan—something that Senator Bob Dole apparently never did in 1996, even though Dole lost by a smaller margin to Clinton that year than Mondale lost to Reagan in 1984:

"Mondale Pulls Closer in a National Poll"[113]
"Poll Shows Better Image for Mondale and Ferraro"[114]
"Mondale Gains Ground, According to Straw Poll"[115]
"Poll Shows Mondale Is Gaining on Reagan"[116]
"Poll Shows Narrowing of Reagan Lead in Race"[117]

The Mondale-Is-Gaining headlines must have been perplexing to loyal *Times* readers, who didn't realize Mondale was ever behind. What about all those jazz musicians living in rent-controlled apartments on the Upper West Side who were "trending for Mondale"? No matter what the facts, it's always the story of the Left's emerging triumph, the swelling chorus of humanity coalescing in a mighty army to support Mondale, Obama, global warming, gun control, abortion rights, the killing of Terri Schiavo, and campaign finance reform.

The Emmy Award winner for spinning identical numbers in opposite ways goes to CBS News's Mike Wallace. In a *60 Minutes* segment about Ward Connerly's ballot initiatives to end racial discrimination by state governments, Wallace said Proposition 209 in California, ending race preferences, passed "narrowly." Describing a similar ballot initiative that lost in Houston, Wallace said that "voters came down heavily in favor of continuing affirmative action in their city."[118] Here are the numbers: California's Proposition 209 passed by 54 percent to 46 percent.[119] The Houston initiative lost by 55 percent to 45 percent.[120] Unless words have no meaning, it is impossible that one of those passed "narrowly" while the other was defeated "heavily."

The voters in Houston weren't even told what they were voting for, because the wording of the initiative was altered to say nothing about racial preferences at all, and instead referred to "affirmative action" and "outreach" programs. Of course, Wallace didn't mention that. Also an African American was running for mayor of Houston that year, thus increasing the black turnout. Wallace didn't mention that, either. But the unavoidable fact is: The votes in California and Houston were nearly identical—and Wallace described one as a crushing defeat and the other as a hair's-breadth victory.

If that's what the media do with virtually identical percentages, one can imagine what they do with more amorphous ideological labels. These are actual *New York Times* headlines describing two Supreme Court nominees:

"An Advocate for the Right" —News story on Bush nominee
    Judge John Roberts, July 28, 2005
"Balanced Jurist at Home in the Middle" —News story on
    Clinton nominee Ruth Bader Ginsburg, June 27, 1993

It used to be that the media could manufacture phony scandals out of whole cloth and destroy a presidency, throw an election, or lose a war without breaking a sweat. With Watergate, the media used a minor scandal—something that would have been a slow afternoon around the Clinton White House—to remove President Nixon from office and turn South Vietnam over to the Communists. With McCarthyism, they vilified an American patriot to hide the Democratic Party's shameful collaboration with Soviet spies. With Dan Quayle's spelling of "potato," they sent a warning shot across the bow to anyone thinking about being a conservative in public.

Today the media can't even falsely report that the Republican vice presidential candidate lied about the birth of her last child without the story falling apart in a day. So naturally, they're upset.

The establishment media can still have a good run with some fake scandals. They can occasionally become so insufferable that a Republican will withdraw from a Senate race (Jack Ryan) or resign from Congress (Mark Foley). They can persuade a few extremely stupid

Americans that their nonsense stories, such as Halliburton and Harken Energy, are major scandals deserving impeachment.

But the media have a much harder row to hoe if they want to throw a presidential election or lose a war these days. CBS's Dan Rather couldn't pawn off his fake Bush National Guard documents on the nation for even a full day. Within hours, conservative blogs had exposed the documents as fakes—as they were later conclusively proved to be by document examiners.

One might think competition would make the dinosaur media better. When Steve Jobs introduced the iPhone, his competitors immediately set to work trying to imitate it. When the TV show *Judge Judy* was a smash hit with viewers, other networks quickly introduced their own courtroom reality shows. When Google swept the Internet and made its founders billionaires, Silicon Valley's best minds went to work to create their own search engines. But when Fox News Channel comes along, presents both sides of the story, and within a few years has the highest ratings on cable news, instead of imitating the wildly successful network, liberals plot to yank Fox News's power.

Talk about the media being victims of the media! The existence of alternative sources of information is even worse than the *Times*'s woefully sparse coverage of Halliburton.

Most of the establishment media continue as they always have, apparently oblivious to the existence of alternative sources of information. The *Times* coverage of the Duke lacrosse players falsely accused of gang rape in 2006 is a perfect example. As Stuart Taylor and K. C. Johnson say in their book about the Duke lacrosse hoax rape case, *Until Proven Innocent*, long after even the originally pro-stripper columnists had come to the conclusion that the lacrosse players were innocent, the *Times* was still hawking the stripper's version of the story. On August 25, 2006, the *Times* ran one of its interminable, Pulitzer-bait articles on the case titled "Files from Duke Rape Case Give Details but No Answers." Within three hours of the article going up online, Taylor and Johnson report, "blogs deftly tore the piece to shreds, exposing the reporters' factual errors, their omission of critical evidence, and their overall pro-[prosecution] Nifong bias."[121]

The problem isn't, pace Paul Krugman and Frank Rich, that the mainstream media's headlines don't have enough exclamation points. It's that the establishment media aren't the only ones who write the news anymore. They still write most of the news, but not all of it. And they've never felt so victimized in their entire lives.

Reporters, editors, and columnists at the *New York Times* felt horribly put upon when Americans reacted with spluttering rage at their publication of a top-secret counterterrorist program tracking the terrorists' finances. The program consisted of a consortium of various countries' financial institutions called the Society for Worldwide Interbank Financial Telecommunication, or Swift, quietly working to follow terrorist money trails. The Treasury Department had voluntarily revealed the basics of the program to various news organizations in the spirit of openness, but with the request that the program not be disclosed to the public.

Two weeks after 9/11, the *Times* had editorialized that "Washington and its allies must also disable the financial networks used by terrorists." It said that "much more is needed" than what the Bush administration had planned, and lectured Americans, "If America is going to wage a new kind of war against terrorism, it must act on all fronts, including the financial one."[122]

But once liberals calmed down and started going to Anna Wintour parties again, they lost all interest in terrorists. Indeed, they forgot there had ever been a terrorist attack. And so the *Times*, privy to a top-secret counterterrorist program it had once demanded that Bush implement immediately, decided to betray its own country and publish details of the program. It wasn't even a particularly interesting story—unless you were the head of counterintelligence for al Qaeda.

When the *Times* was universally condemned for revealing the secret counterterrorist program, it responded with a series of articles and columns criticizing Americans for daring to question the Newspaper of Record. In two consecutive columns claiming that the *Times* was being bullied, Frank Rich smugly announced that other newspapers, including the *Wall Street Journal*, had published stories on the terrorist-tracking program the exact same day. But no one complained about them.

The *Wall Street Journal*, objecting to being used as the *Times*'s wingman, published an editorial explaining what really happened. Yes, the *Journal* and a few other newspapers had the story of the Swift program, not just the *Times*. But it was the *Times* that announced it was running the story—defying requests not to from the Treasury Secretary John Snow, 9/11 commissioners Tom Kean and Lee Hamilton, Democratic congressman John Murtha, and Director of National Intelligence John Negroponte. At that point, the Treasury Department asked the *Wall Street Journal* to go ahead with its story on Swift, so one newspaper would at least have the facts right.[123]

Sadly for them, overpaid reporters at the *Times* intentionally harming their own country do not tear at the heartstrings of most Americans. So the treasonous scribblers were forced to adopt other victims' mantles. In one whimpering column, Rich suggested that the attacks on the *Times* for defiantly publishing covert national security information were grounded in anti-Semitism. He cited with approval MSNBC's Chris Matthews, who complained about attacks on the poor, defenseless *Times*, saying, "It's the old trick, go after New York, go after big, ethnic New York."[124]

Actually, the reason people were attacking the *Times* was that it was the only newspaper that rebuffed the government's request that the terrorist financial monitoring program not be revealed. Other newspapers had the same information, but apparently at other newspapers, you don't become a hero by betraying your country.[125] Even when using the most powerful newspaper in the world to place all Americans in danger, liberals are always the victims.

7

BRAVE, BEAUTIFUL LIBERALS

Why do people become liberals? Perhaps it is because they truly believe socialism would be good for America. Perhaps the idea of a kindergartner saying, "God is good, God is great, thank you, God, for my food" enrages them. Little Kayla Broadus tried to pull the "God is great" scam at snack time in her Saratoga Springs, New York, kindergarten class, but—fortunately—a public school teacher was on hand to stop this outrage, thus narrowly averting a theocratic coup in America.

The other reason people might become liberals is that they enjoy being told how pretty they are. And clever and talented. And don't forget brave. Liberals love being praised for their courage. It's hard to fit in being brave between being called beautiful, brilliant, and talented, but that's the advantage of having the entire mainstream media doing

PR for liberals. You never have to actually be victimized to be considered a victim—a brave victim—by the media.

To the contrary, it's the victimizers who are wildly cheered on by media elites. Thus, for example, after Elián González was taken from his Miami relatives' home at gunpoint in the second military action against American citizens by Attorney General Janet Reno, *New York Times* columnist Thomas Friedman wrote a column titled, not sarcastically, "Reno for President." Friedman said—again, not sarcastically— "Yup, I gotta confess, that now-famous picture of a U.S. marshal in Miami pointing an automatic weapon toward Donato Dalrymple and ordering him in the name of the U.S. government to turn over Elian Gonzalez warmed my heart. They should put that picture up in every visa line in every U.S. consulate around the world, with a caption that reads: 'America is a country where the rule of law rules. . . . '"[1]

Other than liberals' general feeling that Cubans are tacky, Friedman's statement violated every principle of the *Times*, which is normally for children's rights, for illegal aliens, against guns, against the police and against the rule of law. Would a photo of a uniformed American male pointing a gun at any other foreigner warm the heart of a liberal? How about a Mexican drug smuggler or an Islamic terrorist? Would even a gun pointed at Khalid Sheikh Mohammed warm a liberal's heart as much as a gun pointed at a six-year-old Cuban boy?

The number-one rule with liberals is: Whatever they do is courageous, no matter how blatantly power-grabbing, whoring, or publicity-seeking it is.

An extensive study conducted by professors at Smith College and George Washington University confirmed that most liberals exhibit a "narcissistic pathology" marked by "grandiosity, envy, a lack of empathy, illusion of personal perfection, and a sense of entitlement."[2] Liberals are twice as likely to value being popular as conservatives, whereas conservatives are more likely to value "making my parents proud."[3]

So if you've ever wondered, "Does Barack Obama ever get bored with all those fawning profiles?," the answer is: No, liberals never tire of being praised for every desirable human attribute known to man, not least of which is their mind-boggling courage in the face of endless praise.

When Obama materialized, the media were seized by a mass psychosis that hadn't been witnessed since Beatlemania. *OK* magazine raved that the Obamas "are such an all-American family that they almost make the Brady Bunch look dysfunctional." Yes, who can forget the madcap episode when the Bradys' wacky preacher tells them the government created AIDS to kill blacks! Still gushing, *OK* magazine's crack journalists reported, "Mom goes to bake sales, dad balances the checkbook, and the girls love Harry Potter"—and then the whole family goes to a racist huckster bellowing, "God damn America!"[4]

MONTHS BEFORE NETWORK ANCHORS WERE INTERROGATING vice presidential candidate Sarah Palin on the intricacies of foreign policy, here is how NBC's Brian Williams mercilessly grilled presidential candidate Barack Obama: "What was it like for you last night, the part we couldn't see, the flight to St. Paul with your wife, knowing what was awaiting?" Twisting the knife he had just plunged into Obama, Williams followed up with what has come to be known as a "gotcha" question: "And you had to be thinking of your mother and your father." Sarah Palin was memorizing the last six kings of Swaziland for her media interviews, but Obama only needed to say something nice about his parents to be considered presidential material.

The media's fawning over Obama knew no bounds, and yet, in the midst of the most incredible media conspiracy to turn this jug-eared clodhopper into some combination of Winston Churchill and Brad Pitt, you were being a bore if you mentioned the liberal media. *Oh, surely we've exploded that old chestnut.... Look! Look, Obama just lit up another Marlboro! Geez, does smoking make you look cool, or what! Yeah, Obama! ...* The claim that there's no such thing as a left-wing press is a patent lie told for the sole purpose of enraging conservatives. American newspapers read like the press under Kim Jung Il, which, outside of a police state, tends to look foolish. The prose is straight out of the *Daily Worker*, full of triumphal rhetoric with implicit exclamation points. Their chanted slogans fill your brain, like one of those bad songs you can't stop humming.

There is no other explanation for the embarrassing paeans to Obama's "eloquence." His speeches were a run-on string of embarrassing, sophomoric greeting card bromides. It seemed only a matter of time before Obama would slip and tell a crowd what a special dad it had always been to him.

In announcing his candidacy, Obama bravely proclaimed that he believed in "the basic decency of the American people." And let the chips fall where they may! He decried "a smallness of our politics"—deftly offering a challenge to the small-politics advocates. Then, throwing caution to the wind, he stood up to the antihope crowd, saying, "There are those who don't believe in talking about hope." He said we must "disagree without being disagreeable." This was an improvement on the first draft, which read, "It's nice to be important, but it's more important to be nice." This guy is like the ANWAR of trite political aphorisms. There is no telling exactly how many he is sitting on, but it could be in the billions.

Most weirdly, the major theme of Obama's campaign was the audacity of his running for president. A line from his announcement speech was "I recognize there is a certain presumptuousness in this—a certain audacity—to this announcement." He titled his keynote address at the 2004 Democratic National Convention "The Audacity of Hope"—named after a sermon given by his spiritual mentor, Jeremiah Wright, whom we were not allowed to mention without being accused of ugly campaign tactics. (Rejected speech titles from sermons by the Reverend Wright included "God Damn America!," "The U.S. of K.K.A.," and "The Racist United States of America.")

What is so audacious about announcing that you're running for president? Every sitting and former U.S. senator has run for president or is currently thinking about running for president. Dennis Kucinich ran for president. Lyndon LaRouche used to run for president constantly.

But the media were giddy over their latest crush. Even when Obama broke a pledge and rejected public financing for his campaign—an issue more dear to the *New York Times* than even gay marriage—the *Times* led the article on Obama's broken pledge with his excuse. "Citing the specter of attacks from independent groups on the right," the article began, "Senator Barack Obama announced Thursday that he would opt out of the public financing system for the general election."[5] So he had to break his pledge! It was the Republicans' fault.

When Obama broke his word and voted for the Foreign Intelligence Surveillance Act (FISA) bill, the *Times*'s editorial began: *We are shocked and dismayed by Senator Obama's vote on . . . Oh, who are we kidding? We can't stay mad at this guy! Isn't he just adorable? Couldn't you just eat him up with a spoon? Is he looking at me? Ohmigod, I think he's looking at me!!!!!!!!!!!!! Couldn't you just die?*

It has ever been thus. The establishment media function as a Greek chorus, informing the lumpen masses what to think of this or that person. Liberals are described as Adonis and Helen of Troy, while conservatives are described as dog food.

WHICH FEMALE IN POLITICS HAVE THE ESTABLISHMENT MEDIA described as "outspoken," "funny,"[6] a "superstar,"[7] "passionate and smart,"[8] "influential,"[9] "flamboyant,"[10] "colorful"[11] a "female warrior,"[12] with "national stature,"[13] with "flair and style,"[14] with "vitality and independence,"[15] and with "colour and style,"[16] who was "brimming with style"[17] and "funny and also . . . serious,"[18] who had crowds yelling to her: "You're beautiful!"[19]

It's *Bella!* Yes, the late Bella Abzug, the grotesque, foulmouthed member of Congress from New York. An avid supporter of Joseph Stalin, Abzug also supported Hitler—at least until he invaded the glorious Soviet Union, forcing even Stalin to withdraw his support.[20] She supported the Vietcong in the Vietnam War[21] and Jim Jones, the left-wing cult leader who presided over a mass suicide in Guyana.[22]

Notwithstanding hymns to her cultural significance, Abzug's influence was severely limited by the fact that even the liberal voters of New York refused to elevate her beyond the House of Representatives, rejecting her bids for both the U.S. Senate and the New York City mayoralty.

As for her renowned "style," Abzug enclosed her perfectly spherical frame in frumpy thrift-shop, busy-patterned dresses and enormous floppy hats. Her speaking voice was always set at "bellow." But the media insisted on describing Abzug as an American Venus. As she screeched her opposition to the Vietnam War, we were all supposed to concede that she was just as cute as a bug's ear.

In 2006, thanks to careful stage management, the Democratic

Party finally fielded some candidates who had been allowed to play outside as children. The *Washington Post* promptly produced an article gloating about how gorgeous the Democrats were. "Democrats seem to be fielding an uncommonly high number of uncommonly good-looking candidates," the article boasted, noting that the "beauty gap" could determine who controlled Congress.[23]

One would think that a party that has inflicted Rosa DeLauro, Nita Lowey, Dennis Kucinich, Jerry Nadler, and Hunk of Burning Love Henry Waxman on the world would try to downplay looks as an issue, but these wouldn't be the first average-looking Democrats hailed as beauty queens. Among the raft of liberals we're required to pretend are dazzling beauties are Christiane Amanpour, Sandra Bernhard, Bernardine Dohrn, Gloria Steinem, and Tina Fey, who looks a lot more like Elvis Costello than Sarah Palin.

Not being a liberal, I don't particularly care what people look like, but I note that Miss America Pageant winners are almost always from the conservative South. Liberals also demanded that we all pretend the unathletic fat kid from Arkansas was a dreamboat—at least until his wife ran against Obama. For years, we'd been told how unbelievably sexy Bill Clinton is. If a beer belly, bloated cheeks, tiny, close-set eyes, and a big head equals handsome, where the hell is Newt Gingrich's modeling contract?

When a liberal male is described as having "movie-star looks," it apparently means: "hotter than Henry Waxman." When a liberal female is described as the reincarnation of Jackie O, that means: a Democratic woman who is less physically repulsive than Bella Abzug. A conservative female who is compared to Marie Antoinette is a stylish dresser; if she's called a "bimbo," that means she's gorgeous. Reporters use a string of adjectives to describe a presidential candidate's wife not because readers are clamoring to know what Michelle Obama or Cindy McCain looks like. Remember, the purpose of news is not to inform, but to promote the left-wing agenda. Calling a public figure beautiful and stylish is a reporter's way of saying "thank you for supporting socialized health care"—which is at least better than Nina Burleigh's proposed method of thanking Clinton for keeping abortion legal. (It involved a sexual act for which Monica Lewinsky will, ahem, go down in history.)

About once every half-century, the Democrats manage to produce a female who doesn't look like Bella Abzug. This always leads to fainting spells in the pressrooms and we have to hear about "Camelot" for the next half-century (and counting). There are books, operas, and songs about Jacqueline Kennedy's style for her singular accomplishment of looking like a Republican while being married to a Democrat.

The constant stream of put-downs of Republican women and exaggerated glamorization of Democratic women is so much a part of the fabric of news that no one even notices anymore. The identical characteristic will be given an entirely different cast based purely on ideology. Liberals are intelligent, conservatives are bookish; liberals are bubbly, conservatives are airheads; liberals are slender, conservatives are rail-thin; liberals are passionate, conservatives are angry; liberals are good with children, conservatives are suspected pedophiles.

Tipper Gore and Laura Bush were about as similar as any two potential first ladies could be: They were both attractive, of about the same age and body type; both had warm personalities and wore basic, classic clothing. And yet when their husbands were running against each other for president in 2000, a single column comparing their styles produced diametrically opposed adjectives for the two possible first ladies:

Tipper: "bubbly"
Laura: "bookish"

Tipper: "colorful"
Laura: "dowdy"

Tipper: a "soccer mom"
Laura: a "librarian"

Tipper: "a party animal"
Laura: "a hostess in the traditional mold"

Tipper's likely legacy: "a book of first lady photographs"
Laura's likely legacy: "a cookie named after her"

Just in case it still wasn't clear enough that Tipper was an effervescent dynamo likely to produce "a book of first lady photographs," while Laura was a dreary bore, the column stated outright, "'Tipper' Gore has the edge in pizzazz over Laura Bush."[24]

What is the point of the media going into laborious detail about the physical appearance of famous people, anyway? They're famous—we know what they look like. The media try to change that, too. In a stunning presentation, updated yearly, Ron Robinson of Young America's Foundation puts on a slide show of the photos of conservatives and liberals from the covers of *Time* and *Newsweek*. Not only are there more covers with liberals, by about 20 to 1—and that's just covers of Obama—but liberals are always bathed in a beatific light, while conservatives are photographed in lighting that casts a menacing glow and always seem to show five o'clock shadows. (It's even worse for the conservative men!) When Robinson gave his presentation at *Time* magazine itself, one editor admitted they chose a background color for Newt Gingrich that would make him look sinister. The cover shots of Pat Buchanan and Rush Limbaugh were also grim. This is as opposed to their cover shots of Obama, which typically show him riding a flying white stallion while showering the countryside with gold dust.

Laura Bush may have been somewhat more "bookish" than Tipper, probably about the same as Michelle Obama compared with Cindy McCain. But while Laura Bush was repeatedly called "bookish," Michelle Obama was only "intellectual" and "brainy," both of which might come as news to anyone who had read her senior thesis at Princeton. Michelle wrote her thesis on being black at Princeton because blacks attending Ivy League schools are required by law to major in Being Black. She penned such gems as: "In defining the concept of identification or the ability to identify with the black community, I based my definition on the premise that there is a distinctive black culture very different from white culture."[25] As the blog Sweetness & Light says, "No wonder they wanted [her thesis] locked up until after the elections were safely over."[26]

Brainy!

Democratic women will be praised for their fashion sense, while Republicans dressed nearly identically will draw contempt for their outfits. Reviewing the clothing on ABC's *The View*, well-known fashion plate Troy Patterson of *Slate* magazine raved about Michelle Obama's sleeveless black-and-white dress. Patterson approvingly quoted cohost Sherri Shepherd exclaiming to Michelle, "You are setting this trend where everyone wants to go sleeveless!" *The View*'s conservative cohost Elisabeth Hasselbeck was wearing an outfit that would have been appropriate at the exact same cocktail party as Michelle, and yet her one-sleeve blouse came in for sputtering vitriol from Patterson, who said her outfit "treaded a fine line between merely inappropriate and plainly sluttish."[27]

Laura Bush was savaged for her "prim," "schoolmarm" looks with the deepest cut of all: "She's no Jackie O. . . . And that is putting it politely."[28] But guess who was Jackie O? That's right! Michelle Obama. Democrats simply tell the media how they would like to be described, and the media obey. Jackie Kennedy called her husband's presidency "Camelot," so the press called it Camelot. Clinton wanted to be Elvis, so he was Elvis, albeit the fat one. Barack Obama told a meeting of journalists in August 2007 that his wife was "the Jackie O from the hood,"[29] and hundreds of columns poured forth describing Mrs. Obama as the spitting image of Jackie O. At least that was one way the Obamas were very much like the Kennedys: It was all about cultivating an image.

To be fair, Obama probably didn't need to tell anyone what image Michelle Obama was going for. Her obvious imitation of Jackie O's style—the flipped-under hair, the sleeveless A-line dresses, the short strands of fake pearls—would have been laughable if done by anyone other than a media-designated saint.

Republican: creepy!
Democrat: classy.

A column in the *Seattle Times* purred that Michelle Obama proved "Jackie Kennedy didn't close the book on class, grace and style."[30] A McClatchy Newspapers columnist described her as "Clair Huxtable–

meets–Jackie Kennedy."[31] *Philadelphia Inquirer* columnist Karen Heller asked, "You know who looks like Jackie Kennedy? Michelle Obama."[32] She added helpfully, "Jackie Kennedy was the most popular first lady in history."[33] Another columnist said, "When Barack and Michelle Obama take the stage at the Democratic National Convention, comparisons will be invoked with John and Jackie Kennedy."[34] Shelly Branch, author of the book *What Would Jackie Do?*, excitedly reported on the "growing buzz about the striking similarities between [Michelle Obama] and former first lady Jacqueline Kennedy."[35] So, apparently, what Jackie would do is slavishly imitate another person's style, which I believe is the definition of having no innate sense of style. Adopting the Jack-Ryan-divorce-papers standard of what newspaper readers want to know, I think it would be "interesting" to see what the authors of these glowing articles about Ms. Obama look like.

Vogue editor at large André Leon Talley said Michelle Obama had adopted the Jackie O look—"but in her own way."[36] Yes, a way that wouldn't be laughed at by the media, which is as a Democrat. The *Philadelphia Daily News* interviewed various fashion consultants and they agreed: "Jackie Kennedy . . . Of course." Another style expert said, "It's the first thing I thought." But the article quickly added, "There's nothing contrived or tactical about it."[37] Nothing contrived? She looked like she was going treat-or-treating in a Jackie O costume.

While a stylish Democrat sends the media into swooning fits, a stylish Republican sends them into sans-culottes denunciations of the rich. Nancy Reagan came under relentless attack for her expensive designer dresses—despite the fact that they were generally donated by designers who were friends and wanted publicity for their frocks. The Associated Press even interviewed tax attorneys, asking them whether the Reagans would have to pay extra income tax on the designer dresses given to Mrs. Reagan. No-name folksingers were rewarded with write-ups in the *New York Times* for their songs ridiculing Mrs. Reagan's dresses "on the day that people are cutting food stamps."[38] Because if only the first lady went around in a stained housedress from Kmart, no one would ever go hungry in America.

When Mrs. Reagan acquired a new set of china for the White

House, which had not been replaced since the Truman administration, it was noted approximately one million times that she was buying fine Lenox china as her husband was cutting programs for the poor! A designer offered to donate "Rosalynn" (Carter) stoneware, made in Japan, to the White House,[39] which I'm sure was as charming as it sounds—and heaven knows, the White House needed more pig's-foot serving platters—but it turned out Nancy's new china was also donated, by the Knapp Foundation, and it was American-made.[40] That was irrelevant—there was a Republican to attack! Hundreds of articles upbraided Nancy for the new White House china. It got to the point that President Reagan had to defend his wife from the incessant Marie Antoinette comparisons.

Cindy McCain, who not only was proud of her country before her husband won the Republican primaries but dressed well without freakishly imitating famous first ladies in history, was huffily accused of wearing a $300,000 outfit at the Republican National Convention. *Vanity Fair* put its fashion department on the job, and, estimating her diamond earrings at $280,000, came up with the $300,000 figure. The magazine then helpfully listed what $300,000 would mean "to Americans who don't have the luxury of inheriting a gargantuan beer fortune":

> To Cindy McCain, $300,000 is the price of an outfit.
> To most Americans, $300,000 buys . . .
>> . . . one and a half houses, given the national median home price of $206,500.
>> . . . a year's worth of health care for 750 people.
>> . . . the full array of back-to-school supplies and clothes for 500 kids.
>> . . . enough gas to drive cross-country 543 times.[41]

Say, does anyone remember *Vanity Fair*'s estimate of Teresa Heinz Kerry's outfits? No, neither do I.

The claim that Cindy McCain's "outfit" cost $300,000 ignited a volcanic eruption of sanctimony throughout the fourth estate. On the *Los Angeles Times* blog, Monica Corcoran fumed "does she really need four strands of pearls?" Right on schedule, she also compared Mrs. McCain to Marie Antoinette.[42] In short order, outraged letters to the editor were proclaiming that Cindy McCain's dress alone had cost $300,000: "If I, like Cindy McCain, could afford an outfit that cost over $300,000 to wear only one night, maybe I would also be out of touch."[43] I'm pretty sure Cindy McCain did not throw $280,000 diamonds in the garbage after a night's wear. Travis Shiverdecker carped to the *Capital Times* (Madison, Wisconsin) "that one of Cindy McCain's convention outfits was worth over $300,000," before wailing, "I am 23 years old, in graduate school, and already have over $150,000 in student loans."[44] At least the diamonds were actually worth what Cindy McCain paid for them.

In fact, Cindy McCain's dress was estimated to cost about $3,000, while Michelle Obama's convention dress cost about $1,250[45]—not including a team of fashion consultants to advise her on how to look exactly like Jackie O.

But more urgently, can liberals stop telling us Franklin Delano Roosevelt was our greatest president if they're going to keep up the interminable wealth-baiting? How did John Kerry ever become the presidential nominee of these class warriors? What is the point of liberals railing about Enron's Ken Lay—who was a big Clinton backer, by the way[46]—when the Democratic Party is the wholly owned subsidiary of slimy foreign-born billionaire George Soros?

WHILE LIBERALS LOVE BEING PRAISED FOR THEIR LOOKS, THEIR style, their brilliance, and their courage, there's one quality they don't want talked about: their money. Indeed, Democrats constantly boast about how poor they are—as if that's a virtue in a capitalist society with no class barriers. But no matter how much money they have, liberals will be damned if they're giving up the poor's mantle of angry self-righteousness.

Their claims of poverty merely serve to show how out of touch they are with actual incomes in America. At the Democratic National Convention, there were heartfelt tributes to the peerless self-sacrifice of both Barack and Michelle Obama for passing up lucrative private sector jobs to work in "public service"—which apparently is now defined to include "working as a 'diversity coordinator' at a big-city hospital for $300,000 a year." The soft-focus biographical film of the Messiah shown at the convention proclaimed that Barack Obama's classmates at Harvard Law School "would field offers from big law firms and Wall Street, but he felt compelled to serve."[47] Saint Michelle boasted in her convention speech, "In my own life, in my own small way, I have tried to give back to this country that has given me so much. See, that's why I left a job at a big law firm for a career in public service, working to empower young people to volunteer in their communities."

In 2006, Mother Teresa Obama's total income from "public service" was approximately $375,000.[48] The average salary for a lawyer with twenty years' or more experience in the United States is a little more than $100,000.[49] If Michelle Obama doesn't lay off all this "giving back" stuff pretty soon, she's going to find herself in Warren Buffett's tax bracket.

In fact, Michelle Obama's "public service" career advanced in lockstep with the political advancement of her husband. Michelle was only hired by the University of Chicago hospital once her husband had become a state senator. Most intriguingly, after Obama was elected to the U.S. Senate, her salary was nearly tripled from $121,910 to $316,962—whereupon Senator Obama would use the "new politics" earmark process to try to send taxpayer dollars to Michelle's newly generous employer.[50]

Joe Biden was similarly praised by Democrats for being the poorest U.S. senator. Howard Dean, chairman of the Democratic National Committee, touted Biden as "a good example of a working-class kid," adding that, to this day, Biden was "one of the least wealthy members of the U.S. Senate."[51] Only a Democrat would list "never really made anything of myself" on his résumé. On the *Huffington Post,* operated by a woman who acquired her wealth by marrying a rich gay guy connected to Big Oil, liberal blogger Steven Clemons gloated that, unlike John McCain, Biden wouldn't "forget the number of houses he owns," because in 2006, he was ranked the poorest U.S. senator.[52] According to the tax returns for Biden and his public school teacher wife, in 2006, the Bidens' total income was $248,459; in 2007, it was $319,853[53]—putting the couple in the top 1 percent of all earners in the United States.[54] The national median household income was $48,201 in 2006, and $50,233 in 2007.[55] Working for the government pays well.

If liberals are going to demand a Marxist revolution against the rich every time they see a well-dressed Republican, how about taking a peek at the charitable giving of these champions of the little guy? According to their tax returns, in 2006 and 2007, the Obamas gave 5.8 percent and 6.1 percent of their income to charity.[56] (Michelle Obama has to draw the line somewhere with all this "giving back" stuff.) The Bidens gave 0.15 percent and 0.31 percent of their income to charity.[57] For the same years, John McCain gave 27.3 percent and 28.6 percent of his income to charity.[58]

True, McCain has a rich wife—who runs an enormous charitable foundation—but John Kerry also had a rich wife, and as Peter Schweizer points out in his book *Makers and Takers*, in 1995 he gave not one cent to charity. "That same year," Schweizer writes, "he spent $500,000 to buy a half stake in a seventeenth-century Dutch seascape painting by Adam Willaerts." To be fair, 1995 was an off year for Kerry's charitable giving. The year before, he gave $2,039 to charity, and the year before that, a whopping $175.

In 1998, Al Gore gave $353 to charity—one-tenth as much as the national average for charitable giving by people in Gore's income bracket of $100,000 to $200,000. Gore was at the top end of that category, making $197,729 that year. Perhaps Gore's money was tied up in some sort of "lock box." When Senator Ted Kennedy released his tax returns to run for president in the 1970s, it showed that Kennedy gave barely 1 percent of his income to charity—or, as Schweizer says, "about as much as Kennedy claimed as write-off on his fifty-foot sloop *Curragh*." Propelled by the Daily Kos kids and other left-wingers, Ned Lamont beat Senator Joe Lieberman in the 2007 Democratic primary. In 2005, Lamont made almost $2.8 million in income off his inherited $200 million fortune. He gave $5,385 to charity that year, which Schweizer notes was .027 percent of his income.[59]

In 1991, 1992, and 1993, George W. Bush had incomes of $179,591, $212,313, and $610,772. His charitable contributions those years were $28,236, $31,914, and $31,292. During his presidency, Bush gave away more than 10 percent of his income each year. For purposes of comparison, in 2005, Barack Obama made $1.7 million—more than twice President Bush's 2005 income of $735,180—but they both gave about the same amount to charity. That same year, Vice President Cheney gave 77 percent of his income to charity. The following year, in 2006, Bush gave more to charity than Obama on an income one-third smaller than Obama's.[60] Maybe when Obama talks about "change" he's referring to his charitable contributions.

Liberals have no intention of actually parting with any of their own wealth or lifting a finger to help the poor. As liberal intellectual Bertrand Russell explained while scoffing at the idea that he would give his money to charity, "I'm afraid you've got it wrong. [We] are socialists. We don't pretend to be *Christians*."[61]

Democrats prefer to demonstrate their goodness by giving away *your* money. They bash Republicans for favoring "the rich" because of Republicans' general antipathy to socialist wealth-distribution plans. At the same time, they are delighted to let George Soros play the Daddy Warbucks of the Democratic Party, spending millions of dollars to fund phony "grassroots" left-wing organizations such as MoveOn.org, Media Matters, Americans Coming Together, the Association of Community Organizations for Reform Now (ACORN), and America's leading hate group, the ACLU.[62] These are the organizations that call the shots in the Democratic Party. As Eli Pariser of MoveOn.org said of the Democratic Party after the 2004 election, "Now it's our party. We bought it, we own it, and we're going to take it back."[63]

The precise design of the profoundly undemocratic McCain-Feingold bill was to vastly increase the power of plutocrats and the media so that only the fabulously wealthy can run for major offices in the United States—or at least serve as kingmakers to those who run for office. Naturally, Soros was a big backer of McCain-Feingold. Now the Democrats are utterly beholden to him.

Besides the fact that Soros "owns" the Democratic Party, as his minion put it, here is a précis of everything you need to know about George Soros. On September 11, right after the second plane hit the World Trade Center, the markets were closed and remained closed for the rest of the week. A terrified nation anxiously waited to see if the terrorist attack would cause a stock market crash when the exchanges opened the following Monday. If speculators sold short, betting that American stocks would decline, that bet could become a self-fulfilling prophecy. Selling short is the practice of selling stock without owning it, while planning to buy it back later at a cheaper price and pocketing the difference. If short sellers descended on the market after 9/11, that could spark a collapse, destroying the American economy, but making the short sellers very rich.

A "buy American" campaign swept through Wall Street, with banks and traders vowing not to profit from the terrorist attack on America. Letters, e-mails, and public proclamations urged people to produce a stock market rally when the markets opened on the following Monday. As David Horowitz and Richard Poe write in their book *The Shadow Party*, one money manager sent a letter to a hundred of his clients asking them to buy stock on Monday, saying, "The patriot in me thinks nothing would be a better slap in the face of some terrible people than a market rally."

Struggling pensioners, grandmothers from Iowa, and other average Americans from across the country who had never bought a stock before called brokers to find out how to buy $50 worth of stock that Monday. Before the opening bell, there were two minutes of silence to commemorate the dead, followed by the singing of "God Bless America."

And George Soros said: Sell! Sell! Sell! The Dow Jones Industrial Average fell 685 points that Monday. Speculators like Soros became even richer off of America's misfortune, while truckers and waitresses lost their money.[64] But as Soros told Steve Kroft on CBS's *60 Minutes* of his collaboration with the Nazis, helping them confiscate property from Jews, it was "just like in markets—if I weren't there, somebody else would be taking it away anyhow."[65]

You almost can't blame Soros for betting against America when the markets opened after 9/11; it's not as if he's an American. Soros can barely even speak the language. It's curious that the Democrats loudly boast about speaking for the average American, but their three unelected spokesmen—George Soros, Arianna Huffington, and Daily Kos's Markos Moulitsas—all speak in the accents of their foreign upbringings. Couldn't they at least wait a couple of generations and let their grandchildren do the America-bashing? Whatever you can say about Rush Limbaugh, Matt Drudge, and Sean Hannity, they at least grew up in America.

Soros's money was used to defeat Lieberman in his 2006 primary against Ned-the-Red Lamont, forcing Lieberman to run against—and beat—his own now Soros-controlled party. Soros's money was used to publish the "General Betray Us" full-page attack ad on General Petraeus in the *New York Times*. Soros's money was used to propel Obama to victory in the 2008 Democratic primary. When your party is controlled by a billionaire rootless international financier who expresses "no sense of guilt" for collaborating with the Nazis,[66] you might want to ease up on lecturing the rest of us about the evil rich.

IN ADDITION TO BEING BEAUTIFUL, COMPASSIONATE TRIBUNES of the downtrodden, liberals are brave. I know that because they're always telling me how brave they are. Why, five nights a week, MSNBC's Keith Olbermann courageously books guests who completely agree with him! It doesn't get much braver than that. If anyone dissents from the prevailing worship of one of these beautiful and well-dressed liberals who has taken a vow of poverty to fight for the peasants from their beachfront estates, liberals claim they're being attacked. But not to worry: The media will rally to their defense, hailing the rich and powerful for their courage.

If the liberal is a female, the media will portray any mention of their heroine's failings as sexism, even when their heroine is trying to socialize the nation's entire health care system, or alternatively, when their heroine says that "as a black man, you know, Barack can get shot going to the gas station"[67] and calls America a "downright mean" country. (And she dresses like Jackie O!)

In 1996, Dee Dee Myers said Republicans' ferocity on Whitewater was partially explained by sexism.[68] *Baltimore Sun* columnist and emasculated male Mike Littwin said Hillary was a victim of the "strong woman syndrome," noting that for some, "you're not allowed to be a strong woman."[69] Between photos oozing with respect for women, *Playboy* magazine touted Bill Clinton for being "completely unthreatened by the equally strong woman standing beside him."[70] There were more column inches devoted to denouncing the putative sexism of conservative attacks on Hillary than there were column inches delivering the actual attacks.

The media's interest in "strong woman syndrome" seemed to dissipate during the Bush years, but came roaring back for Michelle Obama in 2008. CNN contributor Roland Martin explained away any criticism of her as a psychological failing of conservative men. "I think what you have," he said, is "some weak men on the conservative side who frankly don't like strong women."

Yes, liberals love a strong conservative woman! They love strong conservative women so much that some of them pay hundreds of dollars an hour to be humiliated by one of them because they've been very bad and must be punished.

Where was all the indignation about attacks on a strong woman when Sarah Palin came along? The moment John McCain introduced Palin as his running mate, liberals switched from being the primary advocates for stamping out sexism toward women in politics to being the primary perpetrators of sexism toward women in politics. The media chorus went up that Palin was chosen only because she was a woman. In fact, she was chosen because she was pro-life, pro-gun, pro-drilling, and pro–tax cuts. Also, she didn't have clownish hair plugs and a tendency to make offensive statements on camera. The media hysterically denounced Palin as "inexperienced" even though she had more executive experience than B. Hussein Obama—the guy at the top of the Democrats' ticket.

In Palin's first interview after being chosen as McCain's running mate, ABC's Charlie Gibson had this exchange with her:

GIBSON: You said recently, in your old church, "Our national leaders are sending U.S. soldiers on a task that is from God." Are we fighting a holy war?

PALIN: You know, I don't know if that was my exact quote.

GIBSON: Exact words.

What Gibson claimed were Palin's "exact words" were nothing of the sort. Here are Palin's actual "exact words"—as quoted by NPR, no less: "Pray our military men and women who are striving to do what is right also for this country—that our national leaders are sending them out on a task that is from God. That's what we have to make sure that we're praying for, that there is a plan and that plan is God's plan."[71]

On Gibson's theory of an "exact quote," ABC's Charlie Gibson said, "you're old" and "God, are we fighting a Holy War!" With some selective editing, those are "exact quotes," too.

Gibson came from ABC's morning show *Good Morning America* where he used to demonstrate omelet recipes and offer hints on inexpensive weekend getaways, but now he's an intellectual because he's wearing glasses. Gibson also asked Palin if she agreed with "the Bush doctrine." Palin reasonably responded, "In what respect, Charlie?" Gibson refused to tell her what he meant, requiring her to try to pry it out of him. Eventually Gibson exasperatedly informed Palin that "the Bush doctrine" was that America has "the right of anticipatory self-defense."

Cut to: the Politburo issuing hysterical denunciations of Palin for her alleged inability to identify Charlie Gibson's definition of "the Bush doctrine." Wikipedia, the online encyclopedia, which can be "edited" by anyone, promptly rewrote its entry on "the Bush doctrine" to correspond with Gibson's definition. The *New York Times* claimed Palin "visibly stumbled" and "did not seem to know what he was talking about."[72]

But in short order, columnist Charles Krauthammer, no slouch on foreign policy matters, pointed out that there is no one "Bush doctrine" and named at least three distinct possibilities for the title. The *Washington Post* ran an article quoting a half dozen foreign policy experts from the Carter, Clinton, and Bush administrations, who agreed on one thing: There was no single "Bush doctrine." The only exception was Richard Holbrooke of the Carter and Clinton administrations, who gave a direct quote from a Bush administration strategy document as "the Bush doctrine." But Philip D. Zelikow, one of the principal authors of that very document, told the *Post*, "I actually never thought there was a Bush doctrine."[73]

All the Left's leading intellectual lights expressed their disdain for

Palin. Foreign policy/home video porno star expert Pamela Anderson told Palin to "suck it," while domestic adviser/aspiring lesbian Lindsay Lohan called Palin a "a narrow-minded, media-obsessed homophobe." Tara Reid, rumored to have passed out in a puddle of her own vomit, was unavailable for comment.

Meanwhile, Palin's Democratic counterpart, serial plagiarist Senator Joe Biden, was walking around with bean sprouts coming out of his head, a botched eyelid job, and a son and brother charged with fraud in a lawsuit by a former business partner. But you had to search obscure right-wing blogs to find any negative information about Biden.

Palin was subjected to such an unending stream of abuse that even Mark Penn, Hillary Clinton's chief campaign strategist, told CBS News that the media were losing credibility. "When you see them going through every single expense report that Governor Palin ever filed," he said, "if they don't do that for all four of the candidates, they're on very dangerous ground." Penn added that the media had been "the biggest loser in this race."[74]

Palin wasn't being attacked because she was a woman; she was being attacked because she was conservative.

The media do treat women differently, but it's always different in the same way. Linda Tripp and Coleen Rowley were two almost identically situated government whistle-blowers. Tripp told the truth about a president's felonies, and Rowley told the truth about the FBI's old computers and refusal to racially profile the presumed "twentieth hijacker," Zacarias Moussaoui. Both were about the same age, and I defy anyone to tell me Rowley was better-looking than Tripp. But because Rowley blew the whistle on the FBI during a Republican administration, she was portrayed as a modern-day Joan of Arc. Because Tripp blew the whistle on a Democrat president, she was treated like a female Freddy Krueger.

On the *New York Times* op-ed page alone, Frank Rich called Tripp a "snitch"[75] and "that dulcet-toned human wire Linda Tripp,"[76] Anthony Lewis called her a "malignant gossip,"[77] and Maureen Dowd called her a "dingbat"[78] and a "witch."[79] Even the *Times*'s Russell Baker had no complaint with "satirists"—they're "satirists" when they attack conservatives—who made "fun of her physical appearance," because, he said, "she made her bed, let her lie in it."[80]

The ABC News blog asked this question:

> If there were an Ig-Nobel Peace Prize, who would win it?
> —Slobodan Milosevic
> —Osama bin Laden
> —Saddam Hussein
> —Linda Tripp[81]

But Tripp's liberal doppelgänger, Coleen Rowley, who didn't even have a particularly scandalous story about government malfeasance— FBI computers are old!—was hailed for speaking truth to power. (Rowley also complained that the FBI didn't racially profile a potential terrorist, but the media played down that observation.) Dowd called Rowley "the blunt Midwesterner"[82] and a woman "of ingenuity and integrity."[83] Frank Rich called her "a forthright American woman."[84] Anita Hill, who less than a quarter of Americans believed had told the truth about Clarence Thomas, was called in for a special op-ed in the *Times*. She praised Rowley for rising "through the ranks of male-dominated institutions" and yet having "the conviction to act on values that were apparently in conflict with those of the leaders in their institutions."[85] The *Hotline* did not exaggerate when it titled coverage of Coleen Rowley "A Star Is Born."[86] When that much praise pours forth from powerful media bullhorns about someone speaking the truth to power, only one thing is certain: Truth has not been spoken to power.

Where were the blaring trumpets for Linda Tripp's and Sarah Palin's bravery? Bravery, as used in public discourse, bears no relation to what most people think of as bravery. No matter what liberals do, they are brave. No matter what abuse conservatives take, they deserved it.

And why isn't Bush ever called brave? He has been subjected to more abuse than any president in recent memory—even accounting for the fact that liberals are lying when they say they didn't despise Reagan at the time. Bookstores overflow with anti-Bush books. By my count, roughly one in four books in print in the world at this very moment have the words "Bush" and "Lie" in their title. Barnes & Noble was forced to add an "I Hate Bush" section. I don't believe there are as many anti-Hitler books.

Speaking of which, Al Gore called the Bush administration "digital Brown Shirts." Plutocrat George Soros has compared Bush to the Nazis—which raises the question: If Bush is like the Nazis, why isn't Soros collaborating with him? In the July 2008 *Vanity Fair*, James Wolcott also made the totally novel comparison of Bush to . . . Hitler! Wolcott wrote that Goebbels's reaction to meeting Hitler was similar to Karl Rove's reaction to meeting Bush.[87] (Whereas my reaction to meeting James Wolcott was similar to my reaction when I accidentally walked into a gay bar.)

Liberals produced a mock documentary depicting the assassination of George Bush. That film won the International Critics Prize at the 2006 Toronto Film Festival—not to mention "Best Date Movie of 2006" by *The Nation* magazine. A novel released in 2004 advocated the assassination of President Bush "for the good of humankind." Liberal columnist William Raspberry referred to President Bush as "the Devil." Remember the good old days, during Bush's honeymoon with the press, when he was just Hitler?

Compare Bush's cheery disposition in the face of constant abuse to a recent ex-president who reacts to the mildest criticism with purple-faced rage.

On the campaign trail for his wife in 2008, Clinton bitterly denounced the press for treating him badly, saying, "Ken Starr spent $70 million and indicted innocent people to find out that I wouldn't take a nickel to see the cow jump over the moon."[88] This was a decade after Ken Starr wrapped up his investigation and eight years after Clinton was out of office, but Clinton was still babbling about Starr in moments of stress.

When he was faced with an actual question by Fox News's liberal host Chris Wallace, Clinton erupted in a sociopathic rage worthy of a Keith Olbermann "Special Comment." Wallace asked, "Why didn't you do more to put bin Laden and al Qaeda out of business?" Displaying the grace and dignity for which he was renowned, the former president threw a hissy fit. He said, "First I want to talk about the context in which this arises," saying, "I'm being asked this on the Fox network" and "I think it's very interesting that all the conservative Republicans, who now say I didn't do enough, claimed that I was too obsessed with bin Laden. All of President Bush's neocons thought I was too obsessed with bin Laden. . . . All the right-wingers who now say I didn't do enough said I did too much—same people."

Needless to say, no "right-wingers" or anyone else ever said Clinton was "too obsessed with bin Laden." The *Washington Post* declared in the first paragraph of an article on August 21, 1998, "President Clinton won warm support for ordering anti-terrorist bombing attacks in Afghanistan and Sudan . . . from many of the same lawmakers who have criticized him harshly as a leader critically weakened by poor judgment and reckless behavior in the Monica S. Lewinsky scandal." Republican Speaker of the House Newt Gingrich was quoted saying of the attacks targeting bin Laden and al Qaeda, "I think the President did exactly the right thing. . . . By doing this we're sending the signal there are no sanctuaries for terrorists. . . ." Senate Majority Leader Trent Lott, another Republican, said, "[The attacks are] appropriate and just."[89]

But continuing his finger-wagging rant, Clinton told Wallace, "So you did Fox's bidding on this show. You did your nice little conservative hit job on me."

"Well, wait a minute, sir," Wallace replied, "I want to ask a question. You don't think that's a legitimate question?"

"It was a perfectly legitimate question," Clinton said, "but I want to know how many people in the Bush administration you asked this question of." Later he bleated, "You people ask me questions you don't ask the other side."

Actually, Wallace had asked virtually the same or similar questions of Colin Powell ("Wouldn't we have been better off if we had finished the job in Afghanistan before going into Iraq?")[90] and Donald Rumsfeld ("What do you make of his [Richard Clarke's] basic charge that pre-9/11 this government, the Bush administration, largely ignored the threat from al Qaeda?").[91]

Indeed, just two weeks earlier, Wallace had grilled Bush's secretary of state Condoleezza Rice, asking her:

"Secretary Rice, why didn't we finish the job in Afghanistan?"
"Isn't it a failure to have allowed the Taliban to regroup?"
"Didn't you and the president ignore intelligence that
    contradicted your case?"[92]

Wallace had simply asked Clinton what we in the news business call "a question." Somehow Rice and various other members of the Bush administration had managed to answer Wallace's questions without whining that he was picking on them.

Democrats are more comfortable with nonquestions, accompanied by an apology for even asking something that resembles a question, as Kate Snow did to Bill Clinton on ABC's *Good Morning America*. Snow said to Clinton, "Pretty simple question. *And maybe you don't want to answer it right now and I respect that fully.* But if you want to answer it, do you personally have any regrets about what you did campaigning for your wife?"[93]

I wish I could get a question like that someday.

After Clinton played the victim on Fox News, liberals rallied to his cause, celebrating him for—what else?—his bravery in standing up to the "conservative hit job." Various Democrats paraded through Fox News studios over the next few days to denounce Fox for being a right-wing hit machine, and rudely asking a Democrat the same question that had been asked of Republicans.[94] The indignity.

ALL LIBERALS ARE DYING TO ACT AS IF THEY ARE BEING PER-secuted. These most fawned upon humans in the history of the universe have massive McCarthyism-"victim" envy. It's one thing to be adored, but they want something more: to have courage. Or at least to be admired for having courage. This presents a bit of a problem, inasmuch as liberals will never be subjected to the tiniest criticism. Still and all, they are consumed by the conviction that they have enemies because they are speaking truth to power. Consequently, they are always playacting, simulating a dialogue with imaginary enemies. Liberals do this in public, and they're not endearing little three-year-olds.

The all-time, number-one Academy Award winners for whining liberals being called "brave" are the members of the country music group the Dixie Chicks. According to Nexis, the Dixie Chicks have been mentioned in the same sentence as "courageous" or "brave" hundreds of times in the past few years. Meanwhile, Ron Silver, the actor-turned-patriot after 9/11, who then saw his acting career stall, has been called brave once.

Lead singer Natalie Maines's bold defiance came in 2003, the year of the Dixie Chicks' sixty-city world tour, when Maines sucked up to her Bush-hating London audience by saying, "Just so you know, we're ashamed the president of the United States is from Texas." What an odd coincidence that the only city Maines attacked Bush in was London! In a way, it was lucky for the group that Maines claimed to be embarrassed by Bush in London and not in Asheville, North Carolina. Hey—maybe . . . no it couldn't be . . .

Attacking Bush in London was courageous in the sense that it is courageous when performing in Chicago to openly defy the crowd by shouting, "How about them Bears?!!!" It shows the same raw guts as performers in Gainesville, Florida, wearing hats emblazoned "Go Gators!" It's the sort of crazy let-the-chips-fall-where-they-may valor that stand-up comics exhibit in New York when they say, "Anybody here from Brooklyn?"

Here's a little bravery chart I've worked up:

Insulting President Bush in Fort Worth: Heroic
Insulting President Bush in Missouri: Possibly brave
Insulting President Bush in Austin: Not brave
Insulting President Bush in London: Gushy suck-up

Please, America, don't hate the Dixie Chicks for being anti-Bush. Hate them for being hacks.

Just to be completely clear that there was not one ounce of valor in what Maines did: When she was telling her London audience she was embarrassed about the U.S. president, she had absolutely no reason to imagine anyone in America would ever hear about it. Unlike Jimmy Carter, who can always expect his anti-American remarks abroad to make news back home, a girl band's onstage chitchat doesn't generally receive international coverage. As the *New York Times* reported, for the first several days after the concert, no one mentioned Maines's nasty remark about the president. Bush's ambassador to Great Britain, William S. Farish, attended the show and warmly greeted the Dixie Chicks afterward. Only after the Drudge Report published Maines's America-hating crowd-pleaser about a week later did Americans find out about it. Ten years earlier, Maines could have sucked up to her leftist European audience without anyone in America ever knowing.

Fans were so appalled at Maines for entertaining the antiwar Brits by attacking the U.S. president on the eve of war that country music stations began treating the Chicks the same way the establishment media treats conservatives. Album sales dropped by 42 percent in one week. In response, Maines apologized to Bush for being disrespectful, but explained that, in Europe, they hate Americans: "We are currently in Europe and witnessing a huge anti-American sentiment as a result of the perceived rush to war."[95] So her defense was that it wasn't her fault because she was just telling the audience what it wanted to hear. That, my friends, is what we call "speaking truth to power."

People in small-town America have no access to media bullhorns but exercised their freedom of speech by calling in to country music radio stations. So naturally the Dixie Chicks became First Amendment heroes in places like New York and Los Angeles for defying these tacky Americans. A *Los Angeles Times* columnist primly declared that those protesting Maines's remark were "violating her most important right and the foundation of this country—her freedom of speech."[96] In January 2004, MTV's Rock the Vote awarded the Chicks the Patrick Lippert

Award for their "enduring commitment to preserving and protecting freedom of expression."[97] To liberals, our precious right to speak means rich celebrities get to say whatever they want without being criticized.

Woeful tales of the Dixie Chicks' suffering at the hands of jackbooted Americans living in small towns across the nation turned out to be good for business. The group had the eighth-highest-grossing concert tour of 2003, and "the most lucrative country tour of all time," according to the Associated Press's David Bauder, who then added, incongruously, "despite being dogged by controversy over a remark made about President Bush."[98] No, the word is not "despite"; it's "because."

The deluge of television profiles, magazine cover stories, and newspaper articles about Maines's dauntless courage was irritating enough the first time around. But then Maines did the exact same thing again in 2005—uncannily, just before the release of the Dixie Chicks' next album! This time, she announced to *Time* magazine—oh yes, she got another interview with *Time* magazine for bravely attacking Bush—she was taking back her apology to Bush from two years earlier.

Maines was like the character played by Lili Taylor in the movie *Say Anything*, who wrote sixty-three songs denouncing her exboyfriend Joe. Bush didn't know who Maines was, but years later, Maines was still neurotically writing songs about him—"Joe lies. Joe lies. Joe lies. When he cries. When he cries. Joe lies. . . ."

Maines called her 2005 song to her imaginary ex-boyfriend George Bush "Not Ready to Make Nice." In the song she lamented her martyrdom—"I've paid a price / And I'll keep paying"—and also touted her own courage and resilience: "I'm not ready to back down / I'm still mad as hell."

What price had she paid again? The Dixie Chicks had been a nationally recognized group since 1998, when they released a slew of chart-topping songs, winning a Grammy Award for best country album in 1999 and many more awards over the years. But until they insulted Bush in London, they had been mentioned in the *New York Times* only in passing, making only two headlines in the Arts and Business sections—and never on the op-ed page. After insulting Bush, the Dixie Chicks' coverage in the *Times* doubled overnight. They were in seven headlines, at least two editorials, and roughly 7 million op-ed columns praising them for their bravery. On the op-ed page alone, the Dixie Chicks were mentioned in columns by Maureen Dowd, Tom Friedman, Paul Krugman, Brent Staples, Bob Herbert (twice), and Frank Rich (three times). One *Times* editorial about the brave Dixie Chicks asserted that they "caused trouble (and ultimately earned greater respect)."[99]

Grandstanders are not born, they're made. It's learned behavior. After watching the Dixie Chicks get attention cheaply, soon all sorts of has-been musical groups were trying to outdo one another in the venom they could hurl at President Bush.

A few weeks after Maines made her anti-Bush remarks in London, Eddie Vedder of Pearl Jam smashed a Bush mask onto the stage and stomped on it. Then Madonna made a music video in which she threw a grenade at a President Bush look-alike.[100] Before the year was up, Bruce Springsteen had told a concert audience, "It's time to impeach the president and put in somebody that knows what they're doing."[101] John Mellencamp, R.E.M., Lenny Kravitz, and the Beastie Boys jumped to release antiwar songs.

Madonna later withdrew the grenade video, but quickly made up for lost time with a stream of Bush-bashing in her tour the next year, including a video of Bush and Saddam Hussein impersonators sharing a cigar. This was "true to her rebellious nature," as one newspaper put it.[102] A few years later, Madonna's tour included a video presentation comparing Republican presidential candidate John McCain to Adolf Hitler, while comparing Barack Obama to Gandhi.[103] What will such a rebel do next? Take on . . . global warming? Her courage takes my breath away.

Just before this orgy of anti-Bush mock violence began, the *Chicago Daily Herald* had solemnly intoned, "Fear is in the air."[104] Yes, there was fear that celebrities would not get on the nightly news. Fear that music columnists across the nation would not call them brave. There was deep fear, my friends, that they would not make a bold anti-Bush statement fast enough to make their fellow musicians look like squares. These celebrity suck-ups would claim to be appalled by Abu Ghraib, but they were perfectly willing to torture the rest of us with their bottomless self-righteousness. The cover of the June 2006 issue of the music magazine *Blender* headlined a quote from Billie Joe Armstrong, lead singer of the punk group Green Day, "I'm not afraid to criticize America."[105] How about pulling that in the old Soviet Union? Then I'd be impressed.

Forget gulags—these thin-skinned liberal narcissists can't survive sixty seconds without someone telling them they're fabulous. When a fan booed Pearl Jam's Vedder as he was demonstrating his way with words by stomping on the Bush mask, Vedder was completely taken aback. Then Vedder shouted down the dissenters with a microphone and 50,000 amps, saying, "I don't know if you heard about this thing called freedom of speech, man." This qualified as one of the most profound public statements ever punctuated with the term "man." While complaining that his free-speech rights were being infringed, he announced—in a worldwide exclusive—that the following year Americans would no longer be allowed to speak! "It's worth thinking about [freedom of speech], because it's going away," Vedder said. "In the last year of being able to use it, we're sure as [expletive] going to use it and I'm not gonna apologize."[106]

Soon, Vedder was backpedaling faster than a Dixie Chick. He later said, "Just to clarify . . . we support the troops." To prove it, he cited his short haircut: "How could we not be for the military? I mean, look at this [expletive] haircut." Vedder also said his remarks had been "misconstrued." The band issued a statement saying Vedder had just been talking about "freedom of speech."

Like the Dixie Chicks, Vedder folded like a house of cards at the first note of dissent. Even with the entire mainstream media ready to hail airhead entertainers for their fearless Bush-bashing, the airheads can't take a few boos from the audience. A few years later, Barbra Streisand responded to a lone heckler responding to her anti-Bush sketch by exploding in rage. "Shut the f—k up, would you?" she wittily retorted. "Shut the f—k up if you can't take a joke."[107] These touchy celebrities demand to be simultaneously showered with praise their every waking moment—and also have trumpets blare for their courage. There is only one way to pull that off in America, and that is to be a liberal.

Having been taught by liberal celebrities to seek attention without risking anything, in 2006 a student speaker at the New School's commencement proceedings bravely insulted the official commencement speaker, Senator John McCain. The world gasped in awe at the raw heroism of Jean Rohe for being rude to an invited guest who also happened to be a Republican, a U.S. senator, and a decorated war hero. Not least of those hailing her bravery was Rohe herself—and really, who was in a better position to judge?

Describing her decision to attack the invited guest, Rohe said that as she talked to people on campus the day before her speech, she discovered how overwhelmingly popular it would be to attack McCain. Everywhere Rohe went that day she ran into students and faculty fashioning armbands and preparing to protest McCain. Her mother wept when Rohe read her illiterate speech over the phone. Literally every person Rohe talked to the day before the ceremony opposed the Iraq War and hated McCain with blind fury. At two graduation ceremonies a day earlier, attacks on McCain had brought wild cheers from the audience.

Rohe's resolve to tell the audience what it wanted to hear was only hardened when she was told there would be media at the event. "The situation seemed pretty serious," she said. "It was something I didn't want to do, but knew I had to out of an obligation to my own values"— such as the value of being popular, getting a standing ovation, and being praised for her courage.[108] Liberals' idea of questioning authority is to check with the authorities to see if a "Question Authority" bumper sticker would be popular. See, where I come from, sucking up to the audience is not called "courageous."

Sensing that grandiosity and fake heroism were within her grasp, Rohe lectured McCain, bravely telling him, "We have nothing to fear from anyone on this living planet."[109] Except Osama bin Laden, apparently: Rohe was furious with Bush for not catching him. So I guess she thought we had something to fear from him. Still, she was brave. I know that because she got a standing ovation.

Rohe then fulfilled her final obligation as a brave liberal by bitterly complaining that those who criticized her behavior were trying "to hurt my feelings."[110]

But to be a true ace at the game, Rohe will have to learn to be an utterly opportunistic grandstander *and make a living at it.* For that, we turn to John Kerry, who has managed to secure a Senate career by passing off his antiwar activism as raw courage, rather than the naked self-promotion that it was.

After spending three months in Vietnam, and then returning to discover that that military service would not boost a political career, Kerry did an about-face and became America's most famous antiwar protester. His 1971 Senate testimony against the war catapulted him to media stardom with a virulently antiwar press. He was awarded a long segment on CBS's *60 Minutes* a few weeks later—in which he was asked if he wanted to run for president.

His fellow antiwar activists "viewed Kerry as a power-grabbing elitist."[111] Kerry's undisguised ambition in the antiwar movement turned him into a regular character in Garry Trudeau's "Doonesbury" comic strip. In a 1971 cartoon published in the *Yale Daily News*, a character walks up to two men talking about John Kerry and says, "If you care about this country at all you better go listen to that John Kerry fellow." Next box: "He speaks with a rare eloquence and astonishing conviction. If you see no one else this year, you must see John Kerry!" Last box: "Who was that?" one man asks. "John Kerry," the other says.

And yet, in 2004, liberal columnist Tom Oliphant converted Kerry's grasping antiwar activism into an act of staggering courage. Oliphant wrote, "What Kerry did in the spring of 1971 still amazes me. The power and eloquence of his statement to the Senate Foreign Relations Committee [blah, blah, blah] . . . At the time, Kerry told me that he assumed his actions had precluded a political career, a sentiment experience had taught me to share."[112]

It was such a brazen inversion of the truth, one almost admired Oliphant for allowing those lines to be published under his name. It certainly showed more audacity than anything Kerry had ever done.

As the *Boston Globe* said, Kerry's Senate testimony "made possible his political career."[113] For Kerry and his acolytes in the press to claim that he was spitting into the wind with his antiwar testimony would be like Britney Spears claiming that appearing on stage wearing only a bra would hurt her performing career, but dammit, she had to do it!

It would be one thing if liberal suck-ups said, *Okay, gimme a break. I have to make a living here.* But they demand that their most whoring behavior be described as "brave." *Wearing just a bra on stage is just something I have to do to be true to myself!* These are goody two-shoes apple-polishers—the kids who volunteer for extra work after school and turn in their classmates who talk when the teacher leaves the room. Okay, fine. There have always been wienies groveling toward authority figures, and in modern America the most powerful authority figure is the liberal establishment. But this may be the first time in history that we ever had to suffer the effrontery of the bootlickers telling us, "I'm bad—I clean erasers for teachers after class because I'm *baaad.*"

I don't care what liberals believe, but don't tell me they're courageous when they are saying exactly what every powerful institution in America wants to hear. These people would have collaborated with Hitler. This is not an exact science, but if you've just been on the cover of a magazine or received a standing ovation, you're not being courageous. There's a different word for it— What's the word I'm searching for? Oh yes, it's "ass-kissing."

MOST HILARIOUS ARE LIBERALS WHO COMPLAIN ABOUT "DEATH threats." In the Dixie Chicks' 2005 song "Not Ready to Make Nice," Maines sang:

> *And how in the world can the words that I said*
> *Send somebody so over the edge*
> *That they'd write me a letter?*
> *Sayin' that I better shut up and sing*
> *Or my life will be over. . . .*

My life will be over? I gather Maines is not talking about the grave risk that she will be on the cover of yet another dozen magazines with feature articles about how she's been silenced. In an editorial—yes, an editorial—the *New York Times* described how the group had suffered: "Their music was boycotted and banned by country music stations, their CDs were burned and smashed, and *group members' lives were threatened.*"[114]

Someone has got to make liberals stop telling us their "lives were threatened." Every public figure's life has been threatened. If more than fifty people know your name, you have been proposed to, propositioned, and insulted and have had threats on your life.

Any public figure who complains about hate mail is a scaredy-cat sissy. My proof:

"I know from experience that I have guaranteed myself a barrage of hate mail." —Paul Krugman, wearing women's underwear, January 23, 2000

"Psychoanalyzing a political movement guarantees a fresh wave of hate mail." —Paul Krugman, wearing women's underwear, May 23, 2001

"Spare me the hate mail." —Paul Krugman, wearing women's underwear, May 28, 2004

"After 9/11, if you were thinking of saying anything negative about the president, you had to be prepared for an avalanche of hate mail." —Paul Krugman, wearing women's underwear, May 6, 2003

Krugman probably writes his own hate mail.

The preeminent security specialist Gavin de Becker says attacks on public figures are almost never preceded by a warning,[115] so you're really pathetic if you're whining about "death threats." John Lennon, Ronald Reagan, and Gianni Versace did not receive any warning before they were shot. The "death threats" liberals constantly wail about are less than nothing. On the other hand, publicizing a public figure's address is intentionally putting that person's life in danger. Noticeably, liberals go out of their way to publicize the addresses of conservative public figures.

According to the mainstream media, this nation is a cauldron of right-wing violence. But oddly, it's always liberals caught doing the political violence. At the 2008 Republican National Convention, for example, liberal protesters were arrested for smashing police cars, slashing tires, breaking store windows, and possessing Molotov cocktails, napalm bombs, and assorted firearms.[116] No conservatives protested the Democratic National Convention. Sarah Palin and Condoleezza Rice have been rushed by crazed liberal women in public forums. Conservative speakers on college campuses have been repeatedly physically attacked by liberals. Bill O'Reilly, Matt Drudge, and Sean Hannity, among others, have been harassed at their homes by liberals. Meanwhile liberal luminaries go about their private lives unmolested. But we're supposed to believe Paul Krugman has to ride in cars with windows blacked out for fear that right-wing proponents of Social Security privatization might get violent.

On December 26, 2006, not long before Barack Obama publicly announced that he was running for president, the *Chicago Sun-Times* reprinted an Internet column by Erin Kotecki Vest. The column was a completely insane "open letter" to Michelle Obama.

"I look at my husband and my two beautiful children," Vest wrote, "and I wonder how on earth you and your family will make this decision [to run for president]. It would be a sacrifice, no question. *Possibly the biggest sacrifice a family could make. We all know it wouldn't just be the usual pressures of the job or public life, it could very well mean the word no one wants to say but everyone is thinking: 'assassination.'*" Claiming she had the courage to say what no one else would, Vest identified the "ugly truth" that "some in America may not be ready to see a black family in the White House"—that "the decision to run for president could mean the death of your husband or family member or yourself." Even though she felt that Barack Obama could "change the world," Vest told Mrs. Obama, "I can't ask you to do it for me. I can't ask you to do it for the children or for the future or for the good of mankind. You are a mother, like I am a mother, and I know I can't ask that of you."

After Obama officially announced that he was running for president, liberals were nearly paralyzed by the fear that he would be assassinated.

On CBS's *Early Show,* host Harry Smith slowly spoke these words to Senator Ted Kennedy: "When you see that enthusiasm [for Obama], though, and when you see the generational change that seems to be taking place before our eyes, does it make you at all fearful?"

Kennedy may be a drunken slob, but unlike CBS news anchors, he is not certifiably insane. He ignored Smith's portentous question and chirpily responded that people were saying "they want a new day and a new generation in this country at this time," and so on.

But Smith somberly returned to his nutty assassination scenario, speaking even more distinctly this time: "I just, I think what I was trying to say is, sometimes agents of change end up being targets, as you well know, and that was why I was asking if you were at all fearful of that."

Again, Kennedy blew him off, saying, "Yeah, yeah. No, I think there's—Barack Obama is the kind of candidate for change and I think the people all over the country have been impressed by the breadth and the width . . ."[117]

About the same time, Representative Bennie Thompson, Democrat of Mississippi, wrote to the Secret Service to request extra protection for Obama, saying, "As an African-American who was witness to some of this nation's most shameful days during the civil rights movement, I know personally that the hatred of some of our fellow citizens can lead to heinous acts of violence."[118]

Then, in February 2008, Nobel Prize–winning author Doris Lessing predicted that Obama would be assassinated because he is black, saying an Obama presidency "would certainly not last long, a black man in the position of president. They would murder him."[119]

The *New York Times* ran a front-page article about the "hushed worry" of Obama's supporters that he will be assassinated.[120] By this point, the "worry" that Obama would be knocked off by imaginary right-wing assassins was about as "hushed" as the news of Britney Spears's latest breakdown.

Chris Matthews joined the macabre brigade, saying, "I don't want to get into all the details, but every American knows what happens in these very charismatic moments, when somebody is really the toast of the town, and people are really excited about a campaign. Sometimes, it brings out the loonies."[121]

In early 2008, there were nearly seven times as many documents on Google for "Obama" and "assassination" as there were for "Bush" and "assassination." This is despite the fact that (1) Bush had been president for the past seven and a half years, and (2) liberals had actually produced books and movies about their fantasy of Bush being assassinated.

I wouldn't mention it, but as long as liberals are going to keep acting as if they are under constant threat from right-wing assassins, I note that 90 percent of the political assassins in this country have been liberals. Most of the rest were random nuts. There was only one white-racist nut—and that was four decades ago. Based on history, Sean Hannity is at greater risk of being shot than Obama is.

Every presidential assassin in the history of the nation has been a liberal—or has had no politics at all. None were right-wingers.

Actor/activist John Wilkes Booth shot President Abraham Lincoln on April 14, 1865, because he was opposed to Lincoln's Republican war policies. Booth, the Tim Robbins of his day, left a letter with his family explaining his actions, saying he loved "peace more than life" and denouncing Republicans for foisting the war on the South.[122] He may have even used the word "quagmire" to describe Gettysburg.

Charles J. Guiteau, who shot President James Garfield in 1881, had a long relationship with a utopian commune called the Oneida Community, where free love and communal child-rearing were practiced.[123]

Leon Czolgosz, who killed President William McKinley in 1901, was a socialist and anarchist (okay, that's redundant) who was captivated upon hearing a speech by radical socialist Emma Goldman the year he shot McKinley.[124] If memory serves, Goldman's inspirational speech had something to do with "hope" and "change."

John Schrank, who shot and wounded Teddy Roosevelt in 1912, seemed to have no political beliefs other than a strong opposition to third terms—which Roosevelt was then running for.[125]

Giuseppe Zangara, who narrowly missed shooting President-elect Franklin Roosevelt in 1933, was consumed by envy of the rich and sought to "make even with capitalists" by killing the president. According to the FBI files, even on the way to the electric chair (he had mortally wounded Chicago mayor Anton Cermak) "Zangara was cursing and railing against capitalists."[126] Earlier, Zangara had plotted to kill Republican president Herbert Hoover, because both Hoover and Roosevelt were "capitalists."[127] Yes, you heard me right: This would-be assassin was to the *left* of FDR.

Lee Harvey Oswald, who shot President John F. Kennedy on November 22, 1963, had been a stone-cold Communist ever since he read a Communist pamphlet about Julius and Ethel Rosenberg as a teenager. Incensed by racial discrimination in America, he defiantly rode in the black sections of buses as a child. Oswald studied Russian and moved to the USSR in his late teens, hoping to avoid the rush. When his application for Soviet citizenship was declined, he slit his wrists. Oswald eventually returned to the United States with his Russian wife and child, where he continued to plot an escape to a socialist paradise such as Cuba or Red China.[128]

Ginned up by publications of the Communist Party and the Socialist Workers Party—*The Worker* and *The Militant*, respectively—Oswald first tried to kill Major General Edwin A. Walker, a John Bircher. Ten days before shooting at Walker—and missing—Oswald had posed for a photograph holding his guns and copies of the socialist publications denouncing Walker.[129] Some of you will recognize this photo as Randi Rhodes's screen saver.

Oswald next plotted to kill former vice president Richard Nixon, but got distracted the day Nixon was in Dallas. He spent the next several months passing out "Fair Play for Cuba" leaflets. In between "You never take me anywhere!" arguments with his wife, Oswald tried to talk her into helping him hijack a plane to Cuba so he could fight in defense of the revolution.[130]

When he was arrested for shooting Kennedy, Oswald immediately placed a call to John Abt, lawyer for the American Communist Party, planning to ask Abt to defend him so he could use the trial to showcase his Marxist beliefs.[131] He never got the chance, thanks to Jack Ruby.

Sirhan Sirhan, who shot Democratic presidential candidate Senator Robert Kennedy on June 5, 1968, was a Palestinian extremist angry with Kennedy for his support of Israel.[132] For more on this worldview, see the works of Noam Chomsky.

Arthur Bremer, who shot and paralyzed Democratic presidential candidate George Wallace on May 15, 1972, was enraged by Wallace's support for segregation. A search of Bremer's apartment turned up Black Panther literature and a diary with entries such as "My country 'tis of thee, land of sweet bigotry." A quarter of a century after he shot Wallace, Bremer expressed no remorse, saying he should be paroled because shooting "segregationist dinosaurs" was not like shooting a person. "They are extinct," Bremer wrote, "by an act of God."[133] This mention of God was the only blemish on Bremer's otherwise impeccable liberal credentials.

Lynette "Squeaky" Fromme, who pointed a loaded gun at President Gerald Ford on September 5, 1975, was part of Charles Manson's countercultural hippie cult. She pulled the gun on Ford because she was incensed about the plight of the California redwoods.[134] (Who can ever forget Ford's famous vow to cut down every redwood on earth?)

Sara Jane Moore, who tried to kill Ford seventeen days later, was a five-time divorcée who, like the Code Pink gals, turned to revolutionary politics in her forties. Moore said she wanted to assassinate Ford because "the government had declared war on the left." Sounding like Seymour Hersh with a better editor, she said Nixon and Ford were waging "a continuing assault on America." She tried to kill Ford in order to "allow the winds of change to start."[135]

I know what some of you are thinking: What about would-be Reagan assassin John Hinckley, who shot the president not for political reasons but hoping to impress a girl? Although Hinckley would seem to be an exception to the rule that all presidential assassins have been liberals, recall that a jury later found Hinckley to be "not guilty by reason of insanity," which is as good a definition of liberalism as I've heard.

To be sure, Martin Luther King, though not a presidential candidate, was a major political figure and he was killed by a white racist. I'd put that in the liberal column, but in deference to *New York Times* sensibilities, I'll make it a draw. Oh, what the heck—conservatives are so far ahead, I'll let liberals call the racist a "right-winger."

But if we're going to get into assassinations of nonpresidential political figures, there was also Malcolm X, who was killed by Black Muslims. And there was the massive political violence of the Left throughout the seventies and beyond carried out by such radical organizations as the Weather Underground, the Black Panthers, and the Black Liberation Army—or Obama's "kitchen cabinet."

Thus, another nonpresidential political assassination was the 1981 murder of Waverly "Chipper" Brown, then the only black officer on the Nyack, New York, police force. The much-loved Brown had served his country in the Air Force during the Korean War and had two daughters who followed him into the Air Force. He worked with black schoolchildren, telling them to stay off drugs and make something of themselves. He personally bought turkeys for a dozen poor neighbors on Thanksgiving. But liberal "revolutionaries" with the Weathermen and the Black Liberation Army who claimed to be fighting "white oppression" killed the only black officer on the police force after their robbery of a Brinks truck in 1981—along with Nyack police sergeant Edward O'Grady and Brinks guard Peter Paige.

Then there was Robert Fassnacht, a physics graduate student at the University of Wisconsin who was killed in 1971 by a car bomb set by antiwar protesters that did more than $6 million in damage to university buildings. Liberals operating under various radical umbrella groups planted bombs or attempted to plant bombs at an Army dance hall at Fort Dix, New York City police headquarters, the Harvard international-studies center, various corporate offices, National Guard headquarters, the Pentagon, and the Capitol Building. A string of cops, prosecutors, lawyers, and accountants were killed, maimed, and paralyzed in the seventies and eighties by these peaceful liberals.

The Democratic Party has closer ties to these violent animals than the Republican Party does to Bob Jones University (a Christian college that terrifies liberals). Most notable are Barack Obama's close connections to Weathermen Bill Ayers and Bernardine Dohrn, who were directly involved in bombing the Pentagon and the Capitol. They were so close to two of the Weathermen involved in the 1981 Brinks robbery, David Gilbert and Kathy Boudin, that they took custody of the convicted terrorists' child. And, of course, Obama held his first political coming-out party at the home of Ayers and Dohrn.

In addition to Obama's cozy relationship with these left-wing terrorists, Bill Clinton pardoned a former Weatherman, Susan L. Rosenberg, who was arrested in November 1984 with 740 pounds of dynamite, a submachine gun, and other weapons in her car. Rosenberg also harbored a getaway driver from the Brinks robbery that cost three men their lives.

So spare us the fantasies of right-wing assassins targeting the blessed Obama. Inasmuch as he is the most far-left president the country has ever had, his base is composed of the very groups from which political assassins are generally drawn.

In a country where the vast majority of the population is patriotic, God-believing, and capitalistic, it's telling that nearly all presidential assassins have been left-wing zealots—pacifists, communitarians, Communists, anarchists, Palestinian extremists, and countercultural hippies. It's bad enough that liberals keep producing the nation's assassins. Can they at least stop pretending to believe they are living in a country bristling with right-wing murderers? In return, we'll all pretend to believe that it's brave every time a Hollywood actress comes out against global warming.

It's also interesting that all presidential assassins or would-be assassins are almost all white people—white folks and one Arab. At any one time, there are surely more blacks in the United States than Communists, Palestinian activists, and Weathermen. So why are white liberals always threatening Republicans with black violence? During the 2004 presidential campaign, Al Gore advised black voters in Jacksonville, Florida, not to turn to "angry acts or angry words."[136] That same day, Elizabeth Edwards warned that there might be riots if John Kerry didn't win. In 2008, Sandra Bernhard's act included the warning that if Sarah Palin[137] came to Manhattan, she'd be gang-raped by black men.[138] The *Philadelphia Daily News* columnist Fatimah Ali cautioned, "If McCain wins, look for a full-fledged race and class war."

Liberals are constantly trying to plant subliminal suggestions with blacks to engage in violence against conservatives. They try to make blacks afraid of Republicans, telling them that Republicans are trying to oppress them—and even plotting to murder Obama! Throughout the 2004 presidential campaign, Democrats told blacks that Republicans had denied them the right to vote in the famous 2000 Florida election. This, despite the fact that a year-long investigation by the Civil Rights Commission could not produce one single black person who was prevented from voting in that election.[139] But Soros-funded Americans Coming Together put out a flyer in Missouri warning blacks that Republicans were trying to prevent them from voting, saying, "They put phony cops at polling places. . . . They make African American voters stand in line for hours, then turn them away from the polls. . . . They did it in St. Louis, they did it in Florida, and now they're trying to do it again."[140]

Trying to get blacks to do their fighting for them doesn't seem to be working for liberals, since it's always white liberals engaging in acts of violence. Every attack on a conservative speaker at a college campus has been committed by white assailants. In the 2004 election, a Madison, Wisconsin, homeowner with Bush yard signs found an eight-foot swastika burned into his grass with weed killer. (Madison: 4 percent African American.)[141] A Bush-Cheney campaign office in Bellevue, Washington, was burglarized and had computers and confidential get-out-the-vote files stolen. (Bellevue: 2 percent African American.)[142] That same year, Bush-Cheney headquarters in Orlando, Florida, were ransacked by union protesters with the AFL-CIO. (A sensible, bipartisan gun-control law would prohibit liberals from owning guns.)

In 2008, two white liberals, Daniel Meinecke, twenty-nine, and Cara Hindman, twenty-six, walked into a McCain campaign headquarters in Galax, Virginia, and belligerently demanded "Obama-Biden" yard signs, clinging to the hope that an Obama presidency would usher in a new era of civility. Told the Obama campaign office was up the street, they began yelling and cursing, and accused the office workers, two married couples in their seventies, of stealing Obama yard signs. Besides the rush of excitement that comes with being a victim in modern America, liberals insist on playing the victim to provide a justification for their own insensate violence against conservatives. The office manager responded that they had stolen no signs and ushered the profanity-spewing leftists out the door. Once on the street, the lovely Cara Hindman—protected by a layer of grease and dirt resulting from weeks of scrupulously not bathing—maced the office manager and opened the door to spray Mace back into the office, hitting five McCain staffers in all.[143]

Instead of smugly pleading with blacks not to riot, maybe Democrats could have a word with their white liberal friends.

These counterfeit victims are so full of their own self-righteousness, they believe they can do anything, lie shamelessly, commit wanton violence, steal from their neighbors, and claim they were acting out of some bizarre sense of self-defense.

Liberals claim they are victims—victims of pregnancy, victims of the Republican Attack Machine, victims of foreign words meaning "monkey," victims of Americans angry they have revealed secret counterterrorist programs, victims of "AmeriKKKa's imperialism," victims of redwood assassins, victims of apocryphal right-wing violence. They're not victims—they are guilty.

NOTES

CHAPTER 1 LIBERAL MOTTO:
SPEAK LOUDLY AND CARRY A SMALL VICTIM

1   Adam Lisberg, "New Lung or WTC Cop Dies," *Daily News* (New York), January 16, 2007.

2   "Statement of Senator Hillary Rodham Clinton on President's Meeting Today with Ceasar Borja Jr.," States News Service, February 1, 2007.

3   Ibid.

4   Sewell Chan and Al Baker, "Weeks After a Death, Twists in Some 9/11 Details," *New York Times*, February 13, 2007.

5   Ibid.

6   Ibid.

7   Motoko Rich, "Gang Memoir, Turning Page, Is Pure Fiction," *New York Times*, March 4, 2008.

8   David Mehegan, "Author Admits Making Up Memoir of Surviving Holocaust," *Boston Globe*, February 29, 2008.

9   Luke Crisell, "Luke Crisell Tries to Track Down the Real JT LeRoy," *The Observer*, March 6, 2005.

10   Ed Siegel, "Unpleasantville in Books, Plays, and Songs: America Is Getting Creepier—And More Interesting," *Boston Globe*, August 26, 2001.

11   See, e.g., Jason Horowitz, "Obama's Pocketbook Speech," *The Observer*, May 3, 2008.

12   Jonah Weiner, "Alicia Keys: Unlocked," *Blender*, March 19, 2008. Available at: http://www.blender.com/articles/default.aspx?key=21056&pg=2.

13   Edward Wong, "Long Island Case Sheds Light on Animal-Mutilation," *New York Times*, January 25, 2000.

14   Ibid.

15   Marc Santora, "Columbia Professor in Noose Case Is Fired on Plagiarism Charges," *New York Times*, June 24, 2008.

16   Robert Stacy McCain, "Expulsion Call Follows GW Hoax on Posters," *Washington Times*, October 11, 2007; Robert Stacy McCain, "'Fight Fire with Fire,'" *Washington Times*, October 18, 2007; Editorial: "Nobles and Knaves," *Washington Times*, October 20, 2007; Eric Roper, "GW Students Get Probation for Posters," *GW Hatchet*, November 15, 2007.

17 Douglas J. Guth, "Wooster Vandals Hold Forum to 'Begin the Healing,'" *Cleveland Jewish News*, January 11, 2005; Joe P. Tone, "Woosteria!," *Cleveland Scene*, January 26, 2005.

18 Stuart Silverstein and Peter Y. Hong, "Vandalism Unifies Linked but Distinct Colleges in the Battle Against Hatred," *Los Angeles Times*, March 13, 2004.

19 "Former Claremont Professor Who Faked Vandalism Gets Year in Jail," Associated Press, December 15, 2004.

20 "Top Five Outrages on College Campuses: Collegiate Network Awards Sixth Annual 'Pollys,'" *Human Events* Online, May 11, 2003.

21 Ruma Banerji, "Ole Miss Vandals Put on Probation," *Commercial Appeal* (Memphis), January 17, 2003.

22 "Hate-Crime Hoaxes Unsettle Campuses," *Chronicle of Higher Education*, January 8, 1999; Naomi Schaefer, "Lies Our Students Tell Us: A False Assault Accusation at UMass Amherst Is Part of a Trend," *Weekly Standard*, January 31, 2000.

23 "Elizabeth Edwards: 'Can't Make John Black' or a 'Woman,'" CNN.com, August 8, 2007. Available at: http://politicalticker.blogs.cnn.com/2007/08/08/elizabeth-edwards-cant-make-john-black-or-a-woman/.

24 Jacob Weisberg, "If Obama Loses Racism Is the Only Reason McCain Might Beat Him," *Slate*, August 23, 2008. Available at: http://slate.com/id/2198397.

25 Robert Lipsyte, "Mantle and America: Allies in Vulnerability," *New York Times*, June 11, 1995.

26 Mark Landler, "Philip Morris Revels in Rare ABC News Apology for Report on Nicotine," *New York Times*, August 28, 1995.

27 Elizabeth Kolbert, "NBC News Chief Stepping Down Amid Troubles," *New York Times*, March 3, 1993.

28 "CNN Retracts Tailwind Coverage," CNN.com, July 2, 1998. Available at: http://www.cnn.com/US/9807/02/tailwind.johnson/.

29 Michael Calderone, "Gov. Rendell: Fox Is 'Most Objective' Cable Network,'" *Politico*, March 31, 2008. Available at: http://www.politico.com/blogs/michael calderone/0308/Gov_Rendell_Fox_is_most_objective_cable_network.html.

30 Clinton interview, *Politico*, February 11, 2008.

31 Gwen Ifill, *The Breakthrough: Politics and Race in the Age of Obama* (Random House, 2009).

32 Washington Post–ABC News Poll, washingtonpost.com, Available at: http://www.washingtonpost.com/wp-srv/politics/polls/postpoll_092308.html.

33 CNN Election Center: "Republican National Convention Day Four, 8:00 pm hour," September 4, 2008.

34 Eric Pfeiffer, "House GOP Tries to Force Fairness Vote," *Washington Times*, October 17, 2007.

35 Amy Keller, "Policing Internet Politics?," *Roll Call*, February 14, 2005.

36 Jim Rutenberg and Bill Carter, "CBS Says Producer Violated Policy by Putting Source in Touch with Kerry Aide," *New York Times*, September 22, 2004.

37 Jane Sutton, "Florida Voting Laws Under Fire Again," *Houston Chronicle*, October 6, 2006.

38 Andrew M. Seder, "Secret Service Says 'Kill Him' Allegation Unfounded," *Times Leader*, October 17, 2008. Available at: http://www.timesleader.com/news/breakingnews/Secret_Service_says_Kill_him_allegation_unfounded_.html.

39 Branchflower Report to the Alaskan Legislative Council, October 1, 2008, Volume 1 at 39 & 71.

40 Serge F. Kovaleski, "Alaska Inquiry Concludes Palin Abused Powers," *New York Times*, October 11, 2008.

41 Douglass K. Daniel, "Analysis: Palin's Words Carry Racial Tinge," Associated Press, October 5, 2008.

42 Jason Horowitz, "Black Congressmen Declare Racism in Palin's Rhetoric," *New York Observer*, October 7, 2008.

43 Jake Tapper, "Obama Flack Accidentally Sends Out Pre-Debate Talking Points," ABC News, October 15, 2008. Available at: http://blogs.abcnews.com/politicalpunch/2008/10/obama-flack-acc.html.

44 Available at: http://cofcc.org/.

45 Editorial: "Martin Luther King Jr.'s America," *New York Times*, January 18, 1999.

46 Carl Cameron, "Gephardt Admits Mistake on Race Issues in '70s," FoxNews.com, January 11, 2004. Available at: http://www.foxnews.com/story/0,2933,108068,00.html.

47 Editorial: "Watered-Down Racism Resolution," *New York Times*, March 23, 1999.

48 Francis X. Clines, "A 'Dreadful Day' Unfolds On and Off House Floor," *New York Times*, December 19, 1998.

49 Editorial: "Scraping the Bottom," *New York Times*, October 6, 2008.

50 Gail Collins, "Clearing the Ayers," *New York Times*, October 9, 2008.

51 Allan Turner, "Museum on a Mission to Save Local Gay History," *Houston Chronicle*, August 24, 2004.

52 Shirish Date, "Some Democratic Delegates Peeved by Flier Promoting Diversity," Associated Press, August 22, 1996.

53 James Moore, "Smear Artist," *Salon*, Aug 28, 2004. Available at: http://dir.salon.com/story/news/feature/2004/08/28/moore_rove_swift_boat/index.html.

54 *Hardball*, MSNBC, August 28, 2007.

55 Jonathan Alter, "Last Stop on the 'V'-Train," *Newsweek*, September 10, 2007.

56 William Robbins, "Nebraska Inquiry Is Given File on Sex Abuse of Foster Children," *New York Times*, December 25, 1988.

57 William Robbins, "Omaha Grand Jury Sees Hoax in Lurid Tales," *New York Times*, July 29, 1990.

58 Associated Press, "Omaha Tales of Sexual Abuse Ruled False," *New York Times*, September 27, 1990.

59 "Theya culpe" coined by Jim Downey.

60 John Winthrop, "A Modell of Christian Charity," Collections of the Massachu-

setts Historical Society (Boston, 1838), 3rd series 7:31–48). Available at: http://history.hanover.edu/texts/winthmod.html.

61   Kevin Combest, "Why Conservatives Give More to Charity," *Human Events Online*, November 29, 2006. Available at: http://www.humanevents.com/article.php?id=18253.

CHAPTER 2 VICTIM OF A CRIME? THANK A SINGLE MOTHER

1   Marilyn Gardner, "In the Pursuit of Prosperity, We Have 'Maxed Out,'" *Christian Science Monitor*, April 3, 2007.

2   Mike Wereschagin, "Winter Heating Costs Will Raise Your Temperature," *Pittsburgh Tribune Review*, September 10, 2005.

3   Greg Kratz, "Variable Work Schedules Turn Personal Lives into Challenges," *Deseret Morning News* (Salt Lake City), October 17, 2004.

4   Leta Hong Fincher, "US Poverty," *Voice of America News*, September 7, 2004.

5   "U.S.: Women's Poverty Deepens amid Slow 2003 Recovery," IPS-Inter Press Service, September 3, 2004.

6   Joann Fitzpatrick, "Homeless Shelter in Stoughton," *Patriot Ledger* (Quincy, MA), August 6, 2001.

7   Sheila R. Zedlewski, "Building a Better Safety Net for the *New* New Orleans," The Urban Institute, February 2006. Available at: http://72.14.205.104/search?q=cache:HsG6n9F7dKIJ:www.urban.org/UploadedPDF/900922_safety_net.pdf+percent22single+mothers percent22+percent22hit+hardestpercent22&hl=en&ct=clnk&cd=11&gl=us&lr=lang_en&client=firefox-a.

8   Yves Colon, "Immigration Fees Going Up Next Week," *Miami Herald*, October 6, 1998.

9   Liz Spayd, "Day-Care Needs Unmet, Report Says," *Washington Post*, October 14, 1993.

10   Engendering the Energy and Climate Change Agenda, United Nations Economic and Social Council, May 1–12, 2006. Available here: http://www.wiserearth.org/article/afa47f4f730d6c90f61a4765912f6d59/group/WEA.

11   Diane Weaver Dunne, "When Children Abuse Their Parents," *Hartford Courant* (Connecticut), May 4, 1998.

12   Michele L. Norris, "Big Markets Gone; Southeast Food Costs Soar," *Los Angeles Times*, August 5, 1985.

13   Andrew DeMillo, "Democrats Look to Connect with Female Voters," *Arkansas Democrat-Gazette* (Little Rock), July 29, 2004.

14   Ori Nir, "New Welfare Plan Said to Deal Blow to Single Mothers," *The Forward*, April 25, 2003.

15   The Brookings Institution, "Assessing the Impact of Welfare Reform on Single Mothers, Part 2," March 22, 2004, Table 2. Demographic Characteristics of

Single Mothers, 1980–2002 (data from the Census Bureau's Annual Social and Economic Study).

16   S. McLanahan and G. Sandefur, *Growing Up with a Single Parent: What Hurts, What Helps* (Cambridge, MA: Harvard University Press, 1994).

17   Linda Bird Francke, "Growing Up Divorced," p. 11.

18   Mary Parke, "Are Married Parents Really Better for Children?," Center for Law and Social Policy, May 2003. Available at: http://www.clasp.org/publications/marriage_brief3_annotated.pdf.

19   Jason DeParle, "Raising Kevion," *New York Times*, August 22, 2004.

20   Ibid.

21   Statement of Charles Murray, House Ways and Means Committee, Human Resources, Hearing on Welfare Reform, July 29, 1994.

22   Richard E. Redding, "It's Really About Sex: Same-Sex Marriage, Lesbigay Parenting, and the Psychology of Disgust," *Duke Journal of Gender Law & Policy*, January 1, 2008 (citing David T. Lykken, "Parental Licensure," *American Psychologist*, 56: 885, 887 [2001], and citing C. C. Harper and S. S. McLanahan, "Father Absence and Youth Incarceration," paper presented at the Annual Meeting of the American Sociological Association, San Francisco, August 1998).

23   Wade Horn, "Why There Is No Substitute for Parents," *Imprimis* 26, no. 6 (June 1997), p. 2.

24   Chuck Colson, *How Shall We Live* (Tyndale House Publishers, 2004) p. 323.

25   David T. Lykken, "Reconstructing Fathers," *American Psychologist* 55: 681,681 (2000), quoted in Redding, "It's Really About Sex."

26   Horn, "Why There Is No Substitute for Parents," *Imprimis* 26, no. 6 (June 1997), p. 2.

27   Redding, "It's Really About Sex."

28   Horn, "Why There Is No Substitute for Parents."

29   David Blankenhorn, *Fatherless America: Confronting Our Most Urgent Social Problem* (New York: Harper Perennial, 1996), p. 31.

30   Bob Ray Sanders, "Hey, Y'all, Let's Fill the Hall (of Fame)," *Fort Worth Star-Telegram*, October 28, 2007; Mona Charen, "More Good News Than Bad?" *Washington Times*, March 16, 2001 (citing Bill Bennett, *The Index of Leading Cultural Indicators: American Society at the End of the Twentieth Century* [New York: Broadway Books, 1994]).

31   Chuck Eddy, "The Daddy Shady Show," *Village Voice*, December 31, 2002.

32   In 1990, there were a total of 34,670 parents with children under eighteen years old. Of those, 24,570 were married, compared with 8,779 who were unmarried, most of whom—86 percent—were single mothers. U.S. Census, Table FM-2. All Parent/Child Situations, by Type, Race, and Hispanic Origin of Householder or Reference Person: 1970 to Present (2003). Available at: http://www.census.gov/population/socdemo/hh-fam/tabFM-2.pdf.

33   Steve Schifferes, "Is the UK a Model Welfare?" BBC News, August 4, 2005. Available at: http://news.bbc.co.uk/1/hi/business/4704081.stm.

34   Martin Newland, "Why England Is Rotting," *Maclean's*, June 11, 2007.

35   Isabel V. Sawhill, Statement to the House Committee on Ways and Means, Subcommittee on Human Resources, Hearing, June 29, 1999. Available at: http://www.brookings.edu/testimony/1999/0629poverty_sawhill.aspx?p=1.

36   David Popenoe, "The Future of Marriage in America," Rutgers University, The National Marriage Project, 2007. Available at: http://marriage.rutgers.edu/Publications/SOOU/TEXTSOOU2007.htm (quoted in Emily Yoffe ". . . And Baby Makes Two," *Slate* magazine, March 20, 2008).

37   Popenoe, "The Future of Marriage in America"; "The Frayed Knot—Marriage in America," *The Economist*, May 26, 2007.

38   Colson, *How Shall We Live.*

39   Barry H. Waldman and Steven P. Perlman, "Homeless Children with Disabilities," *The Exceptional Parent*, June 1, 2008 (American Academy of Developmental Medicine and Dentistry: Developmental Medicine and Dentistry Reviews & Reports).

40   DeParle, "Raising Kevion."

41   Sawhill, Statement to the House Committee on Ways and Means, Subcommittee on Human Resources Hearing.

42   DeParle, "Raising Kevion."

43   Theodore Dalrymple, "The Knife Went In," *City Journal*, Autumn 1994.

44   Theodore Dalrymple, "Tough Love," *City Journal*, Winter 1999.

45   Celia W. Dugger, "On the Edge of Survival: Single Mothers on Welfare," *New York Times*, July 6, 1992.

46   Ibid.

47   Editorial: "Dan Quayle's Fictitious World," *New York Times*, May 22, 1992.

48   "The Frayed Knot."

49   "Waiting for What?," *In These Times*, July 2006.

50   Kathleen Kingsbury, "Pregnancy Boom at Gloucester High," *Time*, June 18, 2008. The mayor later tried to deny the story, but that just led to the *Time* reporter going on TV and attesting to her many sources that there was indeed a "pact." See "So-Called Pregnancy Pact in Gloucester Being Questioned," *The Today Show*, NBC News, June 24, 2008.

51   "The Frayed Knot."

52   See, e.g., House Ways and Means Committee, Nonmarital Births to Adults and Teenagers and Federal Strategies to Reduce Nonmarital Pregnancies, Appendix M. Available at: http://waysandmeans.house.gov/media/pdf/greenbook2003/AppendixM.pdf.

53   Patrick F. Fagan and William H. G. Fitzgerald, "Why Serious Welfare Reform Must Include Serious Adoption Reform," *Heritage Foundation Reports*, July 27, 1995. See also Children's Bureau, Administration for Children and Families, U.S. Department of Health and Human Services, Child Welfare Information

Gateway Voluntary Relinquishment for Adoption Numbers and Trends, 2005. Available at: http://www.childwelfare.gov/pubs/s_place.cfm ("Less than 1 percent of children born to never-married women were placed for adoption from 1989 to 1995").

54   Children's Bureau, Administration for Children and Families, U.S. Department of Health and Human Services, Child Welfare Information Gateway Voluntary Relinquishment for Adoption Numbers and Trends, 2005. Available at: http://www.childwelfare.gov/pubs/s_place.cfm.

55   A service of the Children's Bureau, Administration for Children and Families, U.S. Department of Health and Human Services, Child Welfare Information Gateway Voluntary Relinquishment for Adoption Numbers and Trends, 2005. Available at: http://www.childwelfare.gov/pubs/s_place.cfm.

56   Cheryl Wetzstein, "Verdict on Teens Adopted at Birth: The Kids Are Alright," *Insight on the News*, August 8, 1994.

57   Tamar Lewin, "Adopted Youths Are Normal in Self-Esteem, Study Finds," *New York Times*, June 23, 1994.

58   Ibid.

59   Rebbetzin Faige, "New Study Identifies Strengths of Adoptive Famlies," Foundation for Large Families (Study by Peter L. Benson, Anu R. Sharma, and Eugene C. Roehlkepartain). Available at: http://www.foundationforlargefamilies.com/strengthstudy.html.

60   Lewin, "Adopted Youths Are Normal in Self-Esteem."

61   Jeff Katz, "Finally the Law Puts These Kids' Interests First," *Milwaukee Journal Sentinel*, December 28, 1997.

62   See, e.g., Stephanie Cox Wright, "All of God's Children Are Wonderful Creations, Neither Unwanted nor Disposable," *Asheville Citizen-Times*, October 1, 2004.

63   Andrew Hacker, "'In Trouble' in Black and White," *New York Times*, March 29, 1992 (reviewing Rickie Solinger, *Wake Up Little Susie: Single Pregnancy and Race Before Roe v. Wade* [1992]).

64   Bernard Weinraub, "The Talk of Hollywood: After Months of Political Attack, the 'Cultural Elite' Fires Back," *New York Times*, September 1, 1992.

65   Editorial: "Dan Quayle's Fictitious World."

66   Henry David Rosso, "Angry Exchange over Family Values Between Jackson and Robertson," United Press International, June 11, 1992.

67   Text of speech delivered at the Democratic National Convention by Jesse Jackson, *Associated Press*, July 14, 1992.

68   David Reinhard, "No Room at Democratic Inn for Unborn," *The Oregonian* (Portland), July 21, 1992.

69   Editorial: "The Democrats' Conscience," *Boston Globe*, July 16, 1992.

70   Bryant Gumbel, interview with Hadassah Lieberman, *The Early Show*, CBS, August 16, 2000.

71   Bryant Gumbel, interview with Whoopi Goldberg, *The Early Show*, CBS, August 17, 2000.

72   L. Brent Bozell III, "Nobody Runs Against Hollywood," Creators Syndicate, November 2, 2006.

73   Patty Onderko, "Married vs. Single Moms: Who's Got the Better Deal?," *Babytalk,* September 2007.

74   President Bush Delivers Commencement Address at Miami Dade College, Miami Dade College—Kendall Campus, Miami, Florida, Office of the White House Press Secretary, April 28, 2007.

75   Timothy Malcolm, "Sen. Kerry Draws 5,000 at Boston Rally," *Daily Free Press,* September 4, 2003.

76   Dick Feagler, "Political Embarrassment Comes from Ignoring Reality," *Plain Dealer* (Cleveland), August 19, 1994.

77   Bill Walsh and Joe Darby, "Mom Arrested After Clinton Visit," *Times-Picayune* (New Orleans), August 17, 1994.

78   Editorial: "Crime Bill Tragedies—and Follies . . . ," *Washington Times,* August 18, 1994.

79   Renaldo Smith, " 'Phenomenal' Tribute Paid to Mothers," *Miami Herald,* April 10, 2008.

80   David D. Kirkpatrick, "Bush Allies Till Fertile Soil, Among Baptists," *New York Times,* June 18, 2004.

81   Terry Gross, "David Cay Johnston of the *New York Times* Discusses Taxes," *Fresh Air,* NPR, January 7, 2004.

82   Cheryl Meyer, Michelle Oberman, Kelly White, and Michelle Rone, *Mothers Who Kill Their Children: Understanding the Acts of Moms from Susan Smith to the "Prom Mom"* (New York: NYU Press, 2001), p. 106.

83   *Palm Beach Post* (Florida), January 19, 2001; Anna Maria Della Costa, "Death Penalty Sought for Mother, Boyfriend," *Jupiter Courier* (Jupiter, FL), December 24, 2000.

84   Kevin McDermott, "Outrage, Relief After Verdict in Drowning of 3 Guilty? Yes. Murder? No.," *St. Louis Post-Dispatch* (Missouri), December 13, 2006.

85   Gabriel Margasak, "Mother Says 'Spirit' Tricked Her to Kill Baby," *Stuart News/Port St. Lucie News* (Stuart, FL), September 16, 2001; Pat Moore, "Judge: Mom Who Killed Son Was Insane, Found Not Guilty," *Palm Beach Post* (Florida), February 6, 2003.

86   "Colorado Woman Gets 32 Years in Fire Deaths of Children," Associated Press, January 14, 1999; Mike Patty, "Mom Pleads Guilty in Kids' Deaths," *Rocky Mountain News* (Denver, CO), December 3, 1998.

87   "Mother Convicted in Deaths of Two Toddlers Denied Parole," Associated Press, October 22, 1999; "Jail for Mother Who Let Sons Die in Car," *Advertiser,* November 11, 1995.

88   Wendy Hollway, *Mothering and Ambivalence* (Routledge, 1997), p. 115.

89   Barbara Barnett, *Medea in the Media: Narrative and Myth in Newspaper Coverage of Women Who Kill Their Children* (SAGE Publications, 2006).

90 CP-SouthamStar, "Autistic Son Dies, Mother Charged," *Toronto Star*, November 8, 1996.

91 "Waiting for What?," *In These Times*, July 2006.

92 "NWSA Looks at Resistance to Empire," *Off Our Backs*, April 2006.

93 Amy Harmon, "First Comes the Baby Carriage," *New York Times*, October 13, 2005.

94 Patty Onderko, "Married vs. Single Moms: Who's Got the Better Deal?," *Babytalk*, September 2007.

95 Harmon, "First Comes the Baby Carriage."

96 Ibid.

97 Ibid.

98 Ibid.

99 Lisa Rosen, "Dating in a Family Way," *Los Angeles Times*, May 7, 2002.

100 Ibid.

101 "And Baby Makes Two," *Marie Claire*, March 1, 2008.

102 Hacker, "'In Trouble' in Black and White."

103 Harmon, "First Comes the Baby Carriage."

104 Ibid.

105 U.S. Census, Table FM-2. All Parent/Child Situations, by Type, Race, and Hispanic Origin of Householder or Reference Person: 1970 to Present (2003). Available at: http://www.census.gov/population/socdemo/hh-fam/tabFM-2.pdf.

106 Bonnie Angelo, "The Pain of Being Black: Interview with Toni Morrison," *Time*, May 22, 1989. Available at: http://www.time.com/time/community/pulitzer interview.html.

107 Peter Schweizer, *Makers and Takers* (New York: Doubleday, 2008), p. 37. Steinem fish quote in feminist anthologies everywhere.

108 Barbara Ehrenreich, "Oh, Those Family Values," *Time*, July 18, 1994.

109 Ibid.

110 Ibid.

111 Ibid.

112 Department of Justice, Bureau of Justice Statistics, *Intimate Partner Violence in the U.S.*, Victims, Nonfatal Intimate Partner Victimization Rate Per 1,000 Females by Marital Status, 1993–2005.

113 Ehrenreich, "Oh, Those Family Values."

114 Department of Justice, Bureau of Justice Statistics, *Intimate Partner Violence in the U.S.*

115 Ehrenreich, "Oh, Those Family Values."

116 Barbara Ehrenreich, "In Defense of Splitting Up," *Time*, April 8, 1996.

117 Irving Kristol, *Neoconservatism: The Autobiography of an Idea* (New York: Free Press 1995).

118 Maggie Gallagher, "No Stigmas for People Like Us," *Newsday* (New York), June 7, 1994.

119 G. K. Chesterton, "A Defense of Humilities," *The Defendant*, 1901.

120 Kristol, *Neoconservatism*.

121 Fred Siegel, *The Future Once Happened Here* (New York: Encounter Books, 1997).

122 Felicity Barringer, "Hillary Clinton: From Lawyer to Mother; Now, Both of the Above," *New York Times*, October 30, 1992.

123 Susan Chira, "Conversations/Patrick T. Murphy: A Defender of Chicago's Children Refuses to Be Polite About Abuse," *New York Times*, January 30, 1994.

124 Cynthia Tucker, "Solomon and Modern Adoption," *San Francisco Chronicle*, May 15, 1995.

125 Michael Sneed, "Boy's Parents Bring More Discomfort," *Omaha World Herald*, August 6, 1997.

126 *Moriarty v. Greene*, Nos. 1-99-0277 and 1-99-0409, Consolidated, 1st District, June 28, 2000.

127 G. K. Chesterton, *Daily News*, July 29, 1905.

128 Stephanie Coontz, "Illegitimate Complaints," *New York Times*, February 18, 2007 (discussing the sordid business of three "unsavory men who partied with her mother" fighting over the right to custody of Anna Nicole Smith's daughter).

129 Out-of-wedlock births "decline as women's IQ increases." See Robert Gordon, "Everyday Life as an Intelligence Test," *Intelligence*, January 1, 1997 (citing Herrnstein and Murray, *The Bell Curve* [1994], p. 183).

130 Harmon, "First Comes the Baby Carriage."

131 Sarah Ebner, "Lone Stars," *The Guardian* (London), February 22, 2001.

132 Ruthe Stein, "Mommies Dearest: Mothers Raising Daughters Alone Is a Popular Theme in Hollywood," *San Francisco Chronicle*, November 7, 1999.

133 Onderko, "Married vs. Single Moms."

134 Ibid.

135 Susan S. Lang, "Unwed Mothers' Prospects for Marrying Well, or At All, Are Greatly Diminished, Cornell Study Finds," *Cornell University News Service*, September 26, 2005.

136 Nancy Jo Sales, "Sex and the Single Mom," *Vanity Fair*, June 2005.

137 "Sex and the Single Mom," *People*, March 22, 2004.

138 Michelle Tauber, Alison Singh Gee, and Kwala Mandel in Los Angeles and Jennifer Longley, "New Meg: Not So Nice," *People*, November 3, 2003.

CHAPTER 3 RAGE AGAINST OUR MACHINE

1 Laurie Goodstein, "Serenity Prayer Stirs Up Doubt: Who Wrote It?," *New York Times*, July 11, 2008 (quoting Niebuhr biographer Charles C. Brown on recently discovered evidence that Niebuhr did not write the Serenity Prayer: "It is now well established beyond the shadow of any doubt among knowledgeable and fair-minded people," Mr. Brown said, "that Niebuhr did compose it, probably in 1941 or '43.").

2   Patrick Condon, "Republican Blogger Has Al Franken's Senate Campaign Reeling," Associated Press, May 2, 2008.

3   Bill Kownacki, "A Challenge for Republicans," *The Oregonian* (Portland), May 22, 2008.

4   Lateline ABC Transcripts (Australia), February 5, 2008.

5   *American Morning*, CNN, April 17, 2008.

6   "Democratic Debate Wrap-Up," *Larry King Live*, CNN, April 16, 2008.

7   "Blogometer; At What Cost?," *The Hotline,* April 2, 2008.

8   Patrick Healy, "Clinton Treats Obama Pastor with Extreme Caution," *New York Times*, March 21, 2008.

9   Anthony Lewis, "Playing with the Court," *New York Times*, November 8, 1987.

10   Lauren Collins, "The Other Obama," *The New Yorker*, March 10, 2008.

11   Editorial: "Pot, and Public Pieties," *New York Times*, November 11, 1987.

12   Richard D. Friedman, "Sorry, Judge, Maybe in 20 Years or So," *Washington Post*, November 10, 1987.

13   Gerry Braun, "Real Doctors—Not Spin Doctors—Heal Demo Wounds," *San Diego Union-Tribune*, July 16, 1992.

14   *Live with Dan Abrams*, MSNBC, February 27, 2008.

15   Anderson Cooper, *360 Degrees*, CNN, January 4, 2008.

16   Tim Reid, "Insults Hit a New Low as Rivals Face Crucial Showdown," *Times* (London), April 22, 2008.

17   "Voices as Diverse as Their Backgrounds," *Washington Post*, February 10, 2008.

18   Maureen Dowd, "Brush It Off," *New York Times*, April 20, 2008.

19   Maureen Dowd, "Inside the Times," *New York Times*, April 20, 2008.

20   Charles Bakst, "Clinton in Battle for R.I. Voters," *Providence Journal*, February 24, 2008 (quoting Obama supporter Senator Sheldon Whitehouse of Rhode Island).

21   *60 Minutes*, CBS News, February 10, 2008.

22   Rick Pearson and Mike Dorning, "Clinton Blasts Obama's Tactics," *Chicago Tribune*, February 24, 2008.

23   Keith Olbermann, *Countdown*, MSNBC, May 1, 2008.

24   *Late Edition with Wolf Blitzer*, CNN, September 5, 1999.

25   Interview with former president Bill Clinton, *Today*, NBC, September 21, 2006.

26   Jonathan Chait, "Is the Right Right on the Clintons?," *Los Angeles Times*, January 26, 2008.

27   Todd Purdum, "The Comeback Id," *Vanity Fair*, July 2008.

28   *Today*, NBC, December 14, 2007.

29   Interview with presidential candidates, *Late Edition with Wolf Blitzer*, CNN, January 13, 2008. (John McCain does not seem to have been on *Late Edition with Wolf Blitzer*—at least not during the Republican primary.)

30   Ibid.

31   Ibid.

32   Interview with presidential candidates, *Late Edition with Wolf Blitzer*, CNN, May 18, 2008.

33 Interview with presidential candidates, *Late Edition with Wolf Blitzer*, CNN, May 11, 2008.

34 Michael Saul, "Bam Tries Blue Collar On for Size," *Daily News* (New York), May 18, 2008.

35 Obama's Controversial Comments and Impact on the Election," *Charlie Rose Show*, April 14, 2008.

36 H.R. 4892 [106th Congress], Scouting for All Act. Available at: http://www.govtrack.us/congress/vote.xpd?vote=h2000-468.

37 Brian Ross and Rehab El-Buri, "Obama's Pastor: God Damn American, U.S. to Blame for 9/11," ABC News, March 13, 2008. Available at: http://abcnews.go.com/Blotter/Story?id=4443788.

38 Barack Obama, "On My Faith and My Church," *The Huffington Post*, August 16, 2008.

39 Patrick Healy, "Clinton Clearly Outduels Obama," *New York Times*, April 23, 2008.

40 *Countdown*, MSNBC, April 23, 2008.

41 Editorial: "Guns and Bitter," *New York Times*, April 16, 2008.

42 *American Morning*, CNN, March 21, 2008; "McCain Suspends Aide in Video Flap," *Newsday* (New York), March 21, 2008.

43 Frank Rich, "Shoddy! Tawdry! A Televised Train Wreck!," *New York Times*, April 20, 2008.

44 Jennifer Vanasco, "Author, Former Offender Among Speakers," *University of Chicago Chronicle*, November 6, 1997.

45 Catrin Einhorn and Susan Sauln, "Ex–Obama Fund-Raiser Is Convicted of Fraud," *New York Times*, June 5, 2008.

46 Transcript: "Obama's Remarks on Wright," *New York Times*, April 29, 2008.

47 Democratic Presidential Candidates Debate, Moderated by Charlie Gibson and George Stephanopoulos, Federal News Service, April 16, 2008.

48 Dinitia Smith, "No Regrets for a Love of Explosives," *New York Times*, September 11, 2001.

49 Hope Reeves, "The Way We Live Now: 9-16-01: Questions for Bill Ayers," *New York Times*, September 16, 2001.

50 Peter Wallsten, "Allies of Palestinians See a Friend in Barack Obama," *Los Angeles Times*, April 10, 2008.

51 Andrew Sullivan, "Goodbye to All That: Why Obama Matters," *The Atlantic Monthly*, December 2007. Available at: http://www.theatlantic.com/doc/200712/obama. (Italics added by author for emphasis.)

52 Katharine Q. Seelye and Julie Bosman, "Ferraro's Obama Remarks Become Talk of Campaign," *New York Times*, March 12, 2008.

53 Ibid.

54 Robin Abcarian, "Ferraro Quits Clinton Campaign After Obama Remarks," *Los Angeles Times*, March 13, 2008.

55 Michael Luo, "Ready to Attack Obama, if Some Money Arrives," *New York Times*, June 21, 2008.

56 *Hardball*, MSNBC, June 12, 2008.

57 Ibid.

58 Robin Roberts and Chris Cuomo, "The Bottom Line: Fair or Unfair Tactics?" *Good Morning America*, June 13, 2008.

59 "History of Negative Political Advertising," *Weekend Edition*, NPR, October 31, 2004.

60 Ibid.

61 Roberts and Cuomo, "The Bottom Line."

62 Ibid.

63 Joshua Muravchik, "Kerry's Cambodia Whopper," *Washington Post*, August 24, 2004.

64 See, e.g., Zev Chafets, "Tough Audience: If Kerry Can't Win Over Vets, He's in Big Trouble," *Daily News* (New York), September 1, 2004; Michael Barone, "Democrats Take It on the Chin—as Do Their Barkers in the Old Media," *The American Spectator*, December 1, 2004.

65 Michael Dobbs, "After Decades, Renewed War on Old Conflict," *Washington Post*, August 28, 2004.

66 Laura Blumenfeld, "Hunter, Dreamer, Realist: Complexity Infuses Senator's Ambition," *Washington Post*, June 1, 2003.

67 Editorial: "Politics as Usual," *New York Times*, August 19, 2004.

68 Michael Getler, "Swift Boat Shootout," *Washington Post*, August 29, 2004.

69 Jessica Vascellaro, "Kerry's Medals Were Deserved, Says Widow of Slain Comrade," *Boston Globe*, August 27, 2004.

70 Media Matters for America, "The Lies of John O'Neill: An MMFA Analysis; Swift Boat Vets' Founder Has Told Repeated Untruths About Himself, Swift Boat Vets, *Unfit for Command*," August 24, 2004. Available at: http://media matters.org/items/200408250002.

71 Tahman Bradley, "Bush Swift Boats Belgium, Congress," ABC News, April 4, 2007.

72 Sam Wang and Sandra Aamodt, "Your Brain Lies to You," *New York Times*, June 27, 2008.

73 Jim Rutenberg and Julie Bosman, "Book Attacking Obama Hopes to Repeat '04 Anti-Kerry Feat," *New York Times*, August 13, 2008.

74 Ibid.

75 *Hardball*, MSNBC, August 19, 2004.

76 Thomas Lipscomb, "Did Kerry Write Own Report of Disputed Vietnam River Clash?," *Chicago Sun-Times*, October 1, 2004.

It was written by someone designated "TE 194.5.4.4/1."

An operations order by Admiral Hoffman two months earlier set the format for the designation. The operations order procedures, originated by the operational commander of the Coastal 11 An Thoi unit Kerry served with, Cmdr. Adrian Lonsdale, was the basis for the terms of designation used in this kind of report subsequently. Upon seeing the report, Lonsdale, a Swift Boat Veterans for Truth member, recognized it and recalled the procedures it required as being followed in his command.

· "TE" refers to a "task element," which is defined by the numbers to the right, which show the command structure over the task element in action. "194" is Adm. Elmo Zumwalt, commander of U.S. naval forces in Vietnam; "5" is Hoffman's swift boat command; "4" is Lonsdale's command and the last "4" is Capt. George Elliott's swift boat base at An Thoi, where the boats on this mission were based. The last "1" indicates someone other than the commander of the mission. If the report had been submitted by the mission commander, in this case Thurlow, according to the operations order, it would have begun with a "C" for commander of the Task Element, and the sender would have been "CTE 194.5.4.4."

According to a Navy communications expert, Chief Petty Officer Troy Jenkins, who has examined the message traffic, the report in question was sent from the U.S. Coast Guard Cutter *Spencer*, Lonsdale's command ship, at 11:20 that night.

Only three of the officers on the mission that day were on the *Spencer*, John Kerry, Dick Pease, and Donald Droz. Droz took the wounded from the mine explosion to be examined and treated at the *Spencer*, including the third officer, the severely wounded Dick Pease. Since the *Spencer* had no helipad for the evacuation of the wounded, Droz then had to return to the USS *Washtenaw County*, stationed about 25 nautical miles away, leaving only Kerry aboard the *Spencer* at the time the message was sent at 11:20 P.M.

Could Droz have somehow written the report? Lonsdale says command precedence of days in swift boat service alone rules this out. "According to the command procedure I set down, Kerry would have been the only logical candidate. Kerry had been in Vietnam since November. Droz just arrived at An Thoi in February." Thurlow adds, "I never liked the paperwork anyway. I was happy to have Kerry write them up."

77   David Warsh, "Behind the Hootch," *Boston Globe,* October 27, 1996.
78   Ibid.
79   John O'Neill, *Unfit for Command* (Washington: Regnery, 2004), p. 81.
80   Ibid., p. 81.
81   Jim Rutenberg, "A Billionaire Finances Ads Hitting Obama," *New York Times,* August 23, 2008.
82   Patrick Healy, "Let's Call a Lie a Lie . . . Finally," *New York Times,* September 21, 2008.
83   Maureen Dowd, "Mud Pies for 'That One,'" *New York Times,* October 8, 2008.

CHAPTER 4 WITLESS WITNESSES TO HISTORY

1   From the French, "Cet animal est tres mechant: quand on l'attaque, il se defend."

2   Kathleen Parker, "Palin Should Step Aside," *Virginian-Pilot* (Norfolk, VA), September 29, 2008.

3   Judy Mann, "A Report on the GOP's War Against Women," *Washington Post*, January 17, 1996.

4   Dick Polman, "Women Find Fault with GOP and Opt to Sit Out Primaries," *Philadelphia Inquirer*, March 15, 1996.

5   John Nichols, "Do Republicans Hate the Women of America?" *Capital Times* (Madison, WI), January 12, 1996.

6   Frank Rich, "Angry White Woman," *New York Times*, January 3, 1996.

7   See, e.g., Jules Witcover, "Unshining Moments," *Columbia Journalism Review*, January 1998 / February 1998 (reviewing Seymour M. Hersh, *The Dark Side of Camelot*).

8   Nathan Thrall and Jesse James Wilkins, "Kennedy Talked, Khrushchev Triumphed," *New York Times*, May 22, 2008.

9   Ibid.

10 Mary Ann Giordano, "A J.F.K. Comparison for Obama That Is Not a Compliment," *New York Times*, December 6, 2007 (citing Elie Abel, *The Missiles of October*).

11 See, e.g., Jules Witcover, "Unshining Moments."

12 Louis Liebovich, *The Press and the Modern Presidency: Myths and Mindsets from Kennedy to Election 2000* (2001) at 23.

13 John F. Stacks, *Scotty: James B. Reston and the Rise and Fall of American Journalism* (Little, Brown & Co. 2002) at 282.

14 Richard Reeves, "A Man of Charm, Cruelty," *Orlando Sentinel* (Florida).

15 Humberto Fontova, "The Real Story of JFK and the Cuban Missile Crisis," *NewsMax*, July 21, 2005. Available at: http://archive.newsmax.com/archives/articles/2005/7/20/171552.shtml.

16 Editorial: "The J.F.K. File," *New York Times*, November 19, 2002.

17 See, e.g., Paul Johnson, *Modern Times* (1983) at 650–651.

18 See, e.g., William Safire, *Before the Fall* (1975) at 354; Louis Liebovich, *The Press and the Modern Presidency: Myths and Mindsets from Kennedy to Election 2000* (2001) at 23.

19 Andrew Ferguson, *Fools Names, Fools Faces* (*Atlantic Monthly Press*, 1996) at 74–75.

20 Richard E. Meyer, Associated Press, January 26, 1977 ("Bill D. Moyers, a former top aide to President Johnson, is a front-runner to be named CIA director, informed sources said Wednesday").

21 *Tim Russert Show*, "Bob Woodward and Carl Bernstein, Watergate Reporters, Discuss Watergate and Richard Nixon's Resignation 25 Years Ago," CNBC, August 7, 1999.

22 William Safire, *Before the Fall* (1975) at 364.

23 CBS News, GOP Convention coverage, August 1988 (cited in Media Research Center's 1988 "Notable Quotables." Available at: http://www.mediaresearch.org/notablequotables/bestof/1988/best1-3.asp).

24 Exchange on *Face the Nation*, May 15, 1988 (cited in Media Research Center's 1988 "Notable Quotables." Available at: http://www.mediaresearch.org/notablequotables/bestof/1988/best1-3.asp).

25 Connie Chung, *NBC Nightly News*, April 1, 1988 (cited in Media Research Center's 1988 "Notable Quotables. Available at: http://www.mediaresearch.org/notablequotables/bestof/1988/best1-3.asp).

26 Andrew Cohen, "The Savaging of Seymour," *Globe and Mail* (Canada), January 10, 1998.

27 Richard Reeves, "A Man of Charm, Cruelty," *Orlando Sentinel* (Florida).

28 Daniel S. Greenberg, "Oval Office Astrology Isn't Funny," *Chicago Tribune*, May 14, 1988.

29 Ann McFeatters (Scripps Howard News Service), "Clinton Era Fosters Kiss-and-Tell Trend," *Patriot Ledger* (Quincy, MA), March 16, 1999.

30 David Johnston, "Speakes Says He Told Reagan of Bogus Quotes, but Later," *New York Times*, April 19, 1988.

31 Michael Oreskes, "The New York Times/CBS News Poll: Grudging Public Thinks Tax Rise Now Must Come," *New York Times*, May 27, 1990.

32 Editorial: "If They're Serious About the Deficit," *New York Times*, May 15, 1990.

33 Gary Aldrich, *Unlimited Access: An FBI Agent Inside the Clinton White House* (Washington: Regnery, 1996), p. 205.

34 Dick Morris, *Behind the Oval Office: Winning the Presidency in the Nineties* (New York: Random House, 1997).

35 Helen Thomas, "Backstairs at the White House," United Press International, January 15, 1997.

36 George Stephanopoulos, *All Too Human: A Political Education* (Little, Brown and Company, 1999).

37 "Clinton Scandals Update," *Bulletin's Frontrunner*, March 10, 1999.

38 Jeff Baker, "Boy George," *Sunday Oregonian* (Portland), March 21, 1999.

39 Alison Mitchell, "Impeachment: The Overview," *New York Times*, December 20, 1998.

> A few hours after the vote, Mr. Clinton, surrounded by Democrats, walked onto the South Lawn of the White House, his wife, Hillary, on his arm, to pre-empt calls for his resignation. The man who in better days had debated where he would stand in the pantheon of American Presidents said he would stay in office and vowed "to go on from here to rise above the rancor, to overcome the pain and division, to be a repairer of the breach." *Later, Mr. Clinton called off the bombing in Iraq, declaring the mission accomplished.*

40 Clinton scandals update.

41 Stephanopoulos, *All Too Human*, Epilogue.

42   *Hardball*, MSNBC, October 17, 2006.

43   *The Situation Room*, CNN, October 16, 2006.

44   Debra J. Saunders, "Slam Dunk, The Book," *San Francisco Chronicle*, May 8, 2007.

CHAPTER 5 THEY GOT THE SEX, WE GOT THE SCANDAL

1   Kimberly Kindy and Joe Stephens, "Biden's Son, Brother Named in Two Suits," *Washington Post*, August 24, 2008.

2   Chris Matthews, *Hardball*, MSNBC, September 10, 2008.

3   Anderson Cooper, "Should Candidates' Spouses Be Fair Game?," CNN, May 19, 2008.

4   Foon Rhee, "Poll on Presidential Spouses Finds an Edge for Obama," *Boston Globe*, June 19, 2008 (quoting Obama interview with the Christian Broadcasting Network). Available at: http://www.boston.com/news/nation/articles/2008/06/19/poll_on_presidential_spouses_finds_an_edge_for_obama/.

5   Cooper, "Should Candidates' Spouses Be Fair Game?"

6   Ibid.

7   Michael Cass, "Republican Leaders Criticize Video," *The Tennessean* (Nashville), May 21, 2008.

8   Maria Gavrilovic, "Obama: 'People's Families Are Off Limits,'" CBS News, September 1, 2008. Available at: http://www.cbsnews.com/blogs/2008/09/01/politics/fromtheroad/entry4404967.shtml.

9   Ben Wallace-Wells, "Obama's Narrator," *New York Times*, April 1, 2007.

10   Rick Pearson, "Divorce Turns into Albatross of Senate Race; National Issues Take Back Seat," *Chicago Tribune*, March 5, 2004.

11   More viciousness available here: http://www.democraticunderground.com/discuss/duboard.php?az=view_all&address=150x491.

12   Scott Fornek, "Obama: Back Off Divorce Files," *Chicago Sun-Times*, April 3, 2004.

13   Editorial: "Why the Tribune Went to Court," *Chicago Tribune*, June 25, 2004.

14   Michael Martinez and Rick Pearson, "Court Sets Release of Ryan's Divorce File; Judge Admits Son Will Be Harmed," *Chicago Tribune*, June 18, 2004.

15   *In re Marriage of Ryan*, Declaration of Jeri Ryan, June 9, 2000, p. 22.

16   Barbara Brotman, "The Other Woman Has Great Parts, and a Great Part," *Chicago Tribune*, December 14, 1997.

17   Judy Hevrdejs and Mike Conklin, "Congressman Crane Faces Hearing on Petition Challenges," *Chicago Tribune*, December 24, 1997.

18   Girls of FHM: Jeri Ryan, FHM, December 2006. Available at: http://www.fhmonline.com/site/girls/covergirls/article.aspx?picture=1&girlid=34222.

19   See, e.g., Kate Zernike, "Divorced Dads Emerge as a Political Force," *Boston Globe*, May 19, 1998.

20 Raymond Smith, "Family Justice; Perry Mason? Matlock? Not Here, a Place Where Discovering the Truth and Punishing the Guilty Are Not the Highest Priorities," *Press Enterprise* (Riverside, CA), June 18, 1995.

21 Susan Chandler, Robert Becker, and James Janega, "Divorce Records Can Be a Minefield," *Chicago Tribune*, June 26, 2004.

22 Rick Egusquiza, "Sarah Palin's Dark Secrets," *National Enquirer*, September 15, 2008.

23 "Exclusive: Woman Denies Sarah Palin Had Affair with Her Husband," *Us Weekly*, September 5, 2008.

24 Michael M. Phillips, "In Palin's Past, the Personal Got Political," *Wall Street Journal*, September 9, 2008.

25 Jo Becker, Peter S. Goodman, and Michael Powell, "Once Elected, Palin Hired Friends and Lashed Foes," *New York Times*, September 14, 2008.

26 "New Palin Scandal—Charges of Extramarital Affair," Pam's House Blend, September 5, 2008; Alex Koppelman, "More Dirt on Palin on the Way?," *Salon*, September 5, 2008; "Sexy Palin Ethics Investigation Update," *Gawker*, September 5, 2008.

27 Koppelman, "More Dirt on Palin on the Way?"

28 Amanda M. Fairbanks, "Inviting Bloggers into the Tent," *New York Times*, August 24, 2008.

29 Nancy Dillon, "Reports That Track Palin Vandalized School Buses Aren't True, Says Pal," *Daily News* (New York), September 10, 2008. (A "key culprit" said, "Track wasn't with me. Track had nothing to do with it.")

30 Ben Smith, "The Clintonite Who Owns National Enquirer," *Politico*, October 11, 2007.

31 Dan Payne, "Briefing Paper, Wallpaper, Sealed Papers," *Boston Globe*, April 10, 2004.

32 Randy Ludlow, "State Employee Says She Was Ordered to Check Out Joe the Plumber," *Columbus Dispatch*, October 31, 2008.

33 *The O'Reilly Factor*, "Dan Rather Discusses 'The American Dream,'" Fox News Network, September 7, 2001.

34 Glen Johnson, "As Ted Kennedy Seeks Re-election, Joan Tries to Reopen Divorce Settlement," Associated Press, September 30, 1994.

35 John Ellement, "Joan Kennedy Wants Case Heard in Boston," *Boston Globe*, September 20, 1994.

36 Scot Lehigh, "Kennedy, Romney Deadlocked in Poll," *Boston Globe*, September 17, 1994.

37 Ben Bradlee Jr. and Daniel Golden, "Inside the Kennedy-Romney Race," *Boston Globe*, November 10, 1994.

38 Frank Phillips, "Romney Firm Tied to Labor Fight; Jobs, Benefits Slashed at Ind. Paper Plant," *Boston Globe*, September 23, 1994.

39 Sarah Baxter, "Sleaze Scuppers Democrat Golden Boy," Sunday *Times* (London), July 27, 2008.

40   Howard Kurtz, "Bush Angrily Denounces Report of Extramarital Affair as 'a Lie,'" *Washington Post*, August 12, 1992.

41   "Tabloid Journalism: How Print Handled the Story," *Hotline*, August 12, 1992 (quoting John Harwood in the August 12 *Wall Street Journal*).

42   See generally "Tabloid Journalism: How Print Handled the Story"; see also "The 1992 Campaign; Bush Angrily Denies a Report of an Affair," *New York Times*, August 12, 1992.

43   Editorial: "The Sleaze Factor," *New York Times*, August 5, 1992.

44   See generally "Tabloid Journalism: How Print Handled the Story"; see also "The 1992 Campaign; Bush Angrily Denies a Report of an Affair."

45   "Tabloid Journalism: How Print Handled the Story."

46   Scot Lehigh and Michael Kranish, "Angry Bush Calls Affair Story 'a Lie,' " *Boston Globe*, August 12, 1992.

47   Joe Conason, "Reason No. 1 Not to Vote for George Bush: He Cheats on His Wife," *Spy*, July/August 1992.

48   Kurt Andersen, "Falling Out of Love with Bill," *New York*, April 4, 2008.

49   Transcript Part III: "Cheney, Edwards Discuss Qualities of a VP," CNN.com, October 7, 2004. Available at: http://www.cnn.com/2004/ALLPOLITICS/10/05/debate.transcript3/index.html.

50   Wendy Doniger, "All Beliefs Welcome, Unless They Are Forced on Others," *Washington Post–Newsweek*, "On Faith," September 9, 2008. Available at: http://newsweek.washingtonpost.com/onfaith/wendy_doniger/2008/09/all_beliefs_welcome_unless_the.html.

51   The University of Chicago Divinity School, Meet the Faculty, Wendy Doniger. Available at: http://divinity.uchicago.edu/faculty/doniger.shtml.

52   Katha Pollitt, "Lipstick on a Wing Nut," *The Nation*, September 10, 2008. Available at: http://www.thenation.com/doc/20080929/pollitt.

53   "Corrections and Clarifications," *Chicago Tribune*, September 5, 1996.

54   Tim Craig and Michael D. Shear, "Allen Quip Provokes Outrage, Apology," *Washington Post*, August 15, 2006.

55   Editorial: "George Allen's America," *Washington Post*, August 15, 2006.

56   Matthew Continetti, "George Allen Monkeys Around," *The Weekly Standard*, October 2, 2006.

57   Craig and Shear, "Allen Quip Provokes Outrage, Apology."

58   Michael D. Shear, "Allen, Webb Face Scrutiny of the NAACP," *Washington Post*, October 21, 2006.

59   John M. Broder, "Hanging On to Biden's Every Word," *New York Times*, September 12, 2008.

60   See, e.g., Shankar Vedantam, "For Allen and Webb, Implicit Biases Would Be Better Confronted," *Washington Post*, October 9, 2006.

61   Allison Klein, "Webb Aide Tried to Take Gun Into Senate Building, Capitol Police Say," *Washington Post*, March 27, 2007.

62   See, e.g., Michael Barone, "Democrat Protectionism: It Won't Win Elections or Help the Economy," *Washington Post*, September 29, 1985; Clarence Page, "Obama Hurdle Called 'Bubba,'" *Chicago Tribune*, September 24, 2008; "Emerging Democratic Majority After 40 Years of Decline," *Denver Post*, August 24, 2008.

63   Flyer available here: http://sweetness-light.com/archive/how-webb-campaigns-against-fellow-dems.

64   Michael D. Shear, "Webb, Miller Spar on Spending," *Washington Post*, June 10, 2006.

   The other two mentions were here—Tim Craig and Michael D. Shear, "Allen Flap May Give a Boost to Webb," *Washington Post*, August 19, 2006:

   > Allen's campaign has responded to the incident by accusing Webb of tolerating anti-Semitism. During Webb's Democratic primary campaign against lobbyist Harris Miller, Webb's campaign distributed a flier in southwestern Virginia that included a caricature of Miller with wads of money coming out of his pocket. Miller, who is Jewish, decried the flier as anti-Semitic. Webb has said the flier was not intended to be offensive.

   And here—Michael D. Shear, "Allen Says He Embraces His Jewish Ancestry," *Washington Post*, September 20, 2006:

   > [Allen adviser] Wadhams also accused Webb's campaign of mailing an anti-Semitic flier to Virginia voters during the state's Democratic primary this year. That flier depicted Webb's Jewish opponent, Harris Miller, with money coming out of his pockets. "They have been continuing that anti-Semitic strategy through their paid bloggers," Wadhams said. Webb spokeswoman Kristian Denny Todd called that charge "completely false." She said the flier was not anti-Semitic.

65   Deborah Solomon, "The Contender: Questions for Jim Webb," *New York Times Magazine*, June 1, 2008.

66   Amanda B. Carpenter, "Washington Post Launches Campaign Against George Allen," *Human Events*, October 2, 2006.

67   Dana Milbank, "The Senator's Gentile Rebuke," *Washington Post*, September 19, 2006.

68   Associated Press, "Campaign Staffer in House Race Resigns After Allen E-mail," October 4, 2006.

69   James Wolcott, "Fire in the Beltway," *Vanity Fair*, December 2006.

70   Paul Krugman, "Two More Years," *New York Times*, December 4, 2006.

71   Frank Rich, "Has He Started Talking to the Walls?," *New York Times*, December 3, 2006.

72   See the video here: http://www.powerlineblog.com/archives2/2008/09/021475.php.

73 Ibid.

74 Terence Samuel, "Slaughter the Pig," *Slate*, September 10, 2008 (linking to TheRoot.com, as "also in *Slate*").

75 Obama on Letterman: "McCain Policy Is the Pig," CBS.com, September 11, 2008.

76 Frank Gabrenya, "It's Not Exactly Driver's Ed Fare," *Columbus Dispatch* (Ohio), March 20, 1997.

77 Alexander Marquardt and Chris Welch, CNN.com, April 22, 2008. Available at: http://politicalticker.blogs.cnn.com/2008/04/22/bill-clinton-obama-camp-played-the-race-card-on-me/.

78 Juan Cole, "What's the Difference Between Palin and Muslim Fundamentalists? Lipstick," *Salon*, Sept. 9, 2008.

79 Terence Samuel, "Slaughter the Pig," *Slate*, September 10, 2008.

80 E. J. Dionne Jr. ". . . He Didn't Get," *Washington Post*, November 5, 2004.

81 Amy Forliti, "Antiwar March Planned for Last Day of RNC," Associated Press Online, September 4, 2008.

82 David Freddoso, *The Case Against Barack Obama* (Washington: Regnery, 2008), p. 139. See also Sweetness & Light, "Code Pink's 'Sugar Mommy'— Jodie Evans." Available at: http://sweetness-light.com/archive/meet-code-pinks-sugar-mommy-jodie-evans.

83 Phil Davidson, "Hall in Thick of Melee at GOP Convention," *Idaho Falls Post Register*, September 5, 2008.

84 The final tally isn't in yet for the 2008 conventions, but the 2004 Republican Convention in New York cost $154 million. See Michael Slackman, "G.O.P. Convention Cost $154 Million," *New York Times*, October 14, 2004.

85 Davidson, "Hall in Thick of Melee at GOP Convention."

86 Guest host Rachel Maddow, *Countdown*, MSNBC, September 5, 2008.

87 Martin Kasindorf, "Rich, Famous Push for Secrecy in Divorce," *USA Today*, December 8, 2005.

CHAPTER 6 WHEN 95 PERCENT WORLD DOMINATION JUST ISN'T ENOUGH . . .

1 "Is CBS News Fair and Balanced?," *The O'Reilly Factor*, Fox News Network, January 25, 2000.

2 Editorial: "Looking Past Labor Day," *New York Times*, September 2, 2002.

3 N. R. Kleinfield, "As 9/11 Nears, a Debate Rises: How Much Tribute Is Enough?," *New York Times*, September 2, 2007.

4 Kausfiles, "When Laura Snarked Condi," January 8, 2007.

5 Frank Rich, "The Joy of Sex," *New York Times*, February 4, 1998.

6 Paul Krugman, "Sweet Little Lies," *New York Times*, April 9, 2007.

7 Ibid.

8 Susan Schmidt and Dan Morgan, "Starr: Witnessing for the Prosecution; Counsel Gets Forum to Defend Actions," *Washington Post*, November 19, 1998.

9 According to FBI crime statistics, each year there are about five violent crimes and 35 property crimes for every thousand inhabitants. (Available at: http://www.fbi.gov/ucr/cius_04/offenses_reported/property_crime/index.html.) Over eight years, that would amount to 320 violent and property crimes alone for every thousand Americans, not including white-collar crimes such as embezzlement, fraud, tax evasion, insider trading, and so on.

10 Paul Krugman, "The Waiting Game," *New York Times*, July 16, 2007.

11 Peter Schweizer, *Do as I Say (Not as I Do)* (New York: Doubleday, 2005), pp. 107–9.

12 Ibid., pp. 107–9.

13 Seymour M. Hersh, "Colson Pleads Guilty to Charge in Ellsberg Case and Is Expected to Aid Jaworski and Rodino Panel," *New York Times*, June 4, 1974. Available at: http://select.nytimes.com/gst/abstract.html?res=FB0A1EF83F5 B1A7493C6A9178DD85F408785F9&scp=8&sq=colson&st=p.

14 David Johnston, "White House Announces Leave for Official Who Collected Files," *New York Times*, June 18, 1996.

15 L. Brent Bozell III, "The Database Double Standard," *Human Events* Online, May 17, 2006.

16 See, e.g., Don Van Natta Jr., "Coffees at White House Were Called Fund-Raisers," *New York Times*, September 23, 2000; Editorial: "Return of the White House Turnstile," *New York Times*, September 1, 2000 ("Well after the 1996 fund-raising scandals brought charges that President Clinton had effectively 'sold' the Lincoln Bedroom for campaign contributions, big donors continued to gain easy access to the White House in return for their donations").

17 Deborah Orin, "Clinton-Gore Was Crass Act to the End," *New York Post*, January 25, 2001.

18 "President George W. Bush Holds Media Availability Following Meeting with Governors," FDCH Political Transcripts, January 26, 2001.

19 Christopher Marquis, "White House Vandalism Caper Was Overblown, a Report Finds," *New York Times*, May 19, 2001.

20 Ken Fireman, "Dems Revive Vandalism Story," *Newsday* (New York), June 3, 2001.

21 William Raspberry, "No Joking Matter," *Washington Post*, June 11, 2001.

22 Mark Shields, "Hoax Adds to Readers' Skepticism," *Seattle Post-Intelligencer*, June 4, 2001.

23 Henry J. Reske, "Confirmation Hearings, Round II: Senate and Opinion Polls Support Thomas After Harassment Charges Aired," *ABA Journal*, December 1991.

24 Bob Cohn, "Dirt Trail: The Ugly Journey to Truth," *Ottawa Citizen*, January 12, 1992.

25 "Buchanan: Speech Taps 'Heart and Soul' Conservatism," *The Hotline*, August 18, 1992.

26   Patrick J. Buchanan, "The Thankless Mr. Quayle," *San Jose Mercury News* (California), May 10, 1994.

27   See, e.g., Byron York, "The Democratic Myth Machine," *National Review*, April 19, 2004.

28   Tom Daschle, *Two Years That Changed America* (New York: Three Rivers Press, 2004), pp. 261–62.

29   Jonathan Alter, "Citizen Clinton Up Close," *Newsweek*, April 8, 2002.

30   Media Research Center, "Notable Quotables," January 24, 2000 (citing NBC's *McLaughlin Group*, December 25, 1999).

31   Paul Krugman, "Wag-the-Dog Protection," *New York Times*, February 22, 2005.

32   Frank Rich, "The Road to Perdition," *New York Times*, July 20, 2002.

33   Judy Woodruff, *Inside Politics*, CNN, July 16, 2002.

34   George Lardner Jr. reviewing Lois Romano, *The Life of George W. Bush, Washington Post*, July 30, 1999.

35   Lisa Falkenberg, "Halliburton Stock Falls Off amid SEC Investigation," Associated Press, May 30, 2002.

36   Loren Steffy, "Halliburton Wrist-Slapping Ties Loose End, Opens Doors," *Houston Chronicle*, August 6, 2004.

37   Siobhan Hughes, "Cheney Didn't Recall Halliburton Accounting in SEC Interview," Associated Press, October 3, 2007.

38   Paul Krugman, "The Falling Scales," *New York Times*, October 5, 2004.

39   Paul Krugman, "Conquest and Neglect," *New York Times*, April 11, 2003.

40   Paul Krugman, "Three-Card Maestro," *New York Times*, February 18, 2005.

41   Frank Rich, "The White House Stages Its 'Daily Show,'" *New York Times*, February 20, 2005.

42   Ibid.

43   Katharine Q. Seelye, "Democrats Want Investigation of Reporter Using Fake Name," *New York Times*, February 11, 2005.

44   David S. Cloud, "Memo May Aid Leak Probe," *Wall Street Journal*, October 17, 2003 (cited in JustOneMinute.com, "Now Why Did They Listen to the DailyKos?," February 11, 2005. Available at: http://justoneminute.typepad.com/main/2005/02/know_why_did_th.html).

45   Dareh Gregorian and Philip Messing, "Kinky News Network," *New York Post*, April 19, 2008.

46   "How Crazy Are They?," Powerline, February 1, 2005. Available at: http://www.powerlineblog.com/archives/009414.php.

47   Howard Kurtz, "Eason Jordan, Quote, Unquote," *Washington Post*, February 8, 2005.

48   Roderick Boyd, "A CNN Executive Says G.I.s in Iraq Target Journalists," *New York Sun*, February 8, 2005. Available at: http://www.nysun.com/national/cnn-executive-says-gis-in-iraq-target-journalists/8866/.

49   Howard Kurtz, "CNN's Jordan Resigns over Iraq Remarks," *Washington Post*, February 12, 2005.

50 Boyd, "A CNN Executive Says G.I.s in Iraq Target Journalists."

51 Kurtz, "CNN's Jordan Resigns over Iraq Remarks," *Washington Post*, February 12, 2005.

52 Boyd, "A CNN Executive Says G.I.s in Iraq Target Journalists."

53 Ibid.

54 Michelle Malkin, "Easongate: David Gergen Speaks," michellemalkin.com, February 7, 2005 (recounting phone interview with David Gergen).

55 Michelle Malkin, "Easongate: Chris Dodd Speaks," michellemalkin.com, February 7, 2005.

56 Kurtz, "CNN's Jordan Resigns over Iraq Remarks."

57 According to the Nexis archives, the only newspapers in the entire country to report on the Jordan controversy in their news pages during two weeks of shocking accusations, denials, and contradictions were the *Wall Street Journal*, the *Washington Times*, the *Washington Post*, the *New York Sun*, *The Hotline*, *The Frontrunner*, *Investor's Business Daily*, *The Hollywood Reporter*, and the *Atlanta Journal-Constitution*.

58 Rich, "The White House Stages Its 'Daily Show.'"

59 Paul Krugman, "Department of Injustice," *New York Times*, March 9, 2007.

60 Some political appointees are appointed to jobs from which the president can't fire them without cause, such as FTC commissioners, but U.S. attorneys do not have one of those jobs.

61 David Johnston, "Attorney General Seeks Resignations from Prosecutors," *New York Times*, March 24, 1993.

62 Editorial: "Janet Reno Starts Badly," *New York Times*, March 25, 1993.

63 Editorial: "Earth Day's Real Lessons," *Investor's Business Daily*, April 20, 2001; Ben Lieberman; Clinton's Legacy, *National Review*, July 26, 2001.

64 "Arsenic and Water Don't Mix," *San Francisco Chronicle*, August 27, 2001.

65 Editorial: "A Powerful Poison," *News and Observer* (Raleigh, NC), March 28, 2001; Editorial: "Serve Up a Tasty Glass of Arsenic," *Detroit Free Press*, April 1, 2001; Editorial: "Arsenic, Ozone and Lead Are Poison, Not Politics, *South Bend Tribune* (Indiana), May 14, 2001.

66 Noe Coopersmith, Letter to the Editor, *San Francisco Chronicle*, April 19, 2001.

67 James F. Gerrits, M.D., Letter to the Editor, *Times Herald* (Port Huron, MI), April 14, 2001.

68 "Clinton Book: Profile in Courage Under Ire?," *Los Angeles Times*, August 12, 2001.

69 Bob Herbert, "The Mask Comes Off," *New York Times*, March 26, 2001.

70 Paul Krugman, "The Class Warrior," *New York Times*, April 4, 2001.

71 Maureen Dowd, "De Minimis Maximus," *New York Times*, August 5, 2001.

72 Michael Kelly, "Playing the Arsenic Angle," *Washington Post*, August 22, 2001.

73 Katharine Q. Seelye, "E.P.A. to Adopt Clinton Arsenic Standard," *New York Times*, November 1, 2001.

74 Mike Flaherty, "UW AG Dean Challenges Critical Report," *Wisconsin State Journal* (Madison, WI), February 13, 1993.

75 Ron Fournier, "Clinton Rescinds, Reviews Last-Minute Bush Regulations," Associated Press, January 24, 1993.

76 No new rules were to be proposed after June 1, 2008, or final rules after November 1, with exceptions only in special cases. Charlie Savage and Robert Pear, "Administration Moves to Avert Late Rules Rush," *New York Times*, May 31, 2008.

77 Savage and Pear, "Administration Moves to Avert Late Rules Rush."

78 Robert Pear, "Lobby Presses Agenda Before '08 Vote," *New York Times*, December 2, 2007.

79 Michael Barone, "Thoughts in the Wee Hours of Election Night," *Jewish World Review*, November 9, 2006. Available at: http://www.jewishworldreview.com/michael/barone110906.php3.

80 Ibid.

81 Ibid.

82 Robert F. Kennedy Jr., "Was the 2004 Election Stolen?," *Rolling Stone*, June 1, 2006.

83 Tiffany Lu, "U. Penn Professor's Speech, Book Asks if 2004 Election Was Stolen," *Daily Pennsylvanian*, September 20, 2006.

84 Deborah Solomon, "Head of the Class: Questions for Charles Murray," *New York Times*, September 21, 2008.

85 Richard W. Stevenson and Janet Elder, "Poll Finds Concerns That Bush Is Overly Influenced by Business," *New York Times*, July 18, 2002.

86 ABC News Poll: "Terri Schiavo: Federal Intervention in Schiavo Case Prompts Broad Public Disapproval," March 20, 2005. Available at: http://abcnews.go.com/images/Politics/978a1Schiavo.pdf.

87 Marc Caputo, "'Intruders' Viewed Unfavorably," *Miami Herald*, April 14, 2005.

88 Shaila Dewan, "States Taking a New Look at End-of-Life Legislation," *New York Times*, March 31, 2005.

89 Michael Sokolove, "The Believer," *New York Times*, May 22, 2005.

90 Carl Hulse, "Filibuster Fight Is Bruising the Image of Capitol Hill," *New York Times*, May 22, 2005.

91 Ronald Brownstein, "The Death of Terri Schiavo," *Los Angeles Times*, April 1, 2005.

92 Abby Goodnough, "In War Debate, Parents of Fallen Are United Only in Grief," *New York Times*, August 28, 2005.

93 Dave Moniz, "Troops in Survey Back Bush 4-to-1 over Kerry," *USA Today*, October 3, 2004.

94 William Yardley, "Energized Black Voters Flock to Polls to Back Kerry," *New York Times*, November 3, 2004.

95 Sarah Baxter, "Ground Zero 'Guilt Museum' Stirs Fury," *Sunday Times* (U.K.), June 12, 2005. Available at: http://www.timesonline.co.uk/tol/news/world/article532409.ece.

96 David W. Dunlap, "Lofty Ideals of Freedom Meet," *New York Times*, September 25, 2005 (italics added).

97 See the Flat Earth Society, available at: www.alaska.net/~clund/e_djublonskopf/Flatearthsociety.htm.

98 John Leland, "Under Din of Abortion Debate, an Experience Shared Quietly," *New York Times*, September 18, 2005.

99 Richard W. Stevenson, "Bush Campaign Plays Up Pro-Israel Stance," *New York Times*, May 15, 2004.

100 Solomon Moore, "States Restore Voting Rights for Ex-Convicts," *New York Times*, September 14, 2008 ("Surveys have shown that about 70 percent of former convicts lean Democratic, according to Christopher Uggen, a University of Minnesota criminologist").

101 Gregor Peter Schmitz, "Europeans Back Obama but Not Necessarily His Policies," *Der Spiegel*, September 10, 2008. Available at: http://www.spiegel.de/international/world/0,1518,577449,00.html.

102 Phil Gailey, "Poll Finds Blacks United on Political Views," *New York Times*, August 31, 1984.

103 Associated Press, "Chicago Teamsters, in Poll, Prefer Mondale over Reagan," *New York Times*, September 12, 1984.

104 Fay S. Joyce, "Sierra Club Breaks Its Tradition and Backs a Candidate: Mondale," *New York Times*, September 20, 1984.

105 Claude D. Pepper, "The Elderly May Dump Reagan," *New York Times*, September 21, 1984.

106 Associated Press, "Jersey Poll Says Mondale Cuts into Reagan's Lead," *New York Times*, October 13, 1984.

107 Associated Press, "New Mondale Support Seen in New York State," *New York Times*, October 14, 1984.

108 John Herbers, "Church-State Issue May Hurt Reagan's Effort to Attract Jews," *New York Times*, October 18, 1984.

109 Dudley Clendinen, "New Mondale Ads Impress a Skeptic," *New York Times*, September 12, 1984.

110 Associated Press, "Campaign Notes: Poll in Minnesota Shows Mondale Leads Reagan," *New York Times*, October 22, 1984.

111 Bernard Weinraub, "Midwest Crowds Applaud Mondale," *New York Times*, October 25, 1984.

112 Associated Press, "Ivy League Poll Gives Mondale a Clear Lead," *New York Times*, October 30, 1984.

113 "Mondale Pulls Closer in a National Poll," *New York Times*, October 18, 1984.

114 "Poll Shows Better Image for Mondale and Ferraro," *New York Times*, October 17, 1984.

115 "Mondale Gains Ground, According to Straw Poll," *New York Times*, October 15, 1984.

116 United Press International, "Poll Shows Mondale Is Gaining on Reagan," *New York Times*, July 13, 1984.

117 "Poll Shows Narrowing of Reagan Lead in Race," *New York Times*, July 12, 1984.

118 Mike Wallace, "Traitor or Hero?: Controversy over Millionaire Ward Connerly and His Fight for Proposition 209," *60 Minutes*, CBS, November 9, 1997.

119 Robert Pear, "The 1996 Elections: The States—The Initiatives," *New York Times*, November 7, 1996.

120 Sam Howe Verhovek, "The 1997 Elections: Affirmative Action," *New York Times*, November 6, 1997.

121 Stuart Taylor and K. C. Johnson, *Until Proven Innocent* (New York: Thomas Dunne Books, 2007), pp. 263–269.

122 Editorial: "Finances of Terror," *New York Times*, September 24, 2001.

123 Editorial: "Fit and Unfit to Print: What Are the Obligations of the Press in Wartime?," *Wall Street Journal*, June 30, 2006.

124 Frank Rich, "All the News That's Fit to Bully," *New York Times*, July 9, 2006.

125 Rich and others cited as proof that the *Times* was being picked on the fact that other newspapers published stories on the terrorist tracking program the same day. But that's because the other newspapers also had the story but were refraining from publishing it—until the *Times* did. See Gabriel Sherman, "Wall Street Rift: Journal Reporters Reject Gigot Line," *New York Observer*, July 16, 2006. Available at: http://www.observer.com/node/39128. ("On June 22, [*Wall Street Journal* reporter Glenn] Simpson was in Washington when a Treasury source tipped him that *The Times* would be publishing a piece on the subject, according to *Journal* sources. Mr. Simpson delayed a flight back to Belgium and raced to put out a piece on deadline, posting one online minutes after the *Times* story went out. *The Journal*, *The Times*, the *Los Angeles Times*, and *Washington Post* all had Swift stories in the next day's papers.")

CHAPTER 7 BRAVE, BEAUTIFUL LIBERALS

1 Thomas L. Friedman, "Reno for President," *New York Times*, April 25, 2000.

2 Peter Schweizer, *Makers and Takers* (New York: Doubleday 2008), pp. 40–41 (citing Robert S. Lichter and Stanley Rothman, "The Radical Personality: Social Psychology Components of New Left Ideology," *Political Behavior*, 1982).

3 Schweizer, *Makers and Takers*, pp. 40–41 (citing National Cultural Values Survey, Culture and Media Institute, Special Report, 2007).

4 "Inside Obama's Family Life," *OK* magazine, September 2, 2008.

5 Michael Luo and Jeff Zeleny, "Obama, in Shift, Says He'll Reject Public Financing," *New York Times*, June 20, 2008.

6 Sheila Taylor Wells, "Hillary's Hair? Get Over It," *Fort Worth Star-Telegram*, September 1, 1996.

7 Mark Leibovich, "Rights vs. Rights: An Improbable Collision Course," *New York Times*, January 13, 2008.

8   Jon Carroll, "'Bella' Means 'Beautiful,'" *San Francisco Chronicle*, April 3, 1998.

9   Bob Wyss, "Dark Days at City Hall: Carolyn Brassil to the Rescue," *Providence Journal-Bulletin*, April 22, 1998.

10 John Shanahan, Associated Press, August 23, 1977.

11 Ibid.

12 Lee Mitgang, "An AP News Analysis," *Associated Press*, September 9, 1977.

13 Ibid.

14 Wyss, "Dark Days at City Hall."

15 "Queen Bella," *The Economist*, February 26, 1977.

16 Ibid.

17 "The Reliable Source," *Washington Post*, April 9, 1998.

18 Carroll, "'Bella' Means 'Beautiful.'"

19 "Abzug Knocks Off 3 Opponents in Comeback," Associated Press, September 10, 1986.

20 Richard Grenier, "Me Tarzan, You Barbra," *Washington Times*, February 13, 1995.

21 John Waller, "Abzug Molded Conference Agenda," *Washington Times*, September 2, 1994.

22 Kenneth Lloyd Billingsley, "The Lessons of Jonestown," *San Diego Union-Tribune*, November 22, 1998.

23 Shailagh Murray, "Democratic Faces That Could Launch Thousands of Votes," *Washington Post*, October 14, 2006.

24 Julia Watson, "First Ladies' Styles," United Press International, November 14, 2000.

25 Jeffrey Ressner, "Michelle Obama Thesis Was on Racial Divide," *Politico*, February 23, 2008.

26 Sweetness & Light, "Shocker: Michelle Obama Is Race Obsessed," February 23, 2008. Available at: http://sweetness-light.com/archive/shocker-michele-obama-is-race-obsessed-2.

27 Troy Patterson, "Michelle Obama on *The View*," Slate, June 18, 2008.

28 Julie Sevrens Lyons, "Laura Bush Wardrobe Now Subject to Scrutiny," *San Jose Mercury News* (California), December 20, 2000.

29 "The Democrats Keep It Real," *The Hotline*, August 21, 2007.

30 Lynne K. Varner, "The More We Run from Race, the Faster It Chases After Us," *Seattle Times*, January 1, 2008.

31 Margaret Talev, "Spouse vs. Spouse: Clinton and Obama Go for the Unconventional," Knight Ridder, February 1, 2008.

32 Karen Heller, "Clinton, Obama: It's Hard to Choose," *Philadelphia Inquirer*, February 6, 2008.

33 Ibid.

34 Terry Plumb, "Obama Gains Crucial Edge with Youth Vote," *Herald* (Rock Hill, SC), June 8, 2008.

35 Shelly Branch, "Michelle Obama Updates a '60s Look," *Houston Chronicle*, March 9, 2008.

36 "Barack Steady," *The Hotline*, March 3, 2008 (quoting *Vogue*, March 2008).

37 "Clout: If Obama's the New JFK, He Has a Jackie, Too," *Philadelphia Daily News*, February 8, 2008.

38 Barbara Gamarekian, "Retirement Sharpens Singer's Sting," *New York Times*, September 7, 1981.

39 Donnie Radcliffe, "Ham, Grits & Fritz," *Washington Post*, September 22, 1981.

40 Nancy Reagan, *My Turn* (New York: Random House, 1989), pp. 27–29.

41 "How Much Is Cindy McCain's $300,000 Outfit Really Worth?," *Vanity Fair* blog, September 6, 2008. Available at: http://www.vanityfair.com/online/politics/2008/09/last-week-the-vanity-fair.html.

42 Monica Corcoran, "Cindy McCain Wears $300,000 Outfit," *Los Angeles Times* blog, September 4, 2008.

43 Elinor Katz, Letter to the Editor, *Staten Island Advance* (New York), September 12, 2008.

44 Travis Shiverdecker, "Privileged Lifestyle Means McCains Out of Touch," *Capital Times* (Madison, Wisconsin), September 13, 2008.

45 "John McCain Predicting Victory Last Night," CNN, September 5, 2008.

46 Charles R. Smith, "The Real Enron Scandal," *NewsMax*, Jan. 28, 2002 ("In 1992, Enron donated $100,000 to Clinton's inauguration, and Enron's top exec, Ken Lay, stayed at the White House 11 times."). Available at: http://archive.newsmax.com/archives/articles/2002/1/28/155951.shtml.

47 "A Mother's Promise," Barack Obama bio video, available at http://www.barackobama.com/learn/meet_barack.php.

48 "Truth Squad," *Chicago Tribune*, August 27, 2008.

49 Salary Survey Report for Job: Attorney / Lawyer, Payscale.com, September 13, 2008. http://www.payscale.com/research/US/Job=Attorney_percent2f_Lawyer/Salary.

50 See Freddosso, *The Case Against Barack Obama*, p. 117; C. Simon Davidson, "Are There Grounds for a Complaint Against Obama?" *Roll Call*, September 2, 2008.

51 Politifact.com, "Biden Is One of the Least Wealthy Members of the U.S. Senate," *St. Petersburg Times*, August 24, 2008. Available at: http://politifact.com/truth-o-meter/statements/659/.

52 Steven Clemons, "Joe Biden Won't Forget the Number of Houses He Owns," *Huffington Post*, August 22, 2008. Available at: http://www.huffingtonpost.com/steve-clemons/joe-biden-wont-forget-the_b_120539.html.

53 Brian Montopoli, "Biden's Tax Returns Show Modest Wealth," CBS News blog, September 12, 2008. Available at: http://www.cbsnews.com/blogs/2008/09/12/politics/horserace/entry4445194.shtml.

54 Robert Frank, "The Rich-O-Meter," *Wall Street Journal*, February 1, 2007, http://blogs.wsj.com/wealth/2007/02/01/the-rich-o-meter/.

55 "Household Income Rises, Poverty Rate Unchanged, Number of Uninsured Down," U.S. Census Bureau, August 26, 2008, available at: http://www

.census.gov/Press-Release/www/releases/archives/income_wealth/012528.html. See also Abby Goodnough, "Census Shows a Modest Rise in U.S. Income," *New York Times,* August 29, 2007.

56 TaxProf Blog, "McCain Releases 2006 & 2007 Tax Returns, but Not His Wife's," April 18, 2008. Available at: http://taxprof.typepad.com/taxprof_blog/2008/09/biden-releases.html.

57 Tax Prof Blog, "Biden Releases 10 Years of Tax Returns," September 12, 2008. Available at: http://taxprof.typepad.com/taxprof_blog/2008/09/biden-releases.html.

58 TaxProf Blog, "McCain Releases 2006 & 2007 Tax Returns, but Not His Wife's."

59 Schweizer, *Makers and Takers,* pp. 58–62.

60 Ibid., 63–64.

61 Paul Johnson, *Intellectuals* (New York: Harper Perennial, 1990), p. 223.

62 See, e.g., Editorial: "George Soros: The Man, the Mind and the Money Behind MoveOn," *Investor's Business Daily,* September 20, 2007. Available at: http://www.ibdeditorials.com/IBDArticles.aspx?id=275181103776079.

63 Byron York, "Has MoveOn Betrayed the Democratic Party?," *National Review* Online, September 10, 2007.

64 David Horowitz and Richard Poe, *The Shadow Party* (Nashville: Thomas Nelson, 2007), chap. 1.

65 Steve Kroft, interview with George Soros, CBS News Transcripts, December 20, 1998.

66 Interview, George Soros, *60 Minutes,* CBS, December 20, 1998. Available at: http://www.sorosmonitor.com/absolutenm/templates/news.aspx?articleid=33&zoneid=1:

> **KROFT:** My understanding is that you went out with this protector of yours who swore that you were his adopted godson.
>
> **MR. SOROS:** Yes. Yes.
>
> **KROFT:** Went out, in fact, and helped in the confiscation of property from the Jews.
>
> **MR. SOROS:** Yes. That's right. Yes.
>
> **KROFT:** I mean, that's—that sounds like an experience that would send lots of people to the psychiatric couch for many, many years. Was it difficult?
>
> **MR. SOROS:** Not—not at all. Not at all. Maybe as a child you don't—you don't see the connection. But it was—it created no—no problem at all.
>
> **KROFT:** No feeling of guilt?
>
> **MR. SOROS:** No.
>
> **KROFT:** For example that, "I'm Jewish and here I am, watching these people go. I could just as easily be there. I should be there." None of that?
>
> **MR. SOROS:** Well, of course—I could be on the other side or I could be the one from whom the thing is being taken away. But there was no sense that I

shouldn't be there, because that was—well, actually, in a funny way, it's just like in markets—that if I weren't there—of course, I wasn't doing it, but somebody else would—would—would be taking it away anyhow. And it was the—whether I was there or not, I was only a spectator, the property was being taken away. So the—I had no role in taking away that property. So I had no sense of guilt.

67   Interview with Michelle Obama, CBS *60 Minutes*, February 11, 2007.

68   *Crossfire*, CNN, January 28, 1996.

69   Mike Littwin, "Hillary Clinton Could Fight Own Battles, but Her Hands Are Tied Behind Her Back," *Baltimore Sun*, January 15, 1996.

70   Shana Alexander, "The Difficulties of Being Hillary," *Playboy*, January 1, 1994.

71   Barbara Bradley Hagerty, "Examining Palin's Pentecostal Background," NPR Election 2008. Available at: http://www.npr.org/templates/story/story.php?storyId=94332540.

72   Jim Rutenberg, "In First Big Interview, Palin Says, 'I'm Ready,'" *New York Times*, September 12, 2008.

73   Michael Abramowitz, "Many Versions of 'Bush Doctrine,'" *Washington Post*, September 13, 2008.

74   Interview: "Ex–Clinton Aide: Media Tougher on Palin," CBS News, September 12, 2008. Available at: http://www.cbsnews.com/stories/2008/09/11/politics/politicalplayers/main4442492.shtml?source=mostpop_story.

75   Frank Rich, "Mixed Nuts," *New York Times*, February 28, 1998.

76   Frank Rich, "Starr's Secret Helpers," *New York Times*, November 18, 1998.

77   Anthony Lewis, "Politics Dressed as Law," *New York Times*, August 24, 1998.

78   Maureen Dowd, "Truth & Ketchup," *New York Times*, October 4, 1998.

79   Maureen Dowd, "1,000 Points of Lust," *New York Times*, April 8, 1998.

80   Russell Baker, "A Shudder of Disgust," *New York Times*, August 7, 1998.

81   "Terrorist Killer Tripp," Media Research Center, CyberAlert, October 16, 1998. Available at: http://www.mrc.org/cyberalerts/1998/cyb19981016.asp#1.

82   Maureen Dowd, "Dept. of Political Security," *New York Times*, June 9, 2002.

83   Maureen Dowd, "Dump Dem Bums," *New York Times*, June 2, 2002.

84   Frank Rich, "Department of Homeland Insecurity," *New York Times*, June 8, 2002.

85   Anita F. Hill, "Insider Women with Outsider Values," *New York Times*, June 6, 2002.

86   "Intelligence: A Star Is Born," *The Hotline*, June 7, 2002.

87   James Wolcott, "Mad About the Guy," *Vanity Fair*, July 2008.

88   "Bill Clinton Targets Media Coverage of Obama," CNN Politics.com, January 8, 2008. Available at: http://politicalticker.blogs.cnn.com/2008/01/08/bill-clinton-targets-media-coverage-of-obama/.

89   Guy Gugliotta and Juliet Eilperin, "Tough Response Appeals to Critics of President," *Washington Post*, August 21, 1998.

90 Interview with Colin Powell, *Fox News Sunday,* Fox News Network, September 12, 2004.

91 Interview with Donald Rumsfeld, *Fox News Sunday,* Fox News Network, March 28, 2004. Available at: http://www.defenselink.mil/transcripts/transcript .aspx?transcriptid=2376.

92 Interview with Condoleezza Rice, *Fox News Sunday,* Fox News Network, September 10, 2006.

93 *Good Morning America,* ABC, August 4, 2008. Available at: http://news busters.org/blogs/scott-whitlock/2008/08/04/abcs-kate-snow-tells-bill-clinton-feel-free-not-answer-my-question.

94 Lorne Manly, "In Taking on Fox, Democrats See Reward in the Risk," *New York Times,* October 1, 2006.

95 John Berlau, "Antiwar Singers Out of Tune with Public," *Insight,* May 26, 2003.

96 Tamara Conniff, "In Nashville, Dissent Doesn't Play Well," *Los Angeles Times,* March 24, 2003.

97 "Rock the Vote Honors Dixie Chicks," United Press International, January 23, 2004.

98 David Bauder, "The Boss Tops 2003 Concert Earnings List," Associated Press, December 24, 2003.

99 Editorial: "Don't Shut Up and Play," *New York Times,* November 15, 2007.

100 Jon Parele, "Madonna's Real Art: Getting Attention," *New York Times,* April 18, 2003.

101 *Scarborough Country,* MSNBC, October 9, 2003.

102 Jane Stevenson, "Madonna Reinvents Herself," *Edmonton Sun* (Alberta, Canada), May 26, 2004.

103 Joel Ryan, "Madonna Kicks Off 'Sticky and Sweet' Tour in UK," Associated Press, August 23, 2008.

104 Mark Guarino, "Peace Unplugged," *Chicago Daily Herald,* April 22, 2003.

105 "The Incredibles: Billie Joe Armstrong," *Blender,* June 2006. Available at: http://www.blender.com/guide/articles.aspx?id=1944.

106 Mark Brown, "Concert-Goers Jam Exits After Anti-Bush Display," *Rocky Mountain News* (Denver), April 3, 2003.

107 Zachary Pincus-Roth, "Who Told You You're Allowed to Rain on Her Skit?," *New York,* October 10, 2006.

108 Jean Rohe, "Response to McCain's Aide Mark Salter," *Huffington Post,* May 22, 2006. Available at: http://www.huffingtonpost.com/jean-rohe/response-to-mc cains-aide_b_21442.html.

109 Ibid.

110 Ibid.

111 Michael Kranish, "John F. Kerry / Candidate in the Making / Part 3," *Boston Globe,* June 17, 2003.

112 Thomas Oliphant, "The Kerry I Know," *The American Prospect,* August 2004.

113 Kranish, "John F. Kerry / Candidate in the Making."

114 Editorial: "The Courage of Others' Convictions," *New York Times*, February 13, 2007.

115 Oliver Poole, "He Makes Hollywood's Stars Feel Safer," *Vancouver Sun* (British Columbia), May 13, 2002.

116 See, e.g., Rhoda Fukushima, "Man Charged at RNC Had Molotovs, Wanted to "Blow S*** Up," *Pioneer Press* (St. Paul, Minnesota), September 3, 2008; Mara H. Gottfried, "Two GOP Convention Protesters Ordered Held on Firearms Charges: FBI Claims They Had Materials for Molotov Cocktails," *Pioneer Press* (St. Paul, Minnesota), September 11, 2008; Mara H. Gottfried, "Two GOP Convention Protesters Still Held on Firearms Charges," *Pioneer Press* (St. Paul, Minnesota), September 10, 2008; Violent Protest: "56 Arrested Near Convention Site," *Newsday* (New York), September 2, 2008; Amy Forliti, "Some Turn Violent in March to GOP Convention," Associated Press Online, September 2, 2008.

117 Harry Smith, "Senator Ted Kennedy Discusses His Endorsement of Barack Obama," *The Early Show*, CBS News, January 29, 2008.

118 Jeff Zeleny, "In Memories of a Painful Past, Hushed Worry About Obama," *New York Times*, February 25, 2008.

119 "Tasteless Predictions," *The Independent* (London), February 11, 2008.

120 Zeleny, "In Memories of a Painful Past."

121 *Hardball*, MSNBC, May 16, 2008.

122 "The Murder of Mr. Lincoln," *New York Times*, April 21, 1865 (reprinting letter of John Wilkes Booth). Available at: http://query.nytimes.com/mem/archive-free/pdf?_r=1&res=9902E6D81F30EE34BC4951DFB266838E679FDE&oref=slogin.

123 Kenneth D. Ackerman, *Dark Horse: The Surprise Election and Political Murder of President James A. Garfield* (Carroll & Graf Publishers, 2003), p. 135; Douglas O. Linder, "The Trial of Charles Guiteau," University of Missouri–Kansas City School of Law 2007. Available at: http://www.law.umkc.edu/faculty/projects/FTrials/guiteau/guiteauaccount.html.

124 *American Experience: Emma Goldman*, PBS. Available at: http://www.pbs.org/wgbh/amex/goldman/filmmore/pt.html.

125 *This Day in History: October 14, 1912*, Theodore Roosevelt shot in Milwaukee, A&E Television Networks History Channel. Available at: http://www.history.com/this-day-in-history.do?action=Article&id=5436.

126 Federal Bureau of Investigation, United States Department of Justice, Washington, D.C., Franklin D. Roosevelt (Assassination Attempt). Available at: http://digital.library.miami.edu/gov/FDRAssn.html.

127 Report of the President's Commission on the Assassination of President Kennedy, Appendix 7: A Brief History of Presidential Protection at 512. Available at: http://www.archives.gov/research/jfk/warren-commission-report/appendix 7.html.

128 See generally Gerald Posner, *Case Closed: Lee Harvey Oswald and the Assassination of JFK* (New York: Anchor Books, 1994); "Who Was Lee Harvey Oswald?,"

Frontline, PBS. Available at: http://pbs.gen.in/wgbh/pages/frontline/shows/oswald/cron/.

129 Posner: *Case Closed,* pp. 91, 102–8.

130 Ibid., pp. 119–20, 164.

131 Ibid., p. 362.

132 Loren Coleman, *The Copycat Effect: How the Media and Popular Culture Trigger the Mayhem in Tomorrow's Headlines* (New York: Pocket Paperback, 2004), p. 28.

133 Timothy W. Maier, "New Chapters in Assassin's Diary?," *Insight on the News,* December 14, 1998; "Bremer's Release an Unfortunate Reality," *Mobile Register* (Alabama), November 11, 2007; Arthur Bremer Biography, Basic Famous People, available at: http://www.basicfamouspeople.com//index.php?aid=7134.

134 Sandra Salmans, "Leaves from a Family Album," *Newsweek,* September 22, 1975. See video: Lynette "Squeaky" Fromme Discusses Her Assassination Attempt on Ford, Saying "His Life Didn't Mean More Than the Redwoods to Me." Available at: http://minx.cc/?blog=86&post=209933.

135 Eileen Keerdoja, "Squeaky and Sara Jane," *Newsweek,* November 8, 1976; Interview: "Woman Who Tried to Assassinate Ford," ABC7, January 3, 2007. Available at: http://abclocal.go.com/kgo/story?section=news/local&id=4900159.

136 Jerry Seper, "Florida Ballot Chief Warns on 'Observers,'" *Washington Times,* October 26, 2004.

137 "Elizabeth Edwards Says There Will Be No Riots if Kerry Wins," *The Frontrunner,* October 26, 2004.

138 Tim Graham, "Sandra Bernhard: Palin Would Be Gang-Raped by Blacks in Manhattan," *Newsbusters,* September 19, 2008.

139 Peter Kirsanow, "Florida Forever," *National Review,* March 9, 2004. Available at: http://www.nationalreview.com/comment/kirsanow200403090858.asp.

140 Brian Mitchell, "Violence, Fraud Mar '04 Election Already," *Investor's Business Daily,* November 1, 2004.

141 "Population and Housing Profile: Madison, WI," MSA, American Community Service Profile: 2003 (citing 2003 census). Available at: http://www.census.gov/acs/www/Products/Profiles/Single/2003/ACS/Narrative/380/NP38000US4720.htm.

142 Bellevue, Washington, Citidata.com, 2008 (citing 2000 census). http://quickfacts.census.gov/qfd/states/54/5439460.html.

143 Ben Bomberger, "Campaign Workers Attacked," *Galax Gazette,* October 28, 2008. Available at: http://www.galaxgazette.com/cgi-bin/storyviewnew.cgi?055+News.20081027-2025-055-055007.Lead+News

ACKNOWLEDGMENTS

Many of my friends helped with facts, jokes, edits, or titles, so I will get you all disinvited from parties in one fell swoop (they'd be snooze-fests anyway):

Bill Armistead	Mickey Kaus
Hans Bader	Merrill Kinstler
Trish Baker	Harry Liberman
Stephen Bujno	Gary Lawson
Robert Caplain	David Limbaugh
Miguel Estrada	Jay Mann
Sandy Frank	Gene Meyer
Melanie Graham	Jim Moody
John Harrison	Jeremy Rabkin
James Higgins	Jon Tukel
Jim Hughes	Angie Saridakis

Special thanks to Ned Rice, who can produce a joke for any occasion in a minute flat, Steve Gilbert, whom I use as my 24-hour e-mail-able encyclopedia because he knows everything about everything, and Marshall Sella, whose superlative grasp of the English language I attribute to his never having attended public school, as I did, which is why I do not know the rules of grammar.

My Crown editor, Jed Donahue, edited my last two books, but this was the first one I *really* tested him on. He passed with flying colors—and then he collapsed in exhaustion and left Crown. (All this time, I could have been turning in poorly organized books!) So also thank you to my soon-to-be-fully-tested editor Sean Desmond, who took over at the page-proof stage, and my copy editor Toni Rachiele.

I am duly grateful for the always brilliant work of David Tran, who produced another award-winning book cover, aided by the miracle photography of Shonna Valenska. Also thanks to my official agents Mel Berger and Suzanne Gluck and my agent-for-life Joni Evans. Advance thanks to my tireless publicist Diana Banister.

Everyone at Crown was a saint to me through a difficult year, and I'd especially like to express my gratitude to Tina Constable for being so kind and understanding. And thanks to my dear mother for offering to write a note to my publisher explaining why my book was late after a tough week of medical appointments.

INDEX

301

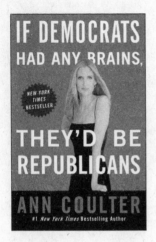